Foucault and Governmentality

Reframing the Boundaries: Thinking the Political

Series editors: Alison Assiter and Evert van der Zweerde

This series aims to mine the rich resources of philosophers in the "continental" tradition for their contributions to thinking the political. It fills a gap in the literature by suggesting that the work of a wider range of philosophers than those normally associated with this sphere of work can be of relevance to the political.

Titles in the Series

Kierkegaard and the Matter of Philosophy, Michael O'Neill Burns
Arendt, Levinas and a Politics of Relationality, Anya Topolski
The Risk of Freedom: Ethics, Phenomenology and Politics in Jan Patocka, Francesco Tava, translated by Jane Ledlie
Nietzsche's Death of God and Italian Philosophy, Emilio Carlo Corriero, translated by Vanessa Di Stefano
Lotman's Cultural Semiotics and the Political, Andrey Makarychev and Alexandra Yatsyk
Axel Honneth: Reconceiving Social Philosophy, Dagmar Wilhelm
Sartre, Imagination and Dialectical Reason: Creating Society as a Work of Art, Austin Hayden Smidt
Ontologies of Sex: Philosophy in Sexual Politics, Zeynep Direk
Reconsidering Cosmopolitanism and Forgiveness: Arendt, Derrida and 'Care for the World', Christopher Peys
Transforming Politics with Merleau-Ponty: Thinking beyond the State, edited by Jérôme Melançon
Derrida and Foucault: Philosophy, Politics, and Polemics, Paul Rekret
Foucault and Governmentality: Living to Work in the Age of Control, Benda Hofmeyr

Foucault and Governmentality

Living to Work in the Age of Control

Benda Hofmeyr

ROWMAN & LITTLEFIELD
Lanham • Boulder • New York • London

Published by Rowman & Littlefield
An imprint of The Rowman & Littlefield Publishing Group, Inc.
4501 Forbes Boulevard, Suite 200, Lanham, Maryland 20706
www.rowman.com

86-90 Paul Street, London EC2A 4NE

British Library Cataloguing in Publication Information Available

Library of Congress Cataloging-in-Publication Data

Names: Hofmeyr, Benda, author.
Title: Foucault and governmentality : living to work in the age of control / Benda Hofmeyr.
Description: Lanham, Maryland : Rowman & Littlefield, 2022. | Series: Reframing the boundaries : thinking the political | Includes bibliographical references and index. | Summary: "Drawing upon political philosophy and political economy, Benda Hofmeyr presents a Foucaultian analysis and historical contextualisation of the rise of neo-liberal governmentality. Historical, sociological and cultural studies help excavate the geneaology of the capitalist subject within the neo-liberal governmental context of the last four decades"—Provided by publisher.
Identifiers: LCCN 2022010165 (print) | LCCN 2022010166 (ebook) | ISBN 9781786611727 (cloth) | ISBN 9781786611734 (ebook)
Subjects: LCSH: Knowledge workers. | Workaholism. | Neoliberalism. | Capitalism—Political aspects. | Foucault, Michel, 1926-1984—Political and social views.
Classification: LCC HD8039.K59 H63 2022 (print) | LCC HD8039.K59 (ebook) | DDC 658.4/038—dc23/eng/20220505
LC record available at https://lccn.loc.gov/2022010165
LC ebook record available at https://lccn.loc.gov/2022010166

Contents

Acknowledgments

Chapter 2 has been published as Hofmeyr 2021a.

Chapter 3 has been published in a shorter version as Hofmeyr 2022a.

Chapter 4 has been published in a truncated format as Hofmeyr 2021b and reprinted here in a longer reworked form.

Chapter 5 has been published in a shorter version as Hofmeyr 2021d.

Chapter 6 has been published in a shorter version as Hofmeyr 2021c.

Chapter 2 and chapter 6 revisit selected arguments developed in Hofmeyr 2005 and Hofmeyr 2008.

CHAPTER ONE

Living to Work in the Age of Control

Knowledge Work Compulsion

Knowledge workers—our generators of game-changing ideas—embody the fuel that powers today's knowledge economy. They are that part of the workforce that thinks for a living, that dreams up the ideas from which new innovations and technologies spring. In neoliberal economies, these workers are known for their diligence, even devotion, to their work, to the point of dependency (Hunnicut 1988; Robin and Dominquez 2008; Schulte 2014). These tireless workers will work regardless of how this compulsion impinges on their private time, or their physical, emotional, and social well-being (Sennett 1998, 2003, 2006; Verhaeghe 2012; Han 2017). Somewhat surprisingly, these highly engaged workers have been reported to experience increased overall well-being, much more so than actively disengaged workers who work far less (Saad 2014)—with the exception of those cases for whom living-to-work has resulted in burnout and stress-related illnesses that confront the worker with the limits of his/her capacities. The living-to-work phenomenon among knowledge workers has seen a concomitant rise in physical and psychological illnesses, which has in turn elicited organisational responses in the form of extensive wellness programmes to mitigate the potentially ruinous knock-on effects of too much work. What animates this study is a desire to get to the heart of *what motivates knowledge workers to work almost all the time*.

Three reasons may account for knowledge workers' work compulsion. The first two are conditions of possibility (they are necessary but not sufficient reasons), whereas the third makes this triad decisive. The first reason is obvious: the performance and outputs relentlessly expected of knowledge workers require them to be unceasingly industrious. Deadlines need to be met. Time-sensitive deliverables call for constant focused attention and for conscious and unconscious problem-solving abilities—as we know, the miraculous human brain keeps on working to solve complex problems, even when our conscious attention is directed elsewhere. The second condition of possibility for this work compulsion is capacity. The connected smart technologies of the present era enable knowledge workers to work any time, any place. They work irrespective of time and place, even while they are seemingly preoccupied with some everyday private responsibility, such as childcare or grocery shopping. The contemporary knowledge worker is always reachable and in touch, enabled to respond in real time to whatever needs to be done. These workers are also inscribed in numerous digital/social platforms that prompt and gently prod to elicit constant responses to keep workers engaged. The latest applications even track and trace, in order to steer workers' movements and habits to optimise their time management. In this process, more or less imperceptible and sometimes even welcome controls are insinuated into the most intimate rhythms of private and professional life—steering the private toward the professional, coaxing online behaviour toward increased consumption of profitable resources. The third and definitive reason for work compulsion—the most decisive side of what I would like to call the golden triangle of the living-to-work phenomenon—is perhaps the most intriguing. Knowledge workers work compulsively because they *want to*. But *why* do they want to work all the time? And what is the link—if there is one—between neoliberal governmentality and this curious wanting-to-work-constantly phenomenon?

Neoliberal Governmentality

Neoliberal governmentality is a complex notion. Michel Foucault coined the term in his lecture series at the Collège de France lecture from 1977 to 1979, published in English in 2007 as *Security, Territory, Population. Lectures at the Collège de France 1977–1978*, and in 2008 as *The Birth of Biopolitics. Lectures at the Collège de France, 1978–79*. His neologism 'governmentality' conjoins a very broadly conceived understanding of government as a technology of power with 'mentality'. For Foucault, this term refers to the rationality that informs the governing regime. In other words, governmentality is one avatar of Foucault's well-known conjunction of power/knowledge. In his lectures, Foucault considers the mid-twentieth-century versions of German and American neoliberalisms as governmentalities. These analyses have variously been used by Foucault scholars to critique or to laud contemporary forms of neoliberalism. The possibility of harnessing his analyses to either side of the debate is made possible by the value-neutral stance that he adopted in the lectures, which appear neither to explicitly support nor to overtly oppose neoliberalism.

In chapter 2, I argue that, in line with Foucault's other work at the time, Foucault's lectures may be read methodologically as a strategics of power/knowledge configurations imbued with what he calls the 'critical attitude'. In other words, I consider them in the spirit of Foucault's analyses as 'problematisations' that seek to interrogate phenomena critically; that is, they seek to unearth the conditions of possibility for discursive formations or 'truths' that legitimise techniques of power, which in turn constitute the 'might' that determines what counts as 'right'. Such 'problematisations' further seek to unearth the weaknesses or fissures in power/knowledge constellations where resistance to power relations which pose an imminent threat of domination becomes possible. If this is indeed the spirit that animates Foucault's analyses of various forms of neoliberalisms as governmentalities, then what some scholars (for example, Zamora and Behrent 2016) have dubbed his 'intrigue with neoliberalism' should not be read simplistically as an uncritical fascination with these phenomena. Rather, I suggest that these 'problematisations' should be recognised as a critical interrogation of a new formation of liberal governmentality that Foucault sensed could become extremely dangerous to human freedom, given that this governmentality relies on the maintenance of various liberties by way of an ever-increasing array of subtle controls of aspects of human existence that previously fell beyond the powers of governmental jurisdiction. It is in this spirit that I bring Foucault's understanding of neoliberal governmentality to bear on the phenomenon of the compulsively working knowledge worker. I therefore attempt, in chapter 3, to explore the phenomenon of knowledge work and the collateral emergence of the knowledge worker as the most important determinant of economic success in the information age, a context permeated, as we shall see, by 'complex control'. (I explain the broad approach in chapter 3 later in this introduction, in my brief discussion on human capital.)

Rationality under neoliberal governmentality consists in the imperative to subject every decision to a cost-benefit calculus: the course of action that a knowledge worker pursues in neoliberal economies is the one that renders the greatest return. For the knowledge worker, leisure and recreation only trump the necessity to work when they optimise the worker's ability to do the work more efficiently. Exercise, such as yoga or meditation, is undertaken for its stress-relieving and wellness benefits, which in turn make the worker more productive at work. Moreover, for knowledge workers, the greatest return is not primarily higher earnings, but rather the quality and content of the work they do (Drucker 1959). What motivates them is a sense of personal achievement, as well as being given greater responsibility, which they see as a sign of recognition. Abraham Maslow (1943) famously places personal achievement that realises the need for self-actualisation, the human need to achieve one's full potential, at the top of the hierarchy of needs in his theory of human motivation. Even learning and self-development, which are, strictly speaking, not *work*, have become a necessary condition for success in the world of work in this era of rapid technological innovation. Continuous learning and upskilling are knowledge work requirements, which implies that, by the very nature of the job, learning and working are to some extent synonymous. It may be reasonable to conclude, then, that knowledge workers willingly, even enthusiastically, work almost all the time, despite the toll it takes on their physical and mental health and social relations.

Thumos

In chapter 4, I go further by delving into a more fundamental philosophical dimension that informs this phenomenon. There appears to be some well-spring of boundless psychic energy that fuels the work compulsion of knowledge workers—what might be called an ambiguous ambition. I put to the test Francis Fukuyama's (1992) contention that dedication to work has a thumotic origin. In other words, we need to ask ourselves to what extent the living-to-work phenomenon may be accounted for by some invisible thumotic satisfaction generated by knowledge work. Fukuyama's argument, in short, is that the adoption of the right market-oriented policy is not in and of itself sufficient to guarantee the success of liberal economies—he posits that the decisive factor in economic success is the persistence of 'irrational' forms of thumos that continue to influence economic behaviour in countless ways that contribute to the wealth of the nation. Some examples that he cites of such 'irrational' forms of thumos include religion, nationalism, and the ability of craft occupations and the professions to maintain standards and to experience pride in their work for its own sake (Fukuyama 1992, 234).

The notion of thumos has its origin in the writings of ancient Greek philosophers and poets, most famously in the work of Homer, Plato, and Aristotle. In the Homeric poems, thumos is associated with the internal psychological process of thought, emotion, volition, and motivation. Homer's various depictions of thumos are invariably attended by a sense of the motivational strength and overmastering urgency of the impulse in question, even when the outcome may be disastrous. Something of the sense of thumos as an interrelated set of motivations re-emerges in Plato's conception of the tripartite soul in *Phaedrus* (circa 370 BCE) and in his *Republic* (circa 375 BCE) (Cairns 2019). For Plato, thumos is one of three innate components of the psyche, along with reason and desire. As in Homer, thumos might be temporarily aligned with or opposed to either reason or desire, or act as an independent agency of sorts. In Plato's *Phaedrus*, thumos is coupled to the love of honour, as well as modesty and self-control, the companion to true glory (§253e). In the *Republic*, thumos refers more explicitly to the spiritedness with which one rises to the defence of someone or something that one holds dear, especially in the face of injustice. For Plato, thumos is the fountainhead of righteous indignation, which, if it is not kept in check, may lead to violent excesses, even self-destruction, on account of the fearless ambition or anger, and the desire for vengeance that thumos fuels. Thumos might be said to account for Icarus' tragic end on account of his insatiable ambition to reach ever greater heights. It is thumos that drives Antigone to bury her brother in defiance of what she views as the intolerable injustice of Creon's refusal to grant him a proper burial, and it is thumos that leads to her suicide, which might be seen as the ultimate act of defiance. It is thumos that fuels Achilles' tireless quest for glory, retribution, and vengeance, but also Hector's courage to overcome his fear and face the apparently invincible Achilles in Homer's *Iliad*.

In the *Republic*, thumos accounts for the 'invincible and unbeatable spirit' (§375b) of the 'guardians' who have to maintain justice in the polis (city-state) (§375a–356c). To perform their duty, they must be quick-tempered, battle-ready, and victory-loving, as well as willing to sacrifice their own good in defence of their polis and their fellow citizens. For Plato, thumos is the very source of bravery, determination, and the desire for justice. However, for Plato, unlike the violent, self-destructive thumos of Homeric epics and Ancient tragedy, thumos has to be balanced by restraint and moderation when the occasion calls for it.

There is no equivalent modern English term that covers the breadth of the scope of the qualities that thumos accounts for in the Greek vision. The absence of such terms in modern English might be interpreted to mean that thumos does not exist now as it did in the Ancient sense, or even that the spirit of thumos is actively suppressed as an undesirable quality that may ignite irrational excesses, such as wars.

In the modern context, then, I take up Fukuyama's linking of thumos and work in chapter 4, and contend that thumos is very much alive in contemporary neoliberal societies. The challenge is then how to localise and concretise the operation of this ephemeral psychic energy associated with the spirit, enterprise, and ambition within neoliberal governmentality. If thumos as determined spiritedness is indeed a force to be reckoned with, may it be said to account for the pervasive global and globalising implementation of neoliberal governmentality? What is it about knowledge workers that sustains their quest for ever-increasing self-improvement and success? If the knowledge worker's drive does indeed emanate from a thumotic source, then it could perhaps account for the paradox in which the engaged compulsive worker *wants to* work all the time and reports an increase in overall well-being, even in the face of the toll that work takes. The next question is then whether neoliberal economic theory has perhaps found a way to harness thumos to the profit incentive, and if so, how.

Human Capital

This line of questioning leads me to interrogate the neoliberal theory of human capital in chapter 5. In his 1978 and 1979 Collège de France lecture series, Foucault mentions—almost as an aside—American economist Gary Becker's (1964) theory of human capital.[1] It is this theory, as we shall see, that recognised that the elusive human spiritedness to work is a resource that cannot merely be exploited, but that work requires the investment by the worker in self-optimisation, as well as the investment by employers in the worker to enable the worker to be optimally efficient and render the most profitable output.

The American brand of neoliberalism, or Anarcho-liberalism, associated with Milton Friedman and the Chicago School, as theorised by Foucault, banks on the realisation that all labour, including wage labour, can be understood as a *voluntary* investment or entrepreneurial activity carried out in the individual pursuit of some sort of surplus value, future return, or wage (Foucault 2008, 224). This theory of human capital recognises that *human* capital differs from other forms of capital in that it requires the human to be present if it is to be converted into surplus wealth. It theorises workers as fundamentally conjoined with their capacities as a kind of assemblage with a dynamic productive potential. This kind of labour—conceived as 'capital-ability' (Foucault 2008, 225)—is not merely a 'factor of production', but has a qualitative and dynamic aspect of its own. Under neoliberalism, the worker is recognised to be 'an active economic subject' in a very real sense, and not just at work, but in everything the person does (Foucault 2008, 223). This working subject is not a partner in a 'process of exchange' as it is traditionally conceived, but a dynamic 'entrepreneur' of her-/himself, constantly balancing costs and benefits, and constantly mindful of the future impact of choices even in seemingly non-economic spheres. Han (2017) conceives of this subject as a 'project' of the self that, in the hope of some return, pursues her/his own transformation through enhancement of her/his basic physical capacities, mental skills, and attitude through the market (Foucault 2008, 226, 229).

To capitalise on this form of labour, the active economic subject requires a very specific organisational logic—one that steers lightly without stifling the worker. In other words, organisations need to control the knowledge worker's conduct *imperceptibly*, not just at work, but in every aspect of the worker's existence. Control needs to be imperceptible, because human capital depreciates in the face of overt coercive measures, because the human capital of knowledge work requires the worker's *voluntary devotion* in order to be optimally effective. It needs to extend to every aspect of the worker's existence because the worker's efficiency depends on her/his mental and physical well-being. This worker needs to buy into the neoliberal governance and accept the premise of the market, which in turn results in the constant development of her/his own human capital in order to survive and prosper. If the worker refuses to submit to the market rationality that inculcates an all-pervasive cost-benefit decision-making process, s/he will experience some measure of discomfort, for example, in the form of unemployability, job loss, or insufficient income, thereby allowing the market to 'correct' the worker's choice calculus. In this sense, the hegemony of neoliberal life appears to preclude the possibility of any alternative mode of existence. It is this broad ontological power of neoliberalism that Foucault (2008) recognises. Does this mean that neoliberalism has succeeded in subsuming the volitional devotion of workers' minds and hands, as well as of their hearts, and not only in neoliberal production, but also in the reproduction of social life? If so, how exactly has this been achieved?

In chapter 3, I draw on the research of Burud and Tumolo (2004) regarding the leveraging of human capital to explore how contemporary organisations have reorganised themselves to achieve optimal power over labour as knowledge work. They maintain that an overtly coercive organisational culture that seeks to constrain, command, or micromanage people smothers the natural human urge to transform progressively, instead of boosting positive self-organisation through spontaneous adaptation. They warn that organisations should not mistake rule to mean order. The order in which human capital thrives arises naturally when self-organising humans are allowed to believe that they are acting spontaneously and to take initiative, to participate in the creation of the cooperative project or deliverable. An important characteristic of highly skilled knowledge workers is that they may know their jobs better than their line managers do, as Burud and Tumolo (2004) point out. One result is that knowledge workers see themselves not as mere orderlies, but as equals, and that they behave like volunteers. They contribute ideas and harness their imagination. For them to do so, they must be actively engaged in their work. As a result, what they look for in the organisations that employ them is a match in their values. What they look for in their work is a job that offers them an opportunity to enhance their own capital. Finally, because knowledge workers carry the means of production with them, they are highly mobile—their work is not confined or confineable to one place, to specific hours or age. If they find themselves in organisations with similar values, ones that afford them ample respect, responsibility, and opportunities for self-development without confining their investment in work to one place or to specific hours, these workers are willing to devote mind, body, and soul to drive results. Highly skilled knowledge workers are therefore quite demanding, and in return, complete devotion is demanded of them. At the same time, they may lack the system of invisible support in the form of an unemployed homemaking spouse that was part and parcel of the traditional one-income household of yesteryear. The optimal organisational culture in which the human capital of the knowledge worker thrives is therefore cognizant of both the private and professional needs of knowledge workers. Such organisations would offer space for initiative and ample freedom and responsibility, flexible working hours, childcare facilities, and paternity as well as maternity leave, to cite but a few examples.

In 1984, George Huber maintained that three processes will become increasingly important in post-industrial organisations: decision-making, innovation, and information acquisition and distribution. He foresaw that one result of this would be that organisations would attempt to ensure routine effectiveness of these processes through increased formalisation: 'In some cases this formalization will have as its purpose ensuring the existence of informal (or at least unstructured) activities, such as experimentation by "self-designing" organizations or acquisition of "soft" information by top managers' (Huber 1984, 928). Huber concludes that during the transition period between the industrial and post-industrial societies, many organisations may be expected to fail due to their resorting to excessive overt management practices ignorant of the 'soft' and stealthy techniques required for post-industrial organisations to respond to the demands of increased decision-making, innovation, and information acquisition and distribution. Soft skills refer to leadership as opposed to managerial skills, the ability to communicate, be flexible, exhibit emotional intelligence, manage conflict, and adapt through resourcefulness and creativity. The post-industrial workplace requires an organisational culture that values soft skills or people skills just as much as, if not more, than hard skills or technical skills, not only to cater to the speed of innovation, but also to the very nature of human capital, which is the driving force of the ideas that fuel innovation and knowledge generation. However, this need for a more flexible, 'soft' organisational culture has not resulted in a more humane or permissive form of control, but in a technologically based network of 'complex control'.

Control

The overarching diagnostics of the present conditions of the subject-formation of knowledge workers under neoliberal governmentality takes as its contextual condition of possibility the fact that these workers find themselves in societies in which, according to Castells (1996), the entire social structure consists of networks powered by microelectronics-based information and communication technologies. He sees networks as grids of interconnected nodes that allow very adaptable, open-ended, and decentralised structures (Castells 1996, 470). The internet has become a decisive facilitator of the increasing globalisation of neoliberalism; since its use has become all-pervasive, it has come to play an indispensable role in practically all areas of human activity. Castells explains that the internet has created a *global*—as opposed to a world—economy, that is, an economy whose constituents are able to work in concert as a whole, in real time or at a specific chosen time on a planetary scale (Castells 1996, 102).

This global economy has three distinct but interrelated features, according to Castells (1996). It is networked, global, and informational. Its informational feature is the fact that the productivity of its constituents fundamentally depends on their capacity to generate, process, and apply knowledge-based information efficiently (Castells 1996, 77). This informational structure recognises the key role played by knowledge workers in the economy. The networked, global structure of the economy is one of the main enabling features of the living-to-work development, since it has created what Castells (1996, 36) calls a 'space of flows' and 'timeless time', which together effectively overcome traditional geographical and temporal boundaries. The 'network logic' links up dominant functions, while fragmenting subordinate functions, and people, in the multiple space of places (Castells 1996, 476). This has brought about significant changes in the formation of identities, which appear as the self's scramble for autonomy in times of instability and the structural changes caused by networks. In these societies, power is exercised by and through networks: the 'power of flows takes precedence over the flows of power' (Castells 1996, 469). This means that power is exercised in 'a complex set of joint action' (Castells 2009, 45) by supranational institutions, multinational corporations, and financial markets.

Importantly, as Castells (1996) also recognises, the rise of global informational capitalism has also led to organisational changes within companies and to a restructuring of labour. The implementation of information and communication technologies requires skilled and self-reliant workers, 'the networkers'. Whereas previous forms of capitalism were characterised by authoritarian and exploitative methods, the Network Society appears to provide greater freedom in the workplace, because 'networkers' need greater autonomy while performing less standardised tasks (Castells 1996, 246). Simultaneous automation, outsourcing, and subcontracting have led to a divide between 'upgraded' information work, which requires a high level of skill and education, and 'downgraded' precarious jobs (Castells 1996, 251). Unions have either been actively disempowered or have not been able to keep up with the restructuring of work toward increased flexibility and the international division of labour in global supply chains. Castells (2000, 380) maintains that global informational capitalism is consequently 'characterized by a tendency towards increased inequality and polarization'. The global division of labour is producing winners—highly skilled information workers—and losers—downgraded service and informal workers, or even unemployed. There are thus structurally excluded populations relegated to regions 'outside' of the network, such as large parts of Africa, but also within developed countries, in slums or ghettos.

In chapter 5, as we shall see, Törnberg and Uitermark (2020) call the form of power operative in and through technologically mediated and informational networks 'complex control'. This form of control operates at the level of micro-interactions, setting up the context and conditions for self-organisation from which the order of things seems to emerge naturally (Törnberg and Uitermark 2020, 1). The fundamental resignation of the self to networked influences beyond its control is not recognised: the world is embracing the era of digital platforms as one of unprecedented freedom because it appears to put the self in the driver's seat against the rigid, top-down configurations of former regimes of governmentality. The digital platforms through which neoliberal governmentality can now exert biopolitical control over the life of the individual and the population is 'open, informal and non-linear' (Törnberg and Uitermark 2020, 2). Like Castells (1996), Törnberg and Uitermark (2020, 2) recognise that self-organisation signals not so much empowerment or freedom, as the worker is being delivered to the rules of the game over which the constituent parts wield no power.

Digital platforms have become essential infrastructure for the organisation of social, economic as well as working life.. User-generated content has become such a standard aspect of new technologies that the 'digital' and social' have become superimposed (Marres 2017 cited by Törnberg and Uitermark (2020, 2)). Social/digital platform engineers hail these platforms as spaces for personal liberation through self-organisation. It is, after all, a 'sharing economy' (Puschmann and Alt 2016), a space of 'commons-based peer production' (Benkler 2002). Mattijssen, Buijs, Elands, and Arts (2018) define the political ideal associated with the term self-organisation as an array of diverse governance arrangements where private actors take their own initiative to act autonomously to pursue public or collective objectives. This is a form of social organisation that is considered disintermediated by means of prosumption, one in which consumers become the producers of what they consume, and hence one that can apparently be liberated from central leadership. Digital and social platforms such as Wikipedia, Airbnb, or Facebook are examples of the purported utopia in which people voluntarily and cooperatively self-organise when the opportunity is presented to them (Benkler 2006; Srnicek 2017). This principle is closely aligned to the way in which complexity theory defines self-organised systems, that is, as systems in which the individual constituents are more or less independent and autonomous in their conduct, while being subject to various direct and indirect interactions (Heylighen, Cilliers, and Gershenson 2006, 125 cited by Törnberg and Uitermark (2020, 3)).

The complicated systems of the past are top-down, hierarchical, and bureaucratic, but complex systems emerge through self-organisation (Törnberg and Uitermark 2020, 3). A complex system's distinct properties arise from the relationships of its many constituents, such as non-linearity, emergence, spontaneous order, adaptation, and feedback loops. A complex digital/social system is set apart from a natural complex system by the fact that the way in which individual constituents may or may not interact is predetermined by the rules of the network. Network governance operates by actively incentivising desired interactions, while discouraging undesired interactions by way of sanctions. It sets the requirements for participation, for example, a level of skill or education, and it rewards interactions that promote competition and entrepreneurial innovation. Whereas natural self-organised systems are resilient because of the inherent redundancy of each individual part belonging to the same class, the constituents of a digital/social self-organised system are differentiated by their unique expertise. What enables the resilience of digital/social self-organised systems is the reserve army of experts waiting in the wings to replace a part who proves inflexible, who fails to keep up with innovation and the ever-changing rules of the game. It is increasingly necessary to display adaptability or plasticity on account of the rapid changes caused by the current crises, including large-scale social and ecological crises (Gunderson and Light 2006). Contemporary neoliberal governmentality, then, creates a resilient social and economic order that is characterised by complex, decentralised, bottom-up governance, which inscribes every aspect of individual and collective life in digital platforms that operate through self-organisation, self-regulation, and self-governance (Helbing 2015, 2 cited by Törnberg and Uitermark (2020, 3)).

This form of biopolitical control of neoliberal governmentality is based on 'tuning and shifting the market competition, using flexible and market-based forms of control, while concealing and de-politicizing through technical coding, which modifies competition within the market, rather than regulating top-down' (Törnberg and Uitermark 2020, 6). The notion of complex power brings to the fore the *appearance of spontaneity*. The fact that phenomena that emerge from mass-interactive systems are hard to trace back to specific causal roots is taken as evidence of their spontaneous emanation, 'as if micro-level causes were not just as much a function of external constraints and conditions' (Törnberg and Uitermark 2020, 6). We know from Foucault's analyses of neoliberal governmentality that the supposedly free market is carefully constructed and maintained, and not actually free or spontaneous in any sense. Likewise, the digital/social platforms that form the predominant working environment of knowledge workers are not disintermediated, as they proclaim themselves to be. These platforms operate by making the social sphere "technically mediated by transforming modes of interaction into quantified and datafied forms that permit control through intervention and manipulation (Van Dijck and Poell 2013 cited by Törnberg and Uitermark (2020, 6)). Törnberg and Uitermark (2020, 6) further explains that digital/social platforms harness quantification that distorts social reality, and they wield ideological choices in their technical codification (Feenberg 2002). The idea of 'nudging' has its origin in behavioural economics (Thaler, Sunstein, and Balz 2013). The strategy is employed in the 'choice architectures' of digital platforms "which drive the users' behaviour by shaping the contexts in which they make decisions" and altering these contexts in predictable ways (Törnberg and Uitermark 2020, 6–7). Various mechanisms are employed, such as altering how and what information is presented, which options are available to users, what the default choices are, or by creating implicit or explicit awards, scores, or rankings (Törnberg and Uitermark 2020, 7). Importantly, digitisation has been proven to bring about the omnipresence of 'highly asymmetric "long-tailed" distributions, in which a few actors receive a majority of the resources of the digital platforms—whether income, attention, or influence' (Törnberg and Uitermark 2020, 7). Much like the neoliberal market, this is conceived as a 'natural' or 'inherent' outcome of digital technology, rather than as the intended result of a political design choice. In this process, the unequal outcomes of self-organising systems are exonerated from any political, conflictual, or power dimensions. This is complex power in action—'the power of *designed self-organization*' (Törnberg and Uitermark 2020, 8). Importantly, self-organisation is imbued with a normative dimension, which casts it as inherently good, in addition to being apparently inevitable, since it seems to result not from any active intention of the actors, but *emerges* on account of some imperceptible synergy co-created among the actors. If 'the new instrument of control is horizontal, decentralised, networked communication' (Törnberg and Uitermark 2020, 9), in which actors not only voluntarily but enthusiastically and constantly engage, to what extent is resistance possible—especially if it is not sought, because control is intangible?

Resistance?

In line with the spirit of Foucault's analyses, I do not intend to proffer solutions. Foucault offers problematisations rather than solutions, as solutions are themselves prone to being co-opted by prevailing relations of power and put to work to further the very agendas they seek to resist. It is important to remember that for Foucault resistance is inherent to the functioning of power relations, that where there is power, there is resistance, conceived as counter-conduct to keep the agonal relationality of the play of power relations from congealing into a rigid form of domination. Resistance is therefore not outside of power. Still, there is a crucial distinction between resistance as *mere* counter-conduct and resistance as truly productive or creative. Productive or creative resistance succeeds in modifying—even if only slightly—the predetermined rules of engagement that orchestrate or pre-arrange the possibilities for action. The possibilities for such resistance within the context of the knowledge organisation are explored by Courpasson, Dany, and Clegg's (2012) analyses of two case studies. In chapter 6, I critically interrogate Courpasson, Dany, and Clegg's argument to plot the risks to which knowledge workers are exposed, the conditions of possibility, as well as the probability of success of productive resistance in the workplace.

What is evident about this documented 'productive' resistance is the fact that it depends on a number of decisive preconditions. It must be initiated by the *right* people in the name of the *right* principles and met by the *right* management in order to succeed. Who are the *right* people, what are the *right* principles, and what constitutes the *right* management? More fundamentally, do these *right* conditions of possibility effectively challenge the underlying rules of the game—the politics of truth—which are at the heart of the regime of power that one seeks to resist? Are these right conditions not already inscribed in the rules, sanctioning certain possibilities of resistance without posing a fundamental challenge to the presiding profit incentive?

Foucault has extensively theorised personal *individual* resistance that entails the use of critique, but how does such individual resistance relate to *collective* resistance, the kind that one would associate with organisational or political change? If personal resistance based on the attitude of critique threatens to uncover the illegitimacy and injustice of the grounds that give the rule of governance its apparent validity, and is premised on the right and obligation to insist on *not* being governed *like that*, is there a place for collective organisational resistance? Perhaps personal individual resistance is a necessary condition for collective resistance, but we might wonder if it is sufficient in the context of the forms of contemporary organisational governance that entail complex mechanisms of control. Resistance that truly risks undermining the validity of the governing logic might be recognised as too dangerous. It may be met by a frontal attack and be put out of commission, or relegated to the margins where it will come to be but one slight variation or negligible exception to the norm. I would wager that in the context of organisations, effective bottom-up resistance would require a certain decisive measure of collective resistance to be effective. But perhaps we should take care not to distinguish too sharply between the individual and the collective. Foucault's conceptualisation of agonal power relations itself implies a network of interconnected forces with no central agency or point of origination of power. If each node in the network of power relations is fundamentally connected to every other node, then every action and every counter-action will necessarily have a ripple effect. One might think of the image of massive spatial objects warping and curving the universe or space-time continuum, resulting in other objects that move on or orbit along those curves. It remains to be seen if the relation holds between individual resistance (as a trigger) and collective resistance (as a domino effect, perhaps), and how it might function in the context of the workplace. Suffice it to say here that Courpasson, Dany, and Clegg (2012) claim to have demonstrated that collective successful or productive resistance is within the capability of the workers, as opposed to change at the sole discretion of management. I also consider a number of other case studies that paint a bleaker picture, exposing the decisive power of management decisions, which prioritise profit regardless of the cost.

In chapter 6, then, I conclude this study by critically interrogating Courpasson, Dany, and Clegg's (2012) analyses by contextualising their argument in favour of the possibility of productive resistance in the workplace against the backdrop of the 'complex' mechanisms of control that operate in the kinds of contemporary neoliberal organisations in which knowledge workers find themselves, and which, I contend, make the success of any proposed method of resistance highly unlikely. Notwithstanding, this improbability is not sufficient cause to surrender to a complete fatalism, as we shall see.

Note

1. Gary S. Becker's *Human Capital: A Theoretical and Empirical Analysis with Specific Reference to Education* is a study of how investment in an individual's education and training is similar to business investments in equipment. Becker looks at the effects of investment in education on earnings and employment, and shows how his theory measures the incentive for such investment, as well as the costs and returns from secondary and tertiary education. Foucault would have referred to the original version, published in 1964. The third edition, published in 1993, and which I cite elsewhere in this book, includes four new chapters, covering recent ideas about human capital, fertility and economic growth, the division of labour, economic considerations within the family, and inequality in earnings.

CHAPTER TWO

Foucault's Analyses of Neoliberal Governmentality

Past Investigations and Present Applications[1]

The quintessential Foucauldian question animating this book throughout is what we are today, in relation to our present, understood as a globalising neoliberal governmentality in which life is reduced to constant work under conditions of strict control. This chapter seeks to elucidate to what extent Foucault's 1978–1979 analyses of governmentality and neoliberalism as a form of governmentality can justifiably be used to come to a critical understanding of present-day neoliberalism(s). I begin by explicating various interpretations of neoliberalism and then specify what I understand 'neoliberalism' to mean. I contextualise Foucault's analyses of neoliberal governmentality in terms of his general thinking of the late 1970s and early 1980s, and especially his insistence on the critical attitude as a virtue and his methodological specifications of philosophical-historical research. I contend that it is inherently justifiable and instructive to consider neoliberalism against this backdrop, and I return to his analyses of the mid-twentieth-century versions of German and American neoliberalisms to critique the neoliberalisms of the 1970s and 1980s—broadly understood—through the lens of governmentality. Such an approach draws its inspiration from—and I would aver, is licenced by—the fact that Foucault's own historiographical ventures were never undertaken primarily for the sake of excavating the past, but explicitly as a revisitation of the past for the sake of a critical understanding of the present. In this regard, Foucault said, concluding his lecture on January 24, 1979:

> I will start with the way in which the elements of this crisis of the apparatus of governmentality have been set out and formulated over the last thirty years and I will try to find in the history of the nineteenth century some of the elements which enable us to clarify the way in which the crisis of the apparatus of governmentality is currently experienced, lived, practiced, and formulated. (Foucault 2008, 70)

Neoliberalism: My Understanding of the Term

I want to set out by explaining what exactly I mean when I speak of neoliberalism. Far too often, the term is mobilised as a vague blanket descriptor of the economic present in the developed world, and in some parts of the developing world, which offers little or no critical purchase. Flew (2014, 49) is clearly aware of this vagueness when he describes the term as an 'oft-invoked but ill-defined' concept. In his article 'Six Theories of Neoliberalism', he taxonomises the uses of the term 'neoliberalism' into six groups:

> (1) an all-purpose denunciatory category; (2) 'the way things are'; (3) an institutional framework characterizing particular forms of national capitalism, most notably the Anglo-American ones; (4) a dominant ideology of global capitalism; (5) a form of governmentality and hegemony; and (6) a variant within the broad framework of liberalism as both theory and policy discourse. (Flew 2014, 49)

He argues that these sprawling definitions are not mutually compatible; moreover, he suggests that the recent status of neoliberalism as a variant of a dominant ideology or hegemony theories is not compatible with Foucault's (2008) uses of the term in his 1978–1979 lectures, *The Birth of Biopolitics* (Flew 2012). I diverge from Flew's contention, in that I note too much overlap in the last four definitions to be convinced that they offer an instructive taxonomy. Neoliberalism, in my reading, is a historical variant of liberalism and of the political development of capitalism that has been implemented on an increasingly global scale. This does indeed make neoliberalism a hegemonic politico-economic programme.

To be sure, at the time when Foucault undertook his analyses of the German and American neoliberalisms that he discusses, they were in their infancy, but he shows that what sets neoliberal governmentality apart from its liberal predecessor is its infiltration into spheres of human existence previously separate from political and economic rule. Admittedly, Foucault's lectures on neoliberalism may justifiably be interpreted as 'value-neutral', but I contend that they should be understood against the backdrop of his contemporaneous conceptualisation of the notion of 'critique', which, as I shall argue, offers a valid reason for using Foucault's analyses of neoliberalism as *governmentality* as a heuristic tool to critique contemporary neoliberal technologies in an incisive and instructive way. To put it differently, Foucault's analyses of specific incarnations of neoliberalisms in terms of *governmentality* uncover key structural elements of neoliberalism generally, which in turn unlocks the secret to neoliberalism's global 'success'—its voracious global implementation—as well as to how it operates to create a peculiar brand of subjectivity.

By way of introduction, let me first briefly specify what I understand under the term 'neoliberalism'. Classical liberalism is a political philosophy that propounds the maximisation of individual liberty while restricting the use of force to achieve this end. With neoliberalism, the emphasis shifts from a political philosophy to a political *programme*. Neoliberalism may be understood as the globalised and globalising political programme (cf. Slobodian 2018) that espouses economic liberalism or *laissez faire* economics as the only means of promoting economic development and securing political liberty. As the dominant mode of contemporary discourse and thought in the developed world—and increasingly including parts of the developing world, thanks to mobile technologies and the internet—neoliberalism has infiltrated our politics and our economy, and also our normalised, 'common sense' way of interpreting, understanding, and relating to the world. It encompasses every sphere of life—the private as well as the public.

Importantly, this global and globalising political programme should not be understood as *one* neoliberalism, with one definitive form and content that holds sway wherever it is implemented. Widely divergent incarnations, hybrid forms, and interpretations of neoliberalism are found across the globe. But as I have stressed, sweeping general definitions invariably prove vacuous and unenlightening. To be of any use, analyses need to be distinct and local studies, ones which are both context- and time-specific.[2] However, what may be said in general about neoliberalism—like its predecessor, liberalism—is that the central value that it propounds is *individual freedom*. A noble ideal indeed, and one which inspired both the American and French Revolutions. For the American revolutionaries, freedom was understood negatively (freedom *from*), as something that needed protection by laws, as posited by Locke (1690),[3] whereas for the French revolutionaries, freedom was a positive achievement (freedom *to*), the freedom of the people without the rule of the sovereign (Rousseau 1762a).[4] What, then, is 'new' about neoliberal freedom? Briefly revisiting the history of neoliberalism as recounted by David Harvey (2005) may prove instructive here.

Harvey (2005) suggests that it was in the name of our unquestionable right to freedom and against 'all its age-old foes'[5] that neoliberalism with its fervent defence of free markets rose to power in the 1970s and 1980s, the era of Thatcherism and Reaganomics. The restructuring of state forms and of international relations after World War II was designed to prevent a return to the catastrophic conditions that threatened the capitalist order in the Great Depression of the 1930s. However, by the end of the 1960s, post-war social consensus was breaking down, which led to a serious crisis of capital accumulation in the Global North, ushering in a global phase of 'stagflation' or the simultaneous and unchecked occurrence of inflation and economic stagnation that lasted throughout the 1970s. Neoliberalism seemed to offer a potential antidote (Harvey 2005). The renowned Austrian political philosopher and economist Friedrich von Hayek, along with an exclusive group of passionate advocates of a similar position—including the economists Milton Friedman and Ludwig von Mises—founded the Mont Pelerin Society in 1947. They depicted themselves as 'liberals' (in the traditional European sense) because of their fundamental commitment to the ideals of freedom. The *neo*liberal label signalled their adherence to the free market principles of neo-classical economics that emerged in the second half of the ninteenth century to displace the seminal theories of Adam Smith, David Ricardo, and Karl Marx. According to Hayek's seminal neoliberal text, *The Constitution of Liberty* (1960), it was a question of displacing an entrenched ideology—that of Marxism, socialism, state planning, and Keynesian state interventionism (which became prominent in the 1930s in response to the Great Depression and was named after John Maynard Keynes)—a battle that would take at least a generation to be won (Harvey 2005, 19–22).

So neoliberalism was a scientifically engineered solution proposed to address a global economic crisis. I want to frame this development in terms of an important rhetorical question Foucault asked in 1978 in his lecture 'What Is Critique?', presented at the same time as his governmentality lectures at the Collège de France: '[F]or what excesses of power, for what governmentalisation, all the more impossible to evade as it is reasonably justified, is *reason* not itself historically responsible?' (Foucault 1978, 37–38, my emphasis). Here Foucault reminds us that even that which is not irrational—what may even be supremely rational, devised by some of the most brilliant minds—may be, or may turn out to be, unreasonable. What is more, the very reason that such 'excesses of power' or 'governmentalization' become so pervasive, and indeed hegemonic, is that these excesses are 'reasonably justified'—as are so many measures to which we have grown accustomed since 9/11 and under the realities of COVID-19. As we shall see later, Harvey already makes this very point in 2005.

Even though neoliberal theory gained academic respectability by the awarding of the Nobel Prize in economics to Hayek in 1974 and to Friedman in 1976, it was not until the end of the 1970s that neoliberalism was consolidated as the new economic orthodoxy regulating public policy at the state level in the developed capitalist world (specifically in the United States and Britain) (Harvey 2005, 22). Since then, we have witnessed a decisive turn to neoliberalism in political-economic practices and thinking in the Global North. According to Harvey (2005, 3), almost all states, ranging from those rising from the ashes of the Soviet Union to entrenched old-style social democracies and welfare states such as New Zealand and Sweden, have succumbed—either voluntarily or in response to coercive pressures—to the neoliberalising trend. One can therefore indeed refer to neoliberalism as the *dominant* mode of contemporary discourse and thought, one which is not limited to politics and the economy, but also characteristic of our common sense (again read normalised) way of interpreting, understanding, and relating to the world, encompassing both the public and the private spheres of human existence. After the global economic crisis of 2007 and 2008, rather than a decline of neoliberalism, we have witnessed what might be termed its 'undeath', due to its remarkable transformative capacity, which defies a demise, as is evident in the post-crisis (re)configuration of neoliberal rationalities and practices of legitimisation (Price 2014).

To explain this normalisation, I would like to quote at length from Harvey's (2005, 5) explanation for the pervasive global implementation of various incarnations of neoliberalism:

> For any way of thought to become dominant, a conceptual apparatus has to be advanced that appeals to our intuitions and instincts, to our values and our desires, as well as to the possibilities inherent in the social world we inhabit. If successful, this conceptual apparatus becomes so embedded in common sense as to be taken for granted and not open to question. *The founding figures of neoliberal thought took political ideals of human dignity and individual freedom as fundamental, as 'the central values of civilization'*. In so doing they chose wisely, for these are indeed compelling and seductive ideals. These values, they held, were threatened not only by fascism, dictatorships, and communism, but by all forms of state intervention that substituted collective judgements for those of individuals free to choose. (my emphasis)

What does this freedom of choice amount to under neoliberalism? First and foremost, it reflects the conviction that individual freedom is guaranteed by *freedom of the market and of trade*. Classical liberals insisted on a strict division between the state and society, but neoliberals subordinate the state to the 'free' market. This market is 'free' because this is a curated freedom that requires intensive maintenance to secure its unfettered operation. This underlying reality subordinates the state to the market, because the state is charged with the responsibility of promoting and facilitating the market's unhindered functioning by way of legislative intervention. As we shall see, the predominance of the market, and the logic that informs it, becomes not merely a fact of life, but a *way* of life. We see that the freedoms attached to profitable capital accumulation—the fundamental goal of neoliberal regimes—reflect the interests of capital (private property owners, businesses, multinational corporations, and financial capital) considered to be the primary sources of wealth creation (Harvey 2005, 7). 'The interests of the community' are only represented indirectly by way of belief in the so-called trickle-down effect, a term I use very loosely here to refer to the conviction that the enrichment of the few will eventually filter down to improve the lives of the poorest of the poor too. While the wealth of the system may increase *in toto*, this line of reasoning does not in fact contain any inherent logic to make provision for how the concentration of wealth might be dispersed throughout the system. Consequently, as the total wealth increases, so does the disparity between rich and poor.

Secondly, neoliberalism sees *competition* as the defining characteristic of human relations. On the one hand, freedom from monopoly is the necessary condition for the possibility of competition. The triumph of one competitor rings the death knell of competition as such. Conversely, increased competition should, at least in theory, optimise market performance and hence contribute to increased freedom. Neoliberalism assumes citizens to be rational, self-responsible, entrepreneurial consumers competing fairly for financial security and success against all others. Their profitable entrepreneurial undertakings finance their consumption; their democratic choices are based on their rational weighing of cost-benefit options; and any failure to obtain and retain financial security is the sole responsibility of the citizens themselves on account of 'irrational' and hence imprudent decision-making. Any lack of profit generation, wealth accumulation, or distribution is thus attributed to the irresponsible actions of the citizens, organisations, and businesses themselves. Again, this line of reasoning in and of itself does not account for the fact that optimal profit generation depends on the wealth already accrued. As a result, there has never been a greater disparity between the rich and the poor in the history of humankind than under the neoliberal regime.[6]

In the service of freedom and competition, distinctive features of neoliberal policy include limited state intervention in the market (in other words, deregulation) except in the form of protection of the freedom of the market and the fostering of unbridled competition. The state is expected to minimise taxation and keep the cost of social provisions (the so-called social safety net) to a minimum. A neoliberal state privatises public services and limits the organisation of labour and collective bargaining of trade unions.

It should therefore be clear that my understanding of neoliberalism is modelled on Harvey's (2005) penetrating Marxist analyses,[7] which expose neoliberalisation as fundamentally an elite project concerned first and foremost with the (re)constitution of class power.[8] Harvey backs up this claim by pointing out the importunate rise in social inequality under neoliberalism, which he regards as structural to the entire project. I am very aware of the fact that Foucault dissociated himself from Marxism and do not intend to suggest that Foucault's lectures on neoliberalism can in any way be read as a Marxist critique of neoliberalism. Indeed, the neoliberalisms of the post-war German *Ordoliberal* School and of the 'Chicago School' that Foucault analysed in 1979 were clearly not the neoliberalism that Harvey explicated in 2005. As will become clear, however, Foucault's incisive analyses throw structural elements of neoliberal governmentality in general into relief in a way that reveals some of these elements still to be operating in present-day incarnations of neoliberalism, without falling into the trap of projecting an anachronistic critique of the neoliberalisms of the twenty-first century onto Foucault's 1979 lectures.

I have often referred to neoliberalism as a politico-economic programme, and that this is the peculiar form that present-day capitalism takes (cf. Hofmeyr 2011). This is arguably true, but one should be careful not merely to conflate neoliberalism and capitalism, as Jason Michael McCann (2016) points out. From its inception, capitalism has been a social and economic mode of living borne out of the Protestant work ethic and its associated belief in personal responsibility (cf. Weber 1905). It is premised on the conviction that people should to some extent be socially and economically free to pursue their own interests, which includes their commercial and financial interests. One might say that, at its best, it affords people the freedom to trade and accumulate wealth, subject to the wider restrictions of a state which safeguards society against the risks that come with capitalist ambition and greed.

Neoliberalism is the political development of capitalism. As we have seen, it is a political and economic ideology that seeks to maximise the freedom of the market by removing all barriers to the private accumulation of wealth. It therefore becomes a kind of power unto itself, not subject to state regulation, but rather a force that mobilises the state to further its primary objective of unmitigated profit accumulation, irrespective of the consequences. Neoliberalism is therefore not against regulation per se, but against regulation over which it has no control and which inhibits its objectives. As a socio-economic paradigm in its purest form, the ruling ethic of capitalism is prudence: it requires circumspection that results in the increase of wealth. The neoliberal pursuit of wealth is an end in itself and it leads to political power—it may be described as a politico-economic means of social control. McCann's (2016) distinction between capitalism and neoliberalism highlights a number of features of Michel Foucault's own analyses in 1978 to 1979 of neoliberalism as 'governmentality'.

Foucault's 1978–1979 Collège de France lecture course (published in English under the title *The Birth of Biopolitics* in 2008) provides a highly nuanced account of the evolution of liberal thought into neoliberalism. In these lectures, Foucault (2007) draws on the notion of 'governmentality' as a combination of the political rationalities of governing and techniques of governmental practice. He already introduced this notion in his earlier 1977–1978 lecture course (published in English as *Security, Territory, Population* in 2007). He identifies the rise of neoliberalism in terms of an intellectual reaction to Keynesian economics and the welfare state on the one hand, and the priority given to the market-enabling and market-conforming economic policies in Germany after World War II on the other. Such ideas, associated with the German *Ordoliberal* school of economists and historians, and authors such as Friedrich von Hayek, were relatively marginal for much of the 1940s and 1950s. However, they gained traction in the 1960s and 1970s. Of particular significance was the intellectual alliance formed with the work undertaken by the Chicago School of economists in the United States, who proposed a more thorough 'generalization of the economic form of the market . . . throughout the social body' (Foucault 2008, 243). Their key concepts, such as human capital theory, monetarism, and the public choice theory of government action, had gained significant international influence by the end of the 1970s (Flew 2014, 59). I will revisit aspects of Foucault's account of neoliberalism in detail; however, my main interest here is not to offer a full elucidation of his account (see Guala 2006; Gane 2008; Hindess 2009; Tribe 2009; Behrent 2009; Flew 2012), but to reassess to what extent Foucault's analyses of neoliberalism as *governmentality* may be used to engage contemporary neoliberalism critically.

The question of whether It is possible to do so has been the subject of heated debate among Foucault scholars over the last decade (see, for example, Dean 2018; Zamora 2014; Behrent 2009; Audier 2015a, 2015b).[9] Although there has been some mention of Foucault's 'neoliberal temptation'

(Zamora 2014; Dean and Zamora 2019), some of these scholars are careful to avoid a simplistic for or against stance—they prudently 'eschew the extremes of presentist and historicist reduction to which it [the debate] has been prone' (Specter 2015, 368). The concomitant presentist temptation would consist in developing a Foucauldian critique of contemporary neoliberalism out of his 1979 lectures, conflating or ignoring the differences between the context of 1979 and that of the (recent) present. In this regard, Wendy Brown (2003, 2014) has indeed drawn strongly on Foucault in her critique of neoliberalism, but she concludes that Foucault's assessment of neoliberalism in 1979 is of very limited usefulness for her purposes, which is to illuminate present-day critical democratic theory: 'Foucault's relative indifference to democracy and to capital constitutes the major limitation in his framework for my specific purposes' (Brown 2014, 50; also quoted in Specter 2015, 368).

To be clear, I do not argue that a Foucauldian critique of neoliberalism is impossible, but rather that the 1979 lectures avoid overt critique, and may in fact have been describing very different terrain, from a very different set of perspectives. The controversy around these lectures concern both Foucault's normative perspective and his methodology, which may be attributed precisely to the fact that here we are looking at public lectures, which were not systematic but rather experimental, exploratory, and provisional. What drew Foucault to his comparative study of German *Ordoliberalism*, American neoliberalism, and French neoliberalism was 'the essential epistemological transformation' of these neoliberal analyses, 'their claim to change what constituted in fact the object, or domain of objects, the general field of reference of economic analysis' (Foucault 2008, 222). He adds:

> In practice, economic analysis, from Adam Smith to the beginning of the twentieth century, broadly speaking takes as its object the study of mechanisms of production, the mechanisms of exchange, and the data of consumption within a given social structure, along with the interconnections between these three mechanisms. Now, for the neo-liberals, economic analysis should not consist in the study of these mechanisms, but in the nature and consequence of what they call *substitutable choices*, that is to say, the study and analysis of the way in which scarce means are allocated to competing ends. (Foucault 2008, 222, my emphasis)

I would argue that it is this epistemological shift in neoliberalism that captured Foucault's attention, which opens one of the most important fissures which would allow these lectures justifiably to be used toward a critical engagement with contemporary neoliberalism without simplistically reducing Foucault's own analyses to an overt rejection of neoliberalism *tout court*. The linchpin that holds together Foucault's analyses of neoliberalism in 1979 and the present incarnation(s) of neoliberalism is neoliberalism's object of economic analysis, which is labour or the 'strategic programming of individual's activity'. Foucault (2008, 222) explains that 'to bring labor into the field of economic analysis, we must put ourselves in the position of the person who works; we will have to study work as economic conduct practiced, implemented, rationalized, and calculated by the person who works'. In short, then, we need to ask this: 'What does working mean for the person who works?' (Foucault 2008, 223). It is beyond the scope of the present chapter to delve into this specific epistemological interest in any detail. Instead, in what follows, the focus is on ascertaining the status of Foucault's lectures on neoliberal governmentality *as a critical toolkit in the present* by contextualising them in terms of his thought in the late 1970s and early 1980s more generally, by revisiting some of his key lectures and his essays from this period. I begin by focusing on the meaning of 'governmentality' as a concept.

Governmentality: Three Senses of the Term

Foucault's work in the latter half of the 1970s and in the early 1980s displays a seemingly divergent two-pronged interest. From 1970 until his death in 1984, Foucault held the Chair of History of Systems of Thought at the Collège de France. While his lecture series at the Collège de France, as well as related articles and interviews at this time, investigated political rationalities and the 'genealogy of the state', his multivolume *Histoire de la sexualité* project, especially Volume II, *L'usage des plaisirs* (1984), and Volume III, *La souci de soi* (1984), displays a paradigm shift away from state-devised strategies of domination towards a 'genealogy of the subject'.

Key to the argument pursued here are the two series of public lectures presented during this time which I have already referred to: the lectures held in 1977 to 1978, collected in *Sécurité, territoire et population* (published in English in 2007) and in 1978 to 1979, collected in *La naissance de la biopolitique* (published in English in 2008). In his 1978 lectures, Foucault traces the genealogy of governmentality from Classical Greek and Roman days via early Christian pastoral guidance through to the notion of state reason and the science of the police.[10] In the 1979 lectures, he focused on the study of liberal and neoliberal forms of government, concentrating in particular on two forms of neoliberalism: German post-war liberalism (*Ordoliberalism* or the Freiburg School), and the liberalism of the Chicago School, which takes neoliberalism a step further, and gives it a more radical form. In these lectures, Foucault deploys the concept of government or 'governmentality' as a guideline for the analysis he offers by way of historical reconstructions embracing a timespan starting from Ancient Greece and following through the topic to modern neoliberalism. In these lectures one finds the key to bridging the gap between the state and the subject:[11] what connects the constitution of the subject and the formation of the state is the problem of government. In an oft-quoted passage from a 1980 Dartmouth lecture, published in 1993, Foucault explains it as follows:

> [I]f one wants to analyze the genealogy of the subject in Western civilization, he has to take into account not only techniques of domination but also techniques of the self. . . . He has to take into account the points where the technologies of domination of individuals over one another have recourse to processes by which the individual acts upon himself. And conversely, he has to take into account the points where the techniques of the self are integrated into structures of coercion and domination. The contact point, where the individuals are driven by others is tied to the way they conduct themselves, is what we can call . . . government. (Foucault 1993, 203–04)

Foucault therefore associates the formation of the state with technologies of domination on the one hand, and the constitution of the subject with technologies of the self on the other.[12] He defines technologies of domination as those practices that determine the conduct of individuals and submit individual conduct to certain ends. Technologies of the self, on the other hand, permit individuals to effect by their own means or with the help of others a certain number of operations on themselves so as to transform themselves. However, he qualifies this binary association by stressing that even technologies of the self are associated with a certain type of domination (Foucault 1982a, 18). The individual, according to Foucault, would be the product of the power imposed and internalised, *as well as* the potential embodiment of resistance. Thus he in part opposes the state to the individual and describes the point of contact between the technologies of domination of others [the state] and those of the self as 'governmentality' (Foucault 1982a, 18–19). Foucault's genealogy of governmentality uncovers, then, the fact that the state and the self do not, in fact, constitute two opposing forces—of domination, on the state's side, and (relative) freedom from domination, on the self side. Rather, the emergence of the apparently 'autonomous' individual and the 'sovereign' state are intricately linked as twin projects extending along the same axis.

The analytical perspective of 'governmentality' does not represent a break in Foucault's work in respect of his earlier analysis of power, but covers a specific type of power, which he terms 'biopower'. This power, as we shall see, is the state's power over life or the practice of modern states and their regulation of their subjects through 'an explosion of numerous and diverse techniques for achieving the subjugations of bodies and the control of populations' (Foucault 1976, 140). Hence, the focus on governmentality enables him 'to tackle the problem of the state and population' in his lecture on February 8, 1978 (Foucault 2007, 116). In his efforts to get to the very heart of the nature of power, Foucault always endeavoured to

> free relations of power from the institution [the army, hospital, school, prison, etc.], in order to analyze them from the point of view of technologies; to distinguish them also from the function, so as to take them up within a strategic analysis; and to detach them from the privilege of the object, so as to resituate them within the perspective of the constitution of fields, domains, and objects of knowledge. (Foucault 2007, 118)

The point, for Foucault, is to uncover the specific technology of power—the 'governmentality'—that operates through the state, because he argues that 'these general technologies of power, [which he has] attempted to reconstruct by moving outside of the institution', and indeed beyond its function as an object, 'ultimately fall under the global, totalising institution that is, precisely, the state' (Foucault 2007, 118). Do we not find beyond the hospital, the prison, the family, the army, etc., yet another institution—an all-encompassing, totalising institution, namely the state? He asks:

> Is it possible to move outside? Is it possible to place the modern state in a general technology of power that assured its mutations, development, and functioning? Can we talk of something like a 'governmentality' that would be to the state what techniques of segregation were to psychiatry, what techniques of discipline were to the penal system, and what biopolitics was to medical institutions? These are the kinds of questions that are at stake [in these lectures]. (Foucault 2007, 120)

Apart from serving as the connective thread linking the constitution of the subject and the formation of the state, the second sense in which the notion of governmentality needs to be understood is etymologically and historically, which enables one to grasp fully its innovative potential for understanding the workings of contemporary neoliberal power. First, the semantic linking of governing (*gouverner*) and modes of thought (*mentalité*) in govern-mentality points to the fact that it is not possible to study the technologies of power without an analysis of the political rationality underpinning them.[13] The concept of governmentality therefore embodies Foucault's belief in the reciprocal constitution of power techniques and forms of knowledge. This implies that governmentality is double-sided: on the one hand, the knowledge side consists in representation, and on the other, the power side entails intervention. Representation refers to a specific discursive field defined by government, which does not simply 'represent' the governing reality in the form of a pure, neutral knowledge, but 'rationalizes' the exercise of power (a pragmatics of guidance). The form in which a problem is represented determines its perception, strategy, and solution. Representation, therefore, structures specific forms of intervention, the power side of government. Political rationality interprets and processes reality in a way that already predetermines the way in which it will be tackled by political technologies (Lemke 2001, 191).

The third sense in which governmentality needs to be understood relates to the fact that Foucault explicitly harks back to the older and more comprehensive meaning of the term, which emphasises the close connection between forms of power and processes of subjectification. Foucault's analyses testify to the fact that up to and well into the eighteenth century the problem of government extended far beyond the political sphere and was conceived as a philosophical, religious, medical, and pedagogical issue. 'Government' did not refer only to management by the state or the administration, but also included managing the self, directing the soul, the family, children, the household, and the community, as he points out in his lecture of February 1, 1978 (Foucault 2007, 93): 'It did not only cover the legitimately constituted forms of political or economic subjection, but also modes of action, more or less considered and calculated, which were destined to act upon the possibilities of action of other people. To govern, in this sense, is to structure the possible field of action of others' (Foucault 1982b, 220–21). Foucault consequently defines government as conduct or 'the conduct of conduct'. To 'conduct', depending on whether one places the stress on the first or second syllable, means both to 'lead' others, which entails mechanisms of coercion, and a way of behaving or conducting oneself within a more or less open field of possibilities. 'The exercise of power consists in guiding the possibility of conduct and putting in order the possible outcome' (Foucault 1982b, 220–21). Crucial in this context, then, is the fact that Foucault endeavours to show in his history of governmentality how the modern autonomous individual and the modern sovereign state co-determine each other's emergence (Lemke 2000, 2–3; 2001, 191). Lemke rightly contends that the concept of governmentality plays a decisive role in Foucault's analytics of power, which Lemke (2000, 3) sums up as follows: '[I]t offers a view on power beyond a perspective that centers either on consensus or on violence; it links technologies of the self with technologies of domination, the constitution of the subject to the formation of the state; finally, it helps to differentiate between power and domination'.

From the foregoing discussion, the critical purchase of conceiving of neoliberalism *as* a form of governmentality appears evident, yet the concerns around the normative status and methodology of Foucault's neoliberal governmentality lectures still need to be addressed.

Foucault's Lectures Contextualised: His Contemporaneous Conceptualisation of Critique

In the first part of his 1978 lecture presented to the French Society of Philosophy, Foucault defines critique as 'an instrument, a means for a future or a truth that it will not know nor happen to be; it oversees a domain it would want to police and is unable to regulate' (Foucault 1978, 25). This definition suggests that critique is a means to an end. However, this end is a future or a truth that remains beyond the grasp of the critique itself, since it is unable to regulate the domain it oversees. It suggests that critique is inherently a responsibility vis-à-vis the future that exceeds the powers of the critique itself. Foucault explains that this means that critique is a function that is subordinated to whatever philosophy, science, politics, ethics, law, literature, etc., positively constitute. For him, the critical attitude is a *virtue* supported by some general *imperative*. Foucault specifically brings this conceptualisation of critique to bear on a historical reconstruction of the art of governing people, starting from the Christian pastoral to the veritably exponential growth of this art in the fifteenth century along a dual trajectory: beyond the religious sphere, expanding into civil society, on the one hand, and a proliferation into a variety of areas, such as how to govern one's mind and body, children, the poor and beggars, a family, armies, cities, and states, on the other (Foucault 1978, 25–26). We are here reminded of the wide scope of activities and areas that 'government' referred to in the fifteenth and sixteenth centuries—precisely the encompassing sense that Foucault draws on in theorising 'governmentality'.

He contends that this 'governmentalization' cannot be dissociated from the question of 'how *not* to be governed' (Foucault 1978, 25–26, my emphasis). Let me clarify that this does not imply that the critical attitude implies a wholesale rejection of governmental rule—in other words, that one does not want to be governed *at all*. Rather, it is to be understood as a perpetual question of 'how not to be governed *like that*, by that, in the name of those principles, with such and such an objective in mind and by means of such procedures, not like that, not for that, not by them' (Foucault 1978, 28).

What Foucault does here is to postulate a necessary partnership between the movement of governmentalisation of both society and individuals and the critical attitude. This alliance entails distrusting and defying the various regimes of governmentalisation that are brought to bear on society and on individuals so as to *develop* the arts of governing. The critical attitude as a way of thinking with a cultural, political, and moral dimension, is 'the art of not being governed like that and at that cost' (Foucault 1978, 29).

Foucault goes on to flesh out this fluid or general definition more precisely. Critique is a legal issue: it means 'putting forth universal and indefeasible rights to which every government . . . will have to submit' (Foucault 1978, 30).[14] Critique is a necessary and certain confrontation of authority: it means not accepting as true 'what an authority tells you is true, or at least not accepting it because an authority tells you that it is true, but rather accepting it only if one considers valid the reasons for doing so' (Foucault 1978, 31). This brings us to the oft-quoted core of this lecture, which is instrumental to the argument that I pursue here. At its core, critique requires a bundle of connected relationships between power, truth, and the subject. Foucault explains:

> And if governmentalization is indeed this movement through which individuals are subjugated in the reality of a social practice through mechanisms of power that adhere to a truth, well, then! I will say that critique is the movement by which the subject gives himself the right to question truth on its effects of power and question power on its discourses of truth. Well, then!: critique will be *the art of voluntary insubordination, that of reflected intractability*. Critique will ensure *the desubjugation of the subject* in the context of what we could call . . . the *politics of truth*. (Foucault 1978, 32, my emphasis)

Here Foucault explicitly echoes Kant's call for courage, *sapere aude!*, to dare to use one's reason without anyone else's direction. In his 1784 essay, 'What is Aufklärung?', Kant contends that it is precisely this 'direction' or exercise of authority that maintains humanity's incapacity to use its own understanding, and humanity's lack of decision, its dependence and subordination. For Kant, as we know, critique meant interrogating the limits of what we can know. Critique is then the reflective examination of the validity and limits of human rational capacity. Enlightenment or autonomy—in the original Greek sense of not involuntarily subordinating oneself to externally imposed laws, but of giving laws or rules to oneself—is located at the point where one has obtained an adequate idea of one's own knowledge and its limits. Only there can obedience be founded on autonomy itself (Foucault 1978, 34–36).

The critical attitude as virtue and imperative therefore conjoins the subject of governmentality and the necessary technologies of power and rationalities of 'truth' that it entails in a conflictual relationship that requires immense courage, but serves as a necessary condition of the possibility of liberty or desubjugation. Foucault's 1978–1979 lectures on governmentality and specifically on neoliberal governmentality were a critical interrogation of the limits of this historically peculiar rationality as a politics of truth, and its subjectification effects. In view of this conjoining, the debate around the status of these lectures—whether they can be read as for or as against neoliberalism—is founded on a false dichotomy. For Foucault, this new form of power/knowledge, neoliberal governmentality, had to be *critically* interrogated, not to establish whether it is to be embraced or rejected, but to ascertain the limits of the politics of truth it is proposing, and its effects of subject formation. Like all these critical analyses, the lectures were open-ended, not complete and definitive, but rather an opening up of an ongoing line of investigation into the contingent episodic outcomes of the relentless will to power. I will return to this shortly. The critical spirit of Foucault's philosophical work—be it his less systematic lectures, or his more methodical published works—offers an indictment of complacency, since as he warns that, even if power is not necessarily bad, it is dangerous. Those scholars who seek to mobilise Foucault's lectures to defend neoliberalism, or at least to interpret them as an embarrassing lapse of judgment in which Foucault was 'tempted' by neoliberalism,[15] risk attempting to interject into the letter of Foucault's word something that flies in the face of the spirit of the critical attitude that he advocates. The spirit of the critical attitude is non-negotiable when it comes to any undertaking that is either archaeological or genealogical in nature, or a 'problematization' of the techniques of the self—a contention on which probably most Foucault scholars would be able to agree.

This brings us to the second contentious issue at the forefront of the debate about the status of Foucault's lectures—their supposed atypical methodology. Some scholars claim that the method Foucault employs is neither archaeological nor genealogical; they also do not see it as a problematisation.[16] Rather, his method appears to be an elusive hybrid of all these 'modes' found in Foucault's histories (Specter 2015, 369). This 'uncategorizability', I surmise, is taken to signify that these particular lectures are somehow anomalous. Hence, it is implied, their insights cannot be considered unambiguous, which further implies that they cannot be put to any critical use unproblematically. I find these concerns puzzling, to say the least, given that Foucault is known for changing his mind, for changing the methods he employed, and for eschewing any label that neatly categorised his thought and confined it to specific allegiances or approaches. That said, such methodological concerns have been raised by distinguished scholars who have devoted themselves to studying Foucault's work, so it would be remiss of me merely to dismiss them. In response to these concerns, then, and in an attempt to allay some of these concerns, I want to consider how Foucault conceived of 'historical-philosophical' research.

Foucault's methodological ruminations are scattered throughout his books, essays, and interviews, but I want to focus on two particular sources. The first is the third part of the lecture 'What Is Critique?' (Foucault 1978, 48–61), in which Foucault specifically addresses the methodological issue of how to conduct historical-philosophical research. The other is the Nietzschean roots of Foucault's approach, which are most succinctly indicated in his 1971 essay 'Nietzsche, Genealogy, History', in which he explicitly draws on Nietzsche's understanding of historical meaning. What interests Foucault is the sense in which Nietzsche opposes *wirkliche Historie* to traditional history: 'The former transposes the relationship ordinarily established between the eruption of an event and necessary continuity. An entire historical tradition (theological and rationalistic) aims at dissolving the singular event into an ideal continuity—as a teleological movement or a natural process' (Foucault 1971, 88).

Wirkliche Historie, then, is an historical tracing that 'deals with *events* in terms of their most unique characteristics, and their most acute manifestations' (Foucault 1971, 88, my emphasis). Moreover, an event is

> the reversal of a relationship of forces, the usurpation of power, the appropriation of a vocabulary turned against those who had once used it, a feeble domination that poisons itself as it grows lax, the entry of a masked 'other'. The forces operating in history are not controlled by destiny or regulative mechanisms, but respond to haphazard conflicts. (Foucault 1971, 88)

An event is therefore a fundamental disruption of the status quo, a re-ordering of the playing field following the irruption of a foreign force.

In section 12 of Nietzsche's second essay in *On the Genealogy of Morals*, 'Guilt, Bad Conscience and Related Matters' (1887), he emphatically dismisses the traditional conflation of origin and purpose, as if the reason for the appearance or emergence of something can be accounted for by the purpose it serves:

> [W]hat causes a particular thing to arise and the final utility of that thing, its actual use and arrangement in a system of purposes, are separate *toto coelo [by all the heavens, i.e. absolutely]*, that something existing, which has somehow come to its present state, will again and again be interpreted by the higher powers over it from a new perspective, appropriated in a new way, reorganized for and redirected to new uses. (Nietzsche 1887, 15–16)

For Nietzsche, all events involve 'overpowering, acquiring mastery' which in turn involve a 're-interpretation, a readjustment' in which the 'sense' and 'purpose' up to then must necessarily be obscured or entirely erased. Here Nietzsche maintains that the usefulness of any organ, for example, an institution, custom, or practice, tells us nothing about its origin. This contention flies in the face of the age-old belief that something's use-value explains its reason for coming onto existence. On the contrary, Nietzsche insists, all purposes or uses are only signs or symptoms that something more powerful has mastered something less powerful and has branded it with its own meaning applied to some function. This implies that the entire history of something is in reality 'a continuing chain of signs of constantly new interpretations and adjustments, whose causes need to be connected to each other' (Nietzsche 1887, 16). The so-called grand scheme of things is nothing but the chronicle of a will to power that animates human action, which translates into the play of power, the victory of the most powerful and retrospective sense-making, despite the contingent circumstances that form the stages of their making. 'Development', then, has nothing to do with progress toward a single goal, 'even less is it the logical and shortest progress reached with the least expenditure of power and resources' (Nietzsche 1887, 16)—which is plain in a mere retrospective glance at the history of humankind. About one quarter into the twenty-first century, in a time of a debilitating global pandemic, in the face of ongoing wars and conflicts, ecological disaster and imminent nuclear Armageddon, with countless children succumbing daily to starvation, the idea of so-called development, reason, and progress following in the wake of the Enlightenment seems like a bad joke, to say the least.[17] Nietzsche offers no reassurances. In 1887, he saw the play of power with uncanny clarity: what accounts for the status quo is

> the sequence of more or less profound, more or less mutually independent processes of overpowering . . . together with the resistance which arises against that overpowering each time, the transformations of form which have been attempted for the purpose of defence and reaction, the results of successful countermeasures. Form is fluid—the 'meaning', however, is even more so. (Nietzsche 1887, 16)

Nietzsche takes it even further into a direction that few of us are inclined to follow: for him, 'the partial loss of utility, decline, and degeneration, the loss of meaning, and purposelessness, in short, death, belong to the conditions of a real progress' (Nietzsche 1887, 16). He contends that '[t]he size of a "step forward" can even be estimated by a measure of everything that had to be sacrificed to it' (Nietzsche 1887, 16–17). For him, the crux of historical methodology, its object of study, which determines its very rationale and methodological logic, is 'a will to power playing itself out in everything that happens' (Nietzsche 1887, 17). It is the 'spontaneous, aggressive, over-reaching, re-interpreting, re-directing, and shaping powers, after whose effects that 'adaptation' [the supposedly purposeful inner adaptation to external circumstances] first follows' (Nietzsche 1887, 17).

We can now better understand Nietzsche's notion of *wirkliche Historie*, which Foucault deals with at some length in his 1971 essay, and defines—echoing Nietzsche—as the tracing of 'the reversal of a relationship of forces, the usurpation of power, the appropriation of a vocabulary turned against those who had once used it' (Foucault 1971, 88).

To come to grips fully with the methodology of historical-philosophical research, we have to venture even further down the path of Nietzschean reasoning. Some years prior to the work discussed earlier, in his second essay in the *Untimely Meditations*, 'The Uses and Disadvantages of History for Life' (1874), Nietzsche already distinguishes between *Historie* and *Geschichte*. This important distinction sheds further light on the object of study of genealogy. *Historie* may be defined as the academic discipline, history, or history as record, whereas *Geschichte* concerns history as *event*. If we grasp the meaning and implications of history as event, we can understand better why in this essay Nietzsche called for a certain forgetfulness of history. Nietzsche was certainly not disavowing the fundamental historicity of human existence (its *Geschichte*). Instead, he was questioning the value of an overly inflated historical sense of life, because of the potentially stultifying effect of such an inflation. If history is a chronicle of arbitrary events resulting from merciless power plays in which the winner momentarily usurps power and reinvents the story of her/his victory to legitimise it and turn it into an honourable and rightful outcome, if history is not animated by a grand scheme that turns the slain into martyrs and heroes, then too much history does not serve life, but guts it of rhyme and reason—the very rhyme and reason that humankind *needs* to survive in the face of non-sensical adversity.

This is the backstory to the seemingly uncharacteristic methodology of Foucault's governmentality lectures. The third section of his 1978 lecture 'What Is Critique?' is specifically focused on the precise nature and procedure of historical-philosophical research. He asks 'under what conditions, at the cost of which modifications or generalizations we can apply . . . the question of the relationships between power, truth and the subject . . . to any moment in history' (Foucault 1978, 47). This method of research would proceed as something that Foucault calls 'an examination of '*eventualiza-*

tion' (événementialisation)' (Foucault 1978, 49). Foucault explains what he means by this 'horrible word' by detailing his now well-known insistence on the imbrication of power and knowledge. But he is careful to qualify what he means by the term in very precise and nuanced terms:

> Hence, the use of the word knowledge (*savoir*) that refers to all procedures and all effects of knowledge (*connaissance*) which are acceptable at a given point in time and in a specific domain; and secondly, the term power (*pouvoir*) which merely covers a whole series of particular mechanisms, definable and defined, which seems likely to induce behaviors or discourse. (Foucault 1978, 51)

He is adamant that for him these two terms only have a *methodological function*. They therefore do not identify some general principle or feature of reality that can be used to legitimise a certain course of action, response, or decision. Rather, methodologically, they function to lay bare those elements or aspects that are pertinent to the analysis at hand. In other words, they function as symptomatic signs, indicators, or fissures—instances of many different entwined incarnations of power/knowledge, as opposed to *one* power and *one* knowledge—where analytical digging is needed, where such digging is bound to unearth some incisive insight into the matter under investigation. Hence, Foucault says this level of excavation may be called approximately the *archaeological* level (Foucault 1978, 53).

Furthermore, it becomes clear that the object of analysis—neoliberal governmentality in this case—is 'not made acceptable by any existing right' (Foucault 1978, 54), irrespective of the habits or routines that have made it familiar to us and have normalised it, irrespective of the forceful workings of power mechanisms or any justifications employed to make it appear natural or legitimate. To understand what could have made such an object of analysis acceptable, one must recognise that it is not in fact at all obvious; we must concede 'its arbitrary nature in terms of knowledge, its violence in terms of power, in short, its energy' (Foucault 1978, 54). What one is dealing with, then, is not a pure form, essence, or foundation, but a 'pure singularity', unique and absolutely arbitrary in its historical emergence. Foucault stresses that '[t]his is without doubt, one of the most important and debatable aspects of this historical-philosophical approach' (Foucault 1978, 55).

By its very nature, a singularity cannot be explained by a unitary, authoritative causal origin that accounts for its unavoidable emergence. The explication of causality in the case of a singularity is much more complex: it has to result from multiple and heterogeneous relationalities. This is where the *genealogical* aspect comes in, in the sense of genealogy as 'something that attempts to restore the conditions for the appearance of a singularity born out of multiple determining elements of which it is not the product, but rather the effect' (Foucault 1978, 57). In other words, a singularity is not the result of a process or action designed with its outcome in mind, but rather it arises as an effect—it is an inadvertent and/or contingent outcome that is more than the sum of its parts, which in some instances unwittingly contribute to a certain effect. Moreover, a singularity is not so much an effect, as it is *effective* (as in *wirklich*), that is, it is still in force and therefore open-ended. The contributing or participating relationships are, at least partly, interactions between individuals and groups involving types of behaviour, decisions, choices, motives, and impulses. By virtue of being *human* interactions, they imply 'always variable margins of non-certainty' (Foucault 1978, 58).

A particularly illuminating aspect of the governmentality lectures is that Foucault dissects the ingenious neoliberal insight that profit, as the outcome of the maximisation of capital, 'a source of future income' (Foucault 2008, 224), is in fact the result of all those 'physical and psychological factors which make someone able to earn this or that wage'. This implies that human labour is not the abstract product of labour power and the time during which it is used, as if such power were an invariable measurable constant that is merely used or not used. Instead, as we know, human capital is contingent on a large variety of factors—not only acquired skills and natural aptitudes, but also complex psychological, emotional, and physical factors that either contribute to, or detract from, the productive output generated by this particular form of labour power, which has a limited lifespan. The pioneers of neoliberalism realised that, to maximise the efficacy and hence the productivity of this labour lifespan, if there is innovation (if new things and forms of productivity are discovered and technological innovations are made), then 'this is nothing other than the income of a certain capital, of human capital,[18] that is to say, of the set of investments we have made at the level of man himself' (Foucault 2008, 231). Foucault's caveat explains the danger that is inscribed in this 'ingenious' neoliberal insight: it implies that every aspect of being human, from the cradle to the grave, is inscribed in, and therefore subjugated to, the neoliberal project of maximising profit—either as a contributing or as a detracting factor.

Now let us return to Foucault's clarification of his historical-philosophical methodology in his 1978 lecture on how to proceed with an examination of 'eventualization'. To account for the 'perpetual mobility, essential fragility or . . . complex interplay between what replicates the same process and what transforms it', he adds a third methodological dimension to archaeology and genealogy. He calls this dimension *strategics* (Foucault 1978, 58). These three dimensions do not represent three successive levels, each derived from the previous one(s), but rather three necessarily contemporaneous dimensions in the same analysis. By simultaneously tracing the conditions of possibility of power/knowledge relations *and* conducting a series of analyses in the form of a strategics, one is able to capture a glimpse of the singularity as an effect of these relationships that are in perpetual slippage vis-à-vis one another. Importantly, Foucault stresses that one has to think about it in such a way that one can see how it is associated with a domain of possibility, but also, and consequently, with reversibility (Foucault 1978, 59–60). The point of this historical-philosophical research would be to ascertain how the indivisibility of knowledge and power, which are caught up in multiple strategic interactions, result in singularities that are simultaneously fixed *and* fragile, and that turn these effects into events. The ephemeral fissure between fixity and fragility that risks destabilising that which appears to be the hard and fast 'way things are' begins with the *decision not to be governed* (Foucault 1978, 60).

From these programmatic reflections on historical-philosophical methodology, voiced in the same period as his governmentality lectures, we can deduce at least two relatively indisputable conclusions for the purposes of the argument that I pursue here. To begin with, despite the claims of a number of Foucault scholars debating the status of these lectures to the contrary, the methodology applied in these lectures is not at odds with the greater scheme of Foucault's *modus operandi.* This is clear if his entire oeuvre is taken into account: in these lectures we can recognise the very same methodological approach that typifies his way of working and thinking in his books, his lectures, and his essays of the late 1970s and early 1980s. Here, too, we see the move from knowledge to a reconceived notion of power that cannot be reduced to domination, but that is inherently annexed to knowledge, and deployed in networks of strategic relationalities, which reveal the potential reversibility of that which seems immutable. To support this first conclusion, I need only briefly remind you of the famous passage from Foucault's essay 'The Subject and Power':

> One can therefore interpret the mechanisms brought into play in power relations in terms of strategies. But most important is obviously the relationship between power relations and confrontation strategies. For, if it is true that at the heart of power relations and as a permanent condition of their existence there is an insubordination and a certain essential obstinacy on the part of the principles of freedom, then there is no relationship of power without the means of escape or possible flight. Every power relationship implies, at least *in potentia*, a strategy of struggle, in which the two forces are not superimposed,

> do not lose their specific nature, or do not finally become confused. Each constitutes for the other a kind of permanent limit, a point of possible reversal. (Foucault 1982b, 225)

The second conclusion that can be drawn from Foucault's reflections on historical-philosophical research is that his investigations were never simply a wholesale dismissal nor a full embrace of any particular regime, be it certain discursive formations, institutions, or a form of the art of government. We find instead painstaking historiographical tracings of mutually responsive power/knowledge relations that resulted in unforeseen eventualisations. The threefold approach—archaeological-genealogical-strategics—exposes the conditions of possibility of the fixity, but also the fragility, of a particular constellation. Like all the objects that caught his interest, neoliberalism intrigued Foucault. But we would miss the point entirely if we mistook this 'intrigue', as Zamora and Behrent (2016) refer to Foucault's fascination with neoliberalism, for some kind of 'temptation', 'defence of', 'apology for', 'flirt[ation] with', or 'an embrace of' neoliberalism (Zamora and Behrent 2016).

I am well aware that this argument can equally be mobilised to contend that Foucault's analyses cannot justifiably be used to critique neoliberalism in its twenty-first-century manifestation. If he was neither for nor against neoliberalism, then his analyses of neoliberal governmentality also cannot be mobilised against it. While these analyses are indeed value-neutral, Foucault contends that 'the critical attitude appears as a specific attitude in the Western world starting with what was historically [he believes], the great process of society's governmentalization' (Foucault 1978, 34). In an attempt to desubjugate the subject in the context of power and truth, Foucault unequivocally made a plea—following Kant—for us to have the courage to use our own reason without the direction of another's tutelage. If 'governmentalization is indeed this movement through which individuals are subjugated in the reality of a social practice through mechanisms of power that adhere to a truth', then 'critique is the movement by which the subject gives himself the right to question truth on its effects of power and question power on its discourses of truth' (Foucault 1978, 32). Governmentalisation then, as I pointed out earlier, cannot be dissociated from the question of 'how not to be governed *like that*, by that, in the name of those principles, with such and such an objective in mind and by means of such procedures, not like that, not for that, not by them' (Foucault 1978, 28). The *letter* of the neoliberal governmentality lectures might be value-neutral, but they throw certain fissures into relief, exposing the fragility of the apparently immutable state of things. In other words, they arm critics with the means to undertake a critique and to adopt the critical attitude itself. Thus the *spirit* animating the lectures not only gives his audience a licence to question and resist a governmental regime when the liberty of the subject is at stake—indeed, the lectures incite their audience to question and resist.

In the final instance, the importance I accord to the critical attitude as a virtue and methodological tool for Foucault may by buttressed by revisiting his lecture of March 7, 1979 (Foucault 2008, 185–214), looking specifically at the two reasons he offers for 'dwelling on these problems of neo-liberalism', referring to the German version, *Ordoliberalismus* between 1930 to 1950.

First, he clarifies his 'methodological reason', and then the 'reason of critical morality' (Foucault 2008, 186). Methodologically, he explains, he has dwelt so long on this problem of German neoliberalism because he wanted to see 'what concrete content could be given to the analysis of relations of power', in other words, to the 'domain of relations' that he calls 'governmentality'. He wanted to investigate whether and how 'this grid of governmentality' or 'analysis of micro-power', which is assumed to be 'valid for the analysis of ways of conducting the conduct of mad people, patients, delinquents, and children, may be equally valid when we are dealing with phenomena of a completely different scale, such as economic policy, for example, or the management of a whole social body' (Foucault 2008, 186). He concludes that 'the analysis of micro-power is not a question of scale, and it is not a question of a sector, it is a question of a point of view' (Foucault 2008, 186).

His second reason for dwelling on the topic is that of 'critical morality'. Here he tries to come to grips with the reasons informing the 'state phobia' at the time. He argues that the state phobia was based on two assumptions that mutually support each other: first, 'that the state has an unlimited force of expansion in relation to its object-target, the civil society, and second, that forms of state give rise to each other on the basis of a specific dynamism of the state'—these seem to him to 'form a kind of critical commonplace frequently found today' (Foucault 2008, 187). These two assumptions 'put into circulation' what he calls 'an inflationary critical value' (Foucault 2008, 187). He offers four reasons for this contention. First, these assumptions are inflationary because

> [they] encourage[ ] the growth, at a constantly accelerating speed, of the interchangeability of analyses. As soon as we accept the existence of this continuity or genetic kinship between different forms of state, and as soon as we attribute a constant evolutionary dynamism to the state, it then becomes possible not only to use different analyses to support each other, but also to refer them back to each other and so *deprive them of their specificity*. (Foucault 2008, 187, my emphasis)

The second reason these assumptions are inflationary, he argues, is that they enable 'a general disqualification by the worst': irrespective of the state's real functioning, its relative scope or whether it is better or worse, by virtue of the state's supposed intrinsic dynamic 'the less can always be disqualified by the more, the better by the worst' (Foucault 2008, 188). The third inflationary mechanism is the fact that these assumptions do away with the need to analyse the actual reality pertaining to a particular state governmentality, because whatever one's grasp of it is or the 'profile of actuality reality presents', an overriding prejudicial suspicion predominates that enables 'one to find something like the fantastical profile of the state' in any actual existing state of affairs. Finally, these assumptions are inflationary inasmuch as they do 'not carry out a criticism or analysis itself'. In other words, he explains, 'it does not seek to know the real source of this kind of anti-state suspicion, this state phobia' (Foucault 2008, 188).[19]

Conclusion: Governmentality as Critique of Neoliberalism

Given the value-neutral stance of Foucault's lectures on neoliberal governmentality and their contested status among Foucault scholars concerned about their 'atypical' methodology, can these lectures justifiably be used to interrogate present-day neoliberal governmentalities critically? Moreover, what is the added value of critically interrogating neoliberalisms *as forms of governmentality* compared to using other forms of critique of neoliberalism?

Critiques of neoliberalism abound—they may be schematically divided into three main lines of argument, according to Lemke (2000). The first is that neoliberalism as an ideology which offers a distorted picture of society and the economy as needing an emancipatory corrective that is scientifically founded. The second is that neoliberalism is an economic-political reality, in other words, the extension of the economy into the domain of politics, the usurpation of the state by capitalism, the globalisation that escapes the political regulations of the nation-state. The third is that neoliberalism is a form of 'practical anti-humanism', wreaking havoc in the lives of individuals, promoting a devaluation of traditional experiences, inciting processes of individualisation that endanger collective bonds, threatening family values and personal affiliations through the imperatives of flexibility, mobility, and risk-taking (Lemke 2000, 6).

These lines of critique certainly hold true and expose important effects of neoliberalism, but analysing neoliberalism as a form of governmentality can augment these arguments in crucial ways. These three lines of critique risk merely relying on the conceptual dualisms that they intend to criticise (knowledge and power; state and economy; subject and power). However, if neoliberalism is understood from the critical vantage point of governmentality, it becomes clear that neoliberalism couples various forms of knowledge, strategies of power, and technologies of the self. This revelation facilitates a more thorough insight into current political and social rearrangements, since it pierces the extensive status of processes of domination and exploitation (Lemke 2000, 7).

The tenor of these lectures by Foucault (2007, 2008) may be considered value-neutral, but Foucault's interest was certainly piqued; he appears to have been keenly and critically intrigued with how self-induced crises fuel creative problem-solving transmutations. Importantly, Foucault's fascination is imbued throughout with his critical attitude, alert to the fact that while the omnipresent workings of power relations are not necessarily bad, they pose a risk. As a chapter in Foucault's historiographical analyses of the liberal and neoliberal arts of government, these lectures proceed as a genealogical excavation of the sources of history (*Historie*) as a discipline in order to reanimate history as an event (historicality or *Geschichtlichkeit*).[20] Foucault suggests that liberalism is a governmental practice that is not satisfied with respecting or guaranteeing this or that freedom, but *consumes* freedom. It can only function insofar as a number of freedoms actually do exist: freedom of the market, freedom of production, the freedom to exercise property rights, freedom of competition, etc. If the practice needs or consumes freedom, it must produce freedom. It must produce freedom, and it must organise freedom. The new art of government therefore appears to involve the 'management of freedom', producing what its subjects need in order to be free (economically). It is intent on ensuring the freedom necessary for freedom, in other words, the management and organisation of the conditions in which one can be free. At the heart of this liberal practice, then, is the tension between the imperative to produce freedoms and the fact that this very act entails the establishment of limitations, controls, forms of coercion, and obligations relying on threats.

Foucault shows that the age of freedoms coincides exactly with the development, dramatic rise, and dissemination throughout society of those famous disciplinary techniques for taking charge of the behaviour of individuals day by day, in all its fine detail. It is for this very reason that in the end this liberal art of government introduces by itself or is the victim from within of what Foucault calls, in his lecture of January 24, 1979, 'crises of governmentality' (Foucault 2008, 68). These crises then arise because the mechanisms for producing freedom ('liberogenic devices') actually produce destructive effects which prevail over the very freedom they are supposed to produce.

It is in this context that Foucault turns his attention to what constitutes a response to this crisis—the German and American neoliberalisms that emerged in the middle of the twentieth century. These early neoliberalisms responded to the crisis induced by too *much* government by returning to a technology of restrained government (Foucault 2008, 322). His analyses uncover, however, that although its operation is less overt than discipline, the neoliberal political programme aimed at limiting state intervention exerts far more effective and insidious control, reaching as far as the intimate recesses of our private lives. Ever since the Great Depression of the 1930s, mechanisms of economic intervention have been deployed to avoid the reduction of freedom that would result from a transition to socialism, fascism, or National Socialism. But Foucault asks in his lecture of January 24, 1979, in a manner unequivocally evidencing the 'critical attitude', 'is it not the case that these mechanisms of economic intervention surreptitiously introduce types of intervention and modes of action which are so harmful to freedom as the visible and manifest political forms one wants to avoid?' (Foucault 2008, 69).

I conclude with a quotation by Thomas Lemke that succinctly captures the critical added value of interrogating neoliberalism as governmentality:

> [T]he concept of governmentality suggests that it is not only important to see if neo-liberal rationality is an adequate representation of society, but also how it functions as a 'politics of truth', producing new forms of knowledge . . . that contribute to the 'government' of new domains of regulation and intervention. (Lemke 2000, 8)

Notes

1. This chapter has been published as Hofmeyr 2021a.
2. Based on the Foucauldian notion of 'governmentality', many subsequent scholars have undertaken what is known as governmentality *studies*. Governmentality studies do not refer to a sweeping social theory, but rather to an angle or analytic perspective. It is not a distinct methodological inventory. Its focus is on technologies and rationalities of (self-)government in distinct fields, and on how these practices and thinking about these practices translate into each other. It entails a local and specific cartography. Importantly, such knowledge of 'government' inevitably fails and is inadequate because it is aimed at the insistent and resistant 'Real'.
3. Locke's theory of freedom is set out in book II, chapter XXI of *An Essay Concerning Human Understanding* (1690).
4. Rousseau's formulation of social contract theory argues against the claim that monarchs are divinely empowered to legislate. In *The Social Contract* (1762),

Rousseau argues that laws are binding only when they are supported by the general will of the people.

5. On the first anniversary of 9/11, in an article entitled 'Securing Freedom's Triumph' in the *New York Times*, then President George W. Bush (2002) wrote: 'Humanity holds in its hands the opportunity to offer freedom's triumph over all its age-old foes' (quoted in Harvey 2005, 5–6).

6. See for example, Cyndi Suarez's (2017) comment that a 'recent article in *Nature* reveals the results of the largest study on inequality in human history, which found that while degrees of inequality have been high in historical societies, they have never been as high as they are now'.

7. Similar analyses are presented by Duménil and Lévy (2011) and Overbeek and Van Apeldoorn (2012).

8. I am aware that theories of neoliberalism as a dominant ideology, such as Harvey's, are open to three criticisms, namely that these theories imply functionalism or attributing widely divergent phenomena to one causal factor; that they instrumentalise or reduce all social and political institutions to instruments that merely further the interests of the ruling class; and that these theories tend to reduce the state to a mere cipher—a passive mechanism controlled from outside the formal political sphere (cf. Flew 2014, 58). As will become clear in the course of my argument, I contend that interpreting neoliberalism as *governmentality* explains neoliberalism as a dominant ideology without falling into these traps.

9. For an archive of this growing body of debate and commentary, see *Foucault News*, http://foucaultnews.com/category/neoliberalism/.

10. Also see the second section of 'What Is Critique?' (Foucault 1978, 36–47).

11. Lemke (2001) also offers a detailed reconstruction of the content of these lectures.

12. On the topic of neoliberal subject formation, also see the well-known Foucault-inspired study by Dardot and Laval (2009).

13. Lemke's argument that the notion of governmentality has to be understood etymologically has been criticised by Michel Senellart in his 'Course Context' (in Foucault 2007, 399–400, note 126). Senellart's argument hinges on the fact that the 'govern' in 'governmentality' is not derived from 'government' like '"musicality" from music'. He contends that Lemke's translation of the word into German as 'Regierungsmentalität' is therefore a mistranslation. The authoritative German-English dictionary, *Langenscheidt*, translates *Regierung* as government, reign, rule, and administration. In various lectures presented in English cited in this chapter, Foucault qualifies his understanding of 'government'. Foucault's conceptualisation of 'government' obviously does not conform to our present-day common understanding of the term, since no alternative term is available to account for the historically encompassing meaning of the term. As with most philosophical concepts, common understandings cannot suffice to comprehend what a term means within the context of a specific philosopher's work. German scholars could possibly have opted to use the verbal form of *Regierung*—*regieren*—translated by *Langenscheidt* as govern, rule, and

reign, which mirrors the different meanings of the noun and the verb in English. The English translators opted for the verb by translating it as 'governmentality' as opposed to 'government-mentality'. However, neither the noun nor the verb encompasses the meaning Foucault attributes to the term. Given Lemke's qualification of his understanding of 'Regierungsmentalität', which I believe to reflect the meaning intended by Foucault, I find Senellart's critique somewhat pedantic, and therefore do not consider it a fundamental point of criticism against Lemke's understanding of Foucault's work.

14. Here I would like to acknowledge Assiter (2021)'s important claim that the concept of right, and specifically the right to freedom is under severe attack in the present period from both the left and the right of the political spectrum. Leftist critics deride it as colonial and Eurocentric, while the right simply denies certain groups and individuals any rights at all. It is important in this context to distinguish between *market* freedom and the individual and collective right to freedom. The right to freedom was enshrined through the UN Declaration of Human Rights in certain forms of governmentality but is increasingly under attack—especially the right to freedom of expression—in certain neoliberal economies and the space for this kind of Kantian critique which I am referring to is becoming more and more attenuated for certain groups.

15. José Luis Moreno Pestaña, for example, argues in *Foucault, la gauche, et la politique* (2010) that Foucault was 'totally convinced by the neoliberal discourse'. Philosopher and sociologist Geoffroy de Lagasnerie in *La dernière leçon de Michel Foucault* (2012) argues that Foucault offered little criticism of neoliberalism, but that, on the contrary, he seemed 'caught up' in it and was prepared to give it his 'tacit assent'.

16. Cf. Flynn (1994) for this tripartite categorisation of Foucault's method.

17. While conceding that this might be true, Assiter (2021) maintains that the notion of a right is still a vital tool to deploy to challenge all forms of power. She argues that the human right to freedom as opposed to market freedom may lie in Ancient Persia and not in the European Enlightenment at all.

18. The main proponent of the theory of human capital was Gary Becker, recipient of the 1992 Nobel Prize in Economic Science. An important reference in this regard is his 1964 book *Human Capital: A Theoretical and Empirical Analysis, with Special Reference to Education*. In this now classic study, he argues that an investment in an individual's education and training is similar to business investments in equipment. As already pointed out, Foucault would have read the 1964 version, not the revised third edition of 1993 which I used.

19. In this regard, an instructive source is Marzocca (2017).

20. The distinction was originally made by Heidegger in *Being and Time* in 1927. See, for example, p. 381 of the 1962 translation: 'The proposition, "Dasein is historical", is confirmed as a fundamental existential ontological assertion. This assertion is far removed from the mere ontical establishment of the fact that Dasein is the basis for a possible kind of historiological understanding which in turn carries with it the possibility of getting a special grasp of the development of historiology as a science'. See especially division II, section V: 'Temporality and Historicality' (Heidegger 1927, 424–55).

CHAPTER THREE

Knowledge Work in the Age of Control[1]

Now that I have addressed the status of Foucault's governmentality lectures as a critical toolkit with which neoliberalism might be interrogated, I can turn to the phenomenon of knowledge work and the concomitant emergence of the knowledge worker in my attempt to undertake a critical ontology of knowledge workers today, broadly construed, taking cognisance of the fact that variations and nuanced differences are sure to exist in different contexts. While my focus is on specific forms of knowledge work that can be performed irrespective of place and time—which, to be sure, does not apply to many other forms of knowledge work, such as the consulting medical professional working in a COVID ward—I do not wish to discount the invaluable role of these other knowledge workers and also non-knowledge workers in the functioning of neoliberal economies. Moreover, my intention here is neither to plot the historical-sociological evolution of (knowledge) work into its present form, nor to suggest that knowledge work in its present incarnation is entirely new or different from previous forms of 'white-collar' work with a significant knowledge component. Rather, I draw on authoritative existing studies on how knowledge work in networked societies may generally be construed in order to come to some broad understanding of how technologies of power as control operate, to determine not only how they work, but also how they are, act, and think. I also consider specific sets of conditions within which knowledge workers conduct their work—conditions which enable them to work while pre-designing how their work may be conducted in networked societies. In short, the main claim that I aim to substantiate in this chapter is that power in the form of control is exerted in a more insidious manner now that knowledge work has become 'networked'. As we shall see, the latest insights in management best practice of knowledge workers confirm "indirect rule" or stealth control to be the most effective way to govern knowledge workers to maximize their efficiency.

In the most general sense, present-day knowledge workers are a modern brand of employee that evolved in response to our technology-dependent and information-driven economy. They play a valuable role in deciding the economic success of organisations and indeed of countries, but there are specific requirements for them to be able do their work well—they have a unique set of needs that must be met for them to thrive and to be as creative and efficient as possible. This implies that the rise of the networked knowledge worker as a decisive element in organisational success in the information age necessitates a new organisational culture, one tailored to the specifications of knowledge work. Importantly, knowledge work cannot be divorced from the worker, and the worker cannot be divorced from the person—life and work have thus become an indivisible whole, precisely because human capital is *human*. Being human, the worker's value and efficiency cannot be divorced from every other aspect of human life—be it mental, physical or emotional. Hence, the ideal organisational culture for a knowledge worker needs to be cognisant of the worker as a whole person, whose work, being networked, is no longer spatially bound—no longer place-specific—but has been transformed into a world of work. This requires the reach of the organisational culture to extend beyond any formal workspace too.

To deploy my argument on the stealth control exerted over knowledge workers, I proceed in the following manner: First, I sketch the broader context of societal control in which knowledge workers are embedded, and which infiltrates knowledge work organizations and further succeeds to erase the boundaries between work and life. To be sure, here I do not engage directly with the management of knowledge work in particular. Instead, I depart from the premise that the work and life of the knowledge worker have become an indivisible whole subject to conditions of macro-level control that has infiltrated the micro-level. Then, I consider the emergence and evolution of the knowledge worker to come to a more precise understanding of what knowledge work is. I proceed by drawing on the research of Burud and Tumolo (2004) to survey the human capital literature to come to a critical understanding of how the literature proposes to leverage human capital to ensure the optimal efficiency of knowledge workers. Understanding this is critical to throw into relief how the subjection of knowledge workers operates under the auspices of greater discretion. In following section, I attempt to plot the implications of the conditions of control for the (self-)governance of the knowledge worker by employing Han's (2017) further specification of control as "smart power" that operates in a benevolent guise. In the final section, I conclude that under conditions of greater autonomy, flexibility and discretion outlined in the human capital literature, governance as "control" insinuates constant work into every aspect of the life of the knowledge worker. The central insight I arrive at is that neoliberalism with its insistence that human capital requires investment has succeeded in spawning an optimally efficient, ever-working subject central to the success of the knowledge economy.

The Age of Control

I start my argument by outlining the broader context of societal control in which knowledge workers are embedded as the decisive driver of the knowledge economy. This is a form of power, as we shall see, that infiltrates both the organizational and private existence of the knowledge worker. One thing that sets the present-day knowledge worker apart from previous incarnations of knowledge workers is that s/he is continuously connected. The knowledge work environment is embedded in what Castells (1996) has characterised as the 'network society'. The invention of electronic and nuclear technologies since the 1940s has coincided with the expansion of an increased number of international corporations beyond physical national boundaries, spreading into hitherto uncommodified areas. Globalised markets, coupled with computer technologies, have transformed the world of work into a deterritorialised network of nodal interfaces, mass consumption, and liquid multinational flows of capital.

In the 1990s, even prior to the current hegemony of the internet, Deleuze predicted that we were moving from a disciplinary society to a society of control. Disciplinary societies, as defined by Foucault (1975), keep individuals "institutionalized"—in the family, schools, barracks, factories or prisons —turning them into docile bodies because of the presence or threat of constant surveillance. The difference, according to Deleuze (1992, 5), is that in disciplinary societies one is always in a position of beginning again. Another institution, the school, for example, takes over from the former (the family) to organize productive labour by distributing bodies in space and ordering them in time. Societies of control extend the environments of control (e.g. the hospital) into continuous free-floating flows of control (operative in and through neighbourhood clinics, hospices, and day care facilities, for example) "where one is never finished with anything" (Deleuze, 1992, 5). A person under control or 'dividual' is 'undulatory, in orbit, in a continuous network (Deleuze 1992, 6). He thus links control to the technological revolution (the machine of control is the computer), and this in turn must inevitably coincide with a "mutation in capitalism" therein that it is now primarily focused on the flow and fluctuations of "stocks", which are nothing more than "coded figures—deformable and transformable", the fluctuations of which imprison the profit-seeker (Deleuze 1992, 6). Deleuze (1992, 4), in short, postulates that the operation of this market made of fluctuating flows of financial capital has become an instrument of social control that is short-term but constant, subject to rapid rates of turnover.

Deleuze wrote at the time of the Third Industrial Revolution; the twenty-first century is the time of the *Fourth* Industrial Revolution. Davis (2016) explains the difference: the Third Industrial Revolution began in the 1950s with the development of digital systems, communication, and rapid advances in computing power, which have enabled new ways of generating, processing, and sharing information. The Fourth Industrial Revolution has inaugurated entirely new capabilities for people and machines with the advent of 'cyber-physical systems' (Davis 2016):

> While these capabilities are reliant on the technologies and infrastructure of the Third Industrial Revolution, the Fourth Industrial Revolution represents entirely new ways in which technology becomes embedded within societies and even within human bodies. Examples include genome editing, new forms of machine intelligence, breakthrough materials and approaches to governance that rely on cryptographic methods such as the blockchain.[2] (Davis 2016, n.p.)

Human subjectivity—our every action and mode of being in networked societies—has therefore become chained to the technology that opens new frontiers of human capability, transcending previously immutable limits, but also insinuating control into the most intimate recesses of human action and being by means of digital surveillance and algorithmic management.

Davis (2016) stresses that all industrial revolutions are ultimately driven by the individual and collective choices and desires of people. And it is not just the choices of the researchers, inventors, and designers developing the underlying technologies that matter, but, even more importantly, those of investors, consumers, regulators, and citizens who adopt, adapt, and employ these technologies in daily life. An important implication of this insight is that knowledge workers operating under the conditions of the Fourth Industrial Revolution find themselves in a world of their own making—a world that humans have created and that is simultaneously creating them and forcing them to create themselves in unpredictable ways in order to function and thrive within it. What this implies, as we shall see, is the active self-inscription of knowledge workers in systems of control.

Understood through the heuristic lens of 'governmentality', we are not simply dealing with the power of technocratic experts and institutions, but also with the way in which human conduct is being conducted (orchestrated), as well as with the methodological application of 'an analytical grid' for assessing the efficacy of this conduct (Foucault 2008, 186). This, then, refers to the relationship between power relations and the conduct of the subject, both in terms of the body of knowledge that provides the criteria for the ideal subject, and in terms of the precise ways in which the actual subject is led to practise itself in satisfying these criteria.

The form of control that operates within and through networks replaces the top-down model associated with the state and institutions (a model which is static and linear) with a form of control (a model which appears open, informal, non-linear); importantly, this new model augurs the spontaneous self-organisation of individuals themselves (Törnberg and Uitermark 2020, 1–2). Here self-organisation should be understood as a political ideal that denotes an array of governance arrangements in which private actors act autonomously and undertake initiatives of their own volition, in pursuit of public, collective, or organisational objectives (Mattijssen et al. 2018).

Törnberg and Uitermark (2020, 1) conceive of this form of control as 'complex control'. Complexity science defines self-organising systems as systems in which the components are relatively independent and thus autonomous in their behaviour, while undergoing direct and indirect interactions (Heylighen et al. 2006, 125). Examples include the sophisticated feats of organisation accomplished by social insects such as bees, ants, and termites, which act without centralised leadership. Each insect follows its own instincts, yet the beehive, ant nest, or termite mound succeeds because of the formation of complex social networks that involve elaborate patterns of communication between individuals within the community. The local mass interactions of the individual ants (or bees or termites) result in the intelligent organisation of the colony (Mitchell 2009; Ball 2012). The ingenuity of complex systems is that their mass of less functionally differentiated components makes each component of the same class (drones or workers, for example) inherently disposable, and easily replaceable. Hence, the organisation is extremely resilient. These systems are malleable and adaptive, as modifying functionality does not require redesigning the entire system (Törnberg and Uitermark 2020, 3).

Neoliberal governmentality operates as such a form of complex and decentralised 'network governance' (Jones, Hesterly, and Borgatti 1997, 911).

This signals a departure from bureaucratic structures within firms and formal relationships between them, to 'organic' or 'informal' connected relationships. Unlike natural complex systems, however, neoliberal complex systems, although self-organised, are neither organic nor informal. Like worker ants, the connected individual nodes are fundamentally individualised. Also, like worker ants, neoliberal working subjects serve the interests of the colony/economy; only neoliberal subjects *believe* that they do so in the name of self-interest, first and foremost. Bauman (2000, 135) describes the 'individual enterprise' as a form of control or governance that expects individuals themselves and individually to use 'their own wits, resources and industry to lift themselves to a more satisfactory condition'. This form of complex control is powerfully bolstered by the digital revolution which allows 'distributed (self-)control, i.e. bottom-up management . . . to create [a] resilient social and economic order by means of self-organisation, self-regulations, and self-governance' (Helbing 2015, 2). Thus what appears to be 'organic' and 'informal' is in fact only the individual's 'freedom to choose' from a curated series of options that are actively rewarded or disincentivised, depending on the extent to which they serve the purpose of furthering the objectives of neoliberal society. This 'designed self-organization' signals an important transition from the kind of control Deleuze described: '[P]ower is now expressed as the subtle tuning of some technical code of a performance indicator, which brings about a cascade of change among . . . networks of interacting players' (Törnberg and Uitermark 2020, 8). Bauman (2000) theorises this form of self-organised control in terms of the *Synopticon*. Unlike the model of the Panopticon, which Foucault describes as the model of disciplinary power where the one watches or guards the many—the Synopticon signifies the many watching or admiring the few, an evolution that came with mass media and television. This form of control operates by enticing the many to emulate the few. It operates not by coercion or explicit command, but by presenting enviable, seductive exemplars.

Törnberg and Uitermark (2020, 5) add a further evolutionary modification of control, one which came with the advent of the internet and pervasive inscription of every aspect of work and personal life in digital platforms. They call this the *social Synopticon*, which is comprised of social media platforms that provide ways to 'share', interact, and give feedback through comments and likes—an immensely powerful feedback mechanism through which the formation of compliant and 'productive' identities is validated and other identities are actively discouraged.

The efficacy of this form of control resides in the fact that it mobilises the freedom of the individual subject. Pettman's (2016) definition of social media offers an excellent illustration of how power as control or the 'conduct of conduct' operates in conjunction with its luminous shadow, freedom:

> '[S]ocial media' names the simultaneously limitless and circumscribed ways we interact via newly enmeshed communications and entertainment technologies. *Limitless* because no two people will navigate the same branching pathways social media affords in the same way (we all have a unique combination of interests and interactions), and *circumscribed* because these are all conducted within the vectors provided by those (increasingly few) entities that own the cables, the satellites, the channels, the sites, the providers, and the applications that funnels us all toward each other, so that we may congregate in the bright light of voluntary and compliant commerce. (Pettman 2016, xi)

Professional life and work are inscribed in and constructed through networking platforms, such as the widely used LinkedIn. Academic networking and sharing platforms such as ResearchGate and Academia.edu similarly function to validate or invalidate, and even benchmark, the self's entrepreneurial efforts and incite constant self-improvement through self-investment. Human capital, after all, requires constant (self-)investment. These professional platforms provide opportunities for almost instant peer evaluation as they 'congregate' experts from around the globe and provide individual users with constantly updated reports on 'reads', 'downloads', and citations. This development has been variously dubbed the 'sharing economy' (Puschmann and Alt 2016) and a 'commons-based peer economy' (Benkler 2002).

Zuboff (2018) uses the term 'surveillance capitalism' to emphasise behaviour modification as an aspect of this digital platform-based control. She maintains that 'surveillance capitalism' is a 'new economic order that claims human experience as free raw material for hidden commercial practices of extraction, prediction, and sales; [comprising a parasitic economic logic in which the production of goods and services is subordinated to a new global architecture of behavioral modification' (Zuboff 2018, 8). Through its 'instrumentarian power', 'surveillance capitalism' mines online users' personal experience, either unbeknownst to them or without their explicit permission,[3] in the form of 'behavioural data' which comprise the basis for predicting users' future online behaviour across a broad spectrum of services and products (Zuboff 2018, 16). Arguing along the same lines as Foucault in his contention of the 'conduct of conduct', Zuboff (2018) stresses that in addition to using technical instruments such as algorithms to anticipate users' behaviour, predictive data are not only based on *monitoring* online behaviour; they are generated by actually *directing* it, for example, Facebook's use of 'subliminal [online] cues' to influence users' emotional states and behaviour.

These inventions were celebrated by their architects for being both 'effective and undetectable' (Zuboff 2018, 16).

With the era of 'surveillance capitalism' came the imperative to be omni-visible and omni-accessible via virtual spaces afforded by advanced communication and information technology. Omni-visibility and omni-accessibility made possible a full cycle of exploitation: it starts with a company's 'incursion' into an unexploited domain of behaviour; it continues with the 'habituation' of users to that incursion, and finally proceeds, unimpeded, with the mining of online behaviour by 'adapting' and 'redirecting any attempts at critique or reform'. 'Nudges' in choice architecture, including surveillance-friendly default settings, take advantage of the fact that users' time and attention are limited. Zuboff (2018) argues that companies such as Facebook and Google are able to do all this because they have monopolised how they are viewed. Here Zuboff (2018) borrows from Émile Durkheim's (1893) work on the division of knowledge production and specialisation, to shed light on how the operation of power in producing knowledge is cut off from how power achieves this knowledge production. The work of digital platforms such as Google and Facebook is hidden in proprietary closed-source code; the platforms use non-disclosure agreements and vertical organisation to obfuscate their practices. The resulting divisions make it hard for anyone other than surveillance capitalists themselves to make authoritative pronouncements about what exactly they do. It is precisely the operation of such an imperceptible, micro-level biopolitical technology of power that Foucault's critical toolkit is designed to take as its object.

As a form of critique, Foucault's theory of governmentality allows for an epistemologically indirect analysis of social institutions, organisations, and societies focusing less on the analysis of its form and more on the abstract 'technology of power' which gives it its functional coherency (Foucault 2007, 117). To understand how working subjectivity is being governed (subjection) and governs itself (subjectivisation), we need to consider the precise nature of work in this network society, which reflects the developments of the Third Industrial Revolution while contributing to the Fourth. Given these developments, it is hardly surprising that 'knowledge workers' are the key propellant of the economy in the neoliberal network society. Their role differs from that of workers in natural complex systems in that these knowledge workers, unlike ants or bees, are functionally differentiated. However, their specialised expertise does not make them irreplaceable, as the imperative of continuous (self)investment in human capital can call on a reserve army of experts ready to step in if any individual knowledge working node fails to deliver. Hence, the resilience of the network remains intact. But what exactly is knowledge work? A review of central literature on the topic proves instructive here. A brief overview of the central literature on the topic allows us to come to a more conceptually precise understanding of what constitutes knowledge work. To this end, I plot the emergence and evolution of the knowledge worker in the next section.

Knowledge Work(-er)

As I have pointed out elsewhere (Hofmeyr 2021b: 250–251), the term 'knowledge worker' was initially formulated by Peter Drucker in *The Landmarks of Tomorrow* (1959). The notions of knowledge work and knowledge workers became noticeable in the literature in the subsequent decade or so (Machlup 1962; Drucker 1969; Bell 1973), and became more pervasive thereafter with the neoliberalisation of economic and political thinking from the end of the seventies. The phenomenon took on its various present forms with the revolutions in the information technology and internet revolutions.

Soete (2001) points out that the pervasiveness of knowledge work in Western labour markets plays a definitive role in what sets globally competitive economies apart from their weaker counterparts. Pyöriä (2005, 117) contends that the 'growth of knowledge work reflects a sea change in the mode of capitalist production'. Gone are the days of 'traditional industrial production based on cheap labour and energy', and on 'heavy material investments as the primary sources of economic productivity' (Pyöriä 2005, 117). Now business success relies on improving efficiency, defined specifically as the maintenance of 'an unbroken flow of human capability to innovate and embody new ideas and knowledge throughout the economy' (Pyöriä 2005, 117). Material (matter/energy) outputs have been supplanted by immaterial (information/knowledge) outputs. Unlike traditional workers, knowledge workers process and manipulate 'information as an end in itself, which means it is the informational content of the job that defines the task, the product, and ultimately the worker' (Schement 1990, cited by Pyöriä 2005, 117). In the evolving definitions of informational labour, key characteristics include 'a high level of education and skills and the use of information technology' (Pyöriä 2005, 117).

Even at the start of the Third Industrial Revolution, Drucker (1959) defined knowledge workers as high-level workers who apply theoretical and analytical knowledge, acquired through formal training, to develop products and services. He already foresaw that knowledge workers would be the most valuable assets of a twenty-first-century organisation, because of their high level of productivity and creativity. Similarly, Bell (1973) interpreted the increasingly 'symbolic and interactive content of work as the fundamental fact about work in a post-industrial society' (Pyöriä 2005, 117). He postulated that the axial principle of the social, political, and cultural logic that marks the end of industrialism is theoretical or abstract knowledge. Post-industrial society, then, is organised around knowledge for the purpose of *social control*:

> What has become decisive for the organization of decisions and the direction of change is the centrality of *theoretical* knowledge—the primacy of theory over empiricism and the codification of knowledge into abstract systems of symbols that, as in any axiomatic system, can be used to illuminate the many different and varied areas of experience. (Bell 1973, 20)

Closer to the end of the twentieth century, Manuel Castells (1996) stressed the application of Weberian rationalisation to the production of knowledge itself. He maintains that the virtuous cycle of knowledge accumulation is the key to prosperity:

> In the new, informational mode of development the source of productivity lies in the technology of knowledge creation, information processing, and symbolic communication. To be sure, knowledge and information are critical elements in all modes of development, since the process of production is always based in some level of knowledge and in the processing of knowledge. However, what is specific to the informational mode of development is the action of knowledge upon knowledge itself as the main source of productivity. (Castells 1996, 17)

Hence, one might derive that what sets post-industrial society apart from industrial society is the importance attached to knowledge as an economic resource. In fact, 'the skill of abstract thinking acquired in formal education has never been more pronounced than in contemporary organizations' (Pyöriä 2005, 122). Although information technology facilitates the informationalisation of work and organisational processes, Pyöriä (2005, 122) further points out that 'the diffusion and use of that technology is not in itself a sufficient criterion for classifying work as informational'. Knowledge work also entails a qualitative difference—it is symbolic-analytical; in other words, it involves 'problem-solving, problem-identifying and strategic brokering activities that are non-standardized' (Reich 1991, cited by Pyöriä 2005, 122). If creativity is emphasized in knowledge at the expense of routines, then the most decisive part of the job description, Pyöriä (2005, 122) maintains, may refer to cognitive processes that are independent of the time or the place where the work is performed, and even of the tools used.

Importantly, the shift described previously, Pyöriä (2005, 122) continues, implies that individual creativity and innovativeness comprise the scarcest and arguably the most valuable resources in an information society. Reich (1991) maintains that the key to the new work processes lies in flexibility, interdisciplinary cooperation, and rapid learning, reskilling, and upskilling at the interface between new technology and human interaction. According to Pyöriä (2005, 122), drawing on Scarbrough (1999), more than occupationally defined norms and practices, the work of knowledge workers is primarily defined by the nature of their work, which is relatively unstructured and organisationally contingent in response to the changing demands of organisations. Non-routine problem-solving is the core of knowledge work that, along with the education criterion, allows one to distinguish knowledge workers not only from traditional workers, but also from routine information technology users, on the basis of the design component in the job (Choi and Varney 1995, cited by Pyöriä 2005, 122).

Drawing on the research of a number of scholars, Pyöriä (2005, 123) continues to throw what may be understood as the ideal-typical knowledge worker into clearer relief. If this worker is expected to use knowledge creatively, then knowledge workers as a class include traditional professionals, but the class is not limited to them (cf. Fincham 1996). McDermott (1995) points out that like craft work, knowledge work in teams is largely individual, *ad hoc*, and it is often invisible. Moreover, because the lifespan of advanced knowledge and new technologies is becoming shorter, the most important skill knowledge workers can possess is the ability to build continuously upon their existing expertise. The requisite life-long learning often builds on extensive formal expertise, although such expertise may have been attained by informal learning, as Hilton (2001) points out. The knowledge worker has access to, learns, and is qualified to practise a body of knowledge that is formal, complex, and abstract (Thompson, Warhurst, and Callaghan 2000).

Who, then, is a knowledge worker, and who is not? Departing from Machlup's (1962) and Porat's (1977) reliance on occupational classifications, more recent studies, Pyöriä (2005, 124) explains, do not place knowledge workers in any particular industry or occupational category. In this regard, Winslow and Bramer (1994) conclude that a knowledge worker is simply someone who interprets and applies information to create and provide value-adding solutions, and to make informed recommendations. Pyöriä (2005, 124) posits that

> the concept of knowledge work is best understood as an ideal-type, because in reality knowledge workers do not constitute an empirically homogeneous category. According to Max Weber's classic definition, ideal-typical concepts are neither empirically detailed descriptions nor theoretically exhaustive elaborations of reality. Instead, their utility lies in the encapsulation of meaning by

capturing essential attributes of certain classes of social phenomena sharing common features or family resemblances.

Knowledge workers, then, are far from evident to pin down in a straightforward definition because they do not fit within an empirically homogenous category. What we might say more generally and by way of summary is that particular aspects of work might be classified as knowledge work if it requires extensive formal *education* and *continuous on-the-job learning* and transferable *skills*. The *nature of the work* is characterised by a low level of standardisation, working with abstract knowledge and symbols. *Organisationally*, it ranges from professional bureaucracies to self-managing teams, job, and task circulation, and the *medium of work* consists of symbols and/or people (Pyöriä 2005, 124). To my mind, however, these characteristics, while they are useful and informative, do not touch on the heart of the matter, which is crucial in determining how to 'manage' knowledge workers for the purposes of maximising their motivation to work and their efficiency.

I would argue that the incisive definition of knowledge work offered by Kelloway and Barling (2000) trumps the definitions summarised earlier. They describe knowledge work as 'discretionary organizational behavior' based on the use of knowledge (Kelloway and Barling 2000, 10). This definition appears to be very broad, but it does draw a line between 'white-collar' workers who manipulate information as part of their job description, and knowledge workers that have to be fully present and ply their creative problem-solving skills to generate knowledge and knowledge-based solutions from the information at their disposal. Specifically, it encompasses, first, the *creation* of new knowledge and innovation; second, the *application* of existing knowledge to current problems; third, the *transmission* of knowledge; and fourth, the *acquisition* of knowledge through teaching and learning (Kelloway and Barling 2000, 10). If knowledge work is indeed 'discretionary behaviour', it is work that may be encouraged, but not demanded. Employees are likely to engage in knowledge work only to the extent that they have the ability, the motivation, and the opportunity to do so (Kelloway and Baring 2000, 10). Whether an employee 'chooses' to engage in knowledge work depends on whether s/he can and wants to do so when the need arises.

This implies that the advent of knowledge work substantially challenges the managerial and organisational practices of the past. Drucker (1999, 84) suggests that increasing knowledge worker productivity 'requires that knowledge workers want to work for the organizations in preference to all other opportunities'. This 'wanting to work' is therefore not merely a cognitive commitment but an affective one (Meyer and Allen 1997). If this argument is correct, then simply increasing the stock of knowledge is not enough. Rather, organisations need to elicit the discretionary use of knowledge actively in a way that maximises it efficiently, which is easier said than done, given the challenges that come with working with people. If knowledge work depends on the disposition and inclination of the working subject, then knowledge workers are not organisational assets, but investors in the organisation (Pfeffer and Sutton 2000). So how then do organisations get knowledge workers to invest in them voluntarily?

Capitalising on Human Capital

Human capital is an intangible yet indispensible asset of every organisation. As is evident from the previous discussion, it is indispensable because it is the definitive *investment* that secures a company's economic growth in the post-industrial information age. Value is vested precisely in workers' ability to perform knowledge work most effectively by being optimally creative, flexible, knowledgeable, and responsive to the changing demands of the problem-solving task at hand. When one understands that human capital cannot be divorced from the human, that knowledge work cannot be divorced from the knowledge worker, and that knowledge work is discretionary, it is clear that rather than mere assets, knowledge workers are themselves investors whose investment needs to be elicited and cannot be commanded. In this section, I largely draw on the research conducted by Burud and Tumolo (2004)[4] on how organisational structures and culture had to adapt to optimally leverage the new human capital.

One of the most successful business books since the millennium that Burud and Tumolo (2004, 10) refer to is Collins' *Good to Great* (2001). It analyses companies that reported fifteen years of returns at or below market norms, followed by fifteen years with cumulative returns at least three times the market average. One of the main reasons these companies went from good to great is that their managers not only understood how important people are to success, but took this awareness one step further. Collins (2001, 13) writes:

> We expected that good-to-great leaders would begin by setting a new vision and strategy. We found instead that they first got the *right people on the bus*, the wrong people off the bus, and the right people in the right seats—and then they figured out where to drive it. The old adage 'People are your most important asset' turns out to be wrong. People are not your most important asset. The right people are.

What Collins (2001) fails to mention is that apart from getting the right people on the bus and in the right seats, one needs to get the right people to *want to* take the bus to bigger and better places. Seven years earlier, Pfeffer (1994) already argued that the right employees are increasingly the best way for companies to achieve and sustain a competitive advantage (Burud and Tumolo 2004, 10). Why? Because the neoliberal business world is one in which deregulation drives prices down, resulting in fiercer competition—one in which communication technology continues to fuel the growth in globalisation, increasing consumers' access to information about products and services around the world (Ohmae 1990, cited by Burud and Tumolo 2004, 12). Communication technology puts these products and services at consumers' disposal, irrespective of physical location, by creating internet-based marketplaces that facilitate e-commerce. Such e-commerce is insidiously bolstered by digital/social platforms that facilitate algorithmically engineered e-connections that pose as self-generated networks. In such a world, it is the skills, relationships, and motivation of employees that determine long-term competitive and sustainable success. Continuous innovation and readiness and responsiveness to changes in existing and potential markets are required to gain a competitive advantage, and people are the only way to achieve that. Although it is computers that are responsible for accumulating data and generating information, it is only people that can make the information usable and turn it into the knowledge sources needed to make impactful business decisions.

The key to maximising knowledge is *human collaboration*. What is called 'social capital' or 'relationship capital' is the sum of the 'trust, mutual understanding, and shared values and behaviors that bind members of human networks and communities and make cooperative action possible' (Cohen and Prusak 2002, 4, cited by Burud and Tumolo 2004, 15). Knowledge work in particular is performed in the context of relationships, as relationships support collaboration, creativity, and interaction, while enhancing commitment and initiative. In fact, knowledge work cannot be done without 'persuasiveness, shared decisions, the pooling of knowledge and the creative sparks people strike off one another', which depend on relationships with others (Cohen and Prusak 2002, 17, cited by Burud and Tumolo 2004, 15). This is a reminder that *what* one knows cannot be divorced from *whom* one knows: efficiency depends on knowing who knows whom, who knows what, and who can be relied upon. Optimal efficiency, moreover, relies on social synergy—something which arguably cannot be emulated or generated by means of screen-mediated meetings (the consequences of which will only become plain in the post-pandemic world after COVID-19).[5]

Relationships depend on *trust*, and trust is honed over time through many social interactions, which is why relationships are hard to replicate quickly. People are inherently social animals, as we know. Hence, mutual and meaningful connections create value to the people that have them. They enable people to gain a sense of purpose, which fuels their commitment, engagement, and initiative, creating a virtuous circle. They are potentially energising and rewarding—relations with others, importantly, improve self-understanding (Walsh, Bartunek, and Lacey 1998, cited by Burud and Tumolo 2004, 16). While relational connections are distinctly individual, organisational culture can provide a habitat in which they either flourish or wither. Relational capital grows when an organisation is stable, and it is destroyed through the volatility of mergers and rapid organisational changes (Burud and Tumolo 2004, 16). Relational capital grows in a hospitable work environment in which there is an ecology of trust, mutuality, shared meanings and goals, and common frames of reference shared by people (Cohen and Prusak 2002, cited by Burud and Tumolo 2004, 16).

Like all forms of capital, human capital can grow or depreciate, depending on the level of investment made. It has become common parlance in the world of business that *investment in human capital* is non-negotiable for economic success. Likewise, human capital depreciates through unemployment, injury, mental decline, or the inability to keep up with innovation. Optimising one's human capital may take the form of employing highly educated, specialised, and skilled employees (getting the right people on the bus) or 'up-skilling' and investing in the continuous development, education, and training of existing employees.

Of equal importance is knowing how to *manage* this form of capital, which is finely attuned to its environment. As pointed out earlier, more so than any other resource, human capital either flourishes or flounders, depending on the networks of relationalities in which it finds itself. This is true for all forms of capital in a globalised marketplace, but the creative, flexible, problem-solving ability of human capital as it is incarnated in the kind of knowledge work that sets one organisation apart from others is a highly sensitive and fragile ecosystem. The optimal functioning of that ecosystem is a complex balance of cognitive, emotional, spiritual, and material factors. Human resilience functions as a mainstay only for as long as this balance is maintained, and it declines, sometimes at an incremental rate, when this balance is off—even if only by a fraction.

Human capital is qualitatively different from machine capital and from financial capital. Drawing on Jean-Jacques Rousseau's 1762 treatise on the nature of man, *Emile, or On Education*, Burud and Tumolo (2004, 16) explain that humans

> are more organisms than mechanisms. They are unpredictable. They are idiosyncratic. . . . Most importantly, people have the innate capacity to 'self-assemble . . . change constantly, reproduce, learn and self-organize' (Ehin 2000:7). They have their own requirements as complex, whole, 'biological systems seeking to fulfil their needs and aspirations' (p. 8). Bio-logic and not machine logic prevails, which is why efforts to control people inevitably fail. Machine logic is mechanistic; you can dissect a machine into parts, and its inputs generate the same outputs every time. Bio-logic is organic: people don't all react the same way, nor do they just react; they act upon and co-create.

As living creatures, people are evolutionary beings, subject to the constant urge to transform progressively. They naturally resist. A coercive organisational culture that seeks to constrain, command, or micro-manage people stunts the natural urge to transform, instead of bolstering positive self-organisation through spontaneous adaptation. That said, coercion can ultimately not suppress that urge completely.

Drucker et al. argues that seeking to manage human beings is the wrong approach (Drucker, Dyson, Handy, Saffo and Senge 1997, cited by Burud and Tumolo 2004, 17). Ehin (2000) urges that organisations should give up any illusion of ruling over human capital and should not confuse rule with order. The order in which human capital thrives arises naturally when self-organising humans are allowed to act spontaneously and to take initiative, in other words, to participate in the creation of the work project. It is this key insight that the human capital literature harnesses to argue against the overt management of knowledge workers in favour of stealth control.

In the context of human capital, attention is a crucial form of currency. In a knowledge economy, 'the delivery of information relies on an exchange of attention, whether to the information itself, to the processes that manage it, or to the people exchanging it. Attention is a highly perishable commodity and in increasingly short supply' (Burud and Tumolo 2004, 17–18). Never before in the history of humankind have we been bombarded by so many simultaneous demands for our attention. The clicking, plugged-in working subject finds her-/himself immersed in endless streams of fleeting information. These constant streams are quick and compact, constantly being updated and everywhere: news feeds, social media posts, emails, podcasts, TED talks, tweets, memes. These streams are fast paced, marked for rapid consumption, with the aid of predictive text, hashtag conventions, emojis, and other acronymic messaging conventions. Pettman (2016, ix) calls this 'the digitilization of distraction'. Apart from causing distraction, information overload undermines effective decision-making because of the individual's limitation of scarce resources to process all the information (Roetzel 2019, cited by Burud and Tumolo 2004, 18). The advent of modern information technology and the subsequent rise of social media and the attention economy have been primary drivers of information overload on multiple fronts: in the quantity produced, the ease of dissemination, and the breadth of the audience that is reached. Apart from the general state of affairs that keeps everyone distracted by way of tweets, posts, memes, TikTok videos, and the like, knowledge workers consume information, as that is precisely what their work entails. Information, in turn, consumes the attention of knowledge workers. Half a century ago, in 1971, Nobel prize–winning economist Herbert Simon already maintained that 'a wealth of information creates poverty of attention' (Simon 1971, 40).

Human attention, as Burud and Tumolo (2004) remind us, is a physiological phenomenon prioritised along a hierarchy of needs, as theorised by Abraham Maslow (1943). His basic motivation theory postulates that human needs may be ordered along five levels, and that satisfying the more basic needs is a necessary condition for the possibility of satisfying the remaining needs. First and foremost, we have physiological needs, which include food, shelter, sex, and the protection of our offspring. Then come safety needs, our need for love and belonging, and our need for esteem (our need for respect, status, recognition, and the drive to achieve). Only once all of the aforementioned needs have been met can human beings tend to the need for self-actualisation—the drive to become the most that one can be. Maslow (1943, 394–95) explains this as follows:

> These basic goals are related to each other, being arranged in a hierarchy of prepotency. This means that the most prepotent goal will monopolize consciousness and will tend of itself to organize the recruitment of the various capacities of the organism. The less prepotent needs are minimized, even forgotten or denied. But when a need is fairly well satisfied, the next prepotent ('higher') need emerges, in turn *to dominate the conscious life and to serve as the center of the organization of behaviour*, since gratified needs are not active motivators. (my emphasis)

What we have come to understand about knowledge work speaks to the fact that it cannot be done effectively if the worker's conscious life is dominated by some unsatisfied basic physiological or psychological need. Moreover, I would argue that knowledge work is intrinsically tied to self-fulfilment needs in a circular fashion. By its very nature, knowledge work is optimally suited to cater to the worker's need for prestige and accomplishment, as well as the need for self-actualisation. Solving a difficult problem creatively is a powerful booster of a sense of accomplishment—arguably much more so than work of a repetitive nature, such as working a cash register at a local supermarket or performing a specific task for a predetermined amount of time as an assembly line worker.[6] Similarly, a sense of accomplishment and self-actualisation must already be in place for knowledge work to be done optimally. Solving a difficult problem requires a minimum level of confidence—the conviction that one will be able to solve it, because one has been able to solve other problems that are almost as or equally difficult. A worker is more likely to rise to the occasion of resolving a complicated task or problem more effectively when that worker's attention is wholly devoted to the task as an end in itself than if the worker must solve the problem only for the purposes of gaining a promotion, for example.

These insights are of crucial importance to the optimal 'management' of knowledge workers. Burud and Tumolo (2004, 19) explain it as follows:

> When basic needs are met, people can focus attention elsewhere. But when their jobs are insecure (which threatens their basic sense of safety), or when their children are in worrisome care, when a spouse or close friend is in crisis, it consumes their attention. It cannot do otherwise. (Children draw instinctive attention because both men and women have a primal drive to protect their progeny.) When managers understand this dynamic as a biological and psychological reality, they can make better decisions about how to maximize attention to work goals. They may realize the pointlessness of punitive approaches and see the value of providing resources that help remove chronic worries about children's care or of giving employees time to deal with family emergencies. They can also better appreciate the importance of reducing the complexity that compromises focused attention—information overload, work interruptions, crisis mode, lack of downtime, and the like.

Drucker (1999) identifies a host of characteristics of knowledge workers that shed light on how they should be 'managed'. Perhaps the most important is that they see themselves as the equals to their managers and behave like volunteers. This 'entitlement' springs from the fact that they know their jobs better than their supervisors do. What they contribute are ideas and imagination, so they must be engaged in their work. For them, work is more than a mere source of income—for them, work is a source of *meaning*. As a result, they seek a match between their values and those of the organisation. Moreover, knowledge workers tend to choose work that enhances their own capital. Finally, since knowledge workers carry the means of production with them, they are highly mobile—not confined or confineable to one place, to specific hours or age (Burud and Tumolo 2004, 25).

'The ideal worker in today's economy is a technically skilled individual willing to devote heart and mind—as well as hands—to drive results' (Burud and Tumolo 2004, 25). This description of the knowledge worker, along with the aforementioned characteristics, reveals two sides of human capital. One side of the coin is that these ideal workers expect a lot—they are 'high-maintenance', if you will—in that their level of expertise makes them demanding and entitled, perhaps even insubordinate, in terms of the rules of the human resources game that applied during the industrial age. The other side of the coin is that everything is being demanded of them—complete devotion of their heart, mind, and hands. As I pointed out in the introductory chapter, they now often have to work without the system of invisible support that takes care of their basic physiological needs, which in the Western industrialised world until around 1960 were often met by a non-working, homemaking spouse in a lower- or middle-class one-income household, or by servants in wealthier households, and the psychological needs met by family. Burud and Tumolo (2004) describe this simultaneous preoccupation with work and the demands of the private life of the knowledge worker as a 'dual-focus' mode.

I will return to this contention shortly, but first I want to come to a more precise understanding of this 'bio-logic investor' called a knowledge worker and how the latest human resources management and development philosophy panders to the *people* behind products and services in such a way that it insinuates subjection ever more aggressively into subjectivisation. As we shall see, knowledge workers are subject not only to the complex control operative through social/digital platforms, but also to an organisational logic of 'stealth' control that likewise seeks to co-opt and profit from self-organisation and the human urge toward self-actualisation.

What drives most knowledge workers is purpose, not profit. For them, profit is not in and of itself purpose. As Drucker (2010, 5) explains: 'Profits for a company are like oxygen for a purpose. If you don't have enough, after a while you are out of the game'. However, 'people who think life is about breathing have missed something' (Drucker 2010, cited by Senge in Burud and Tumolo 2004, 5). The same can be said for organisations that think that profit is their sole purpose. What they are missing is a purpose that generates the buy-in of their people, a purpose that engenders their people's passion, gets their knowledge workers' creative juices flowing, and their minds, hearts, and hands committed. In other words, organisations need to 'tap the power to fully engage people, and, in turn, to command loyalty, commitment, patience, and perseverance' (Burud and Tumolo 2004, 5).

Apart from purpose, knowledge workers—as employees that consider themselves equals and that act like volunteers—require a very particular managerial style. This style mobilises influence, rather than positional power. It is driven by the insight that giving orders is an indication of leadership failure. As VISA International's founding chief executive officer, Dee Hock—cited by Burud and Tumolo (2005, 6)—puts it: 'Ordinances, orders, and enforcement . . . are an attempt to compel the kind of behaviour that organizations fail to induce' (Hock 1999, 89–90).

To manage equals or partners, traditional hierarchies, Burud and Tumolo (2004) maintains, have to make way for organic and flexible organisational structures. Newel et al. (2002) identify adhocracy (an *ad hoc* or fluid approach) to be the best structure for this purpose. An adhocracy de-emphasises bureaucracy and replaces it with a dynamic environment of self-formed and self-managed work teams with few formal roles and procedures, where decision-making is decentralised to the workers themselves (Mintzberg 1993, cited by Burud and Tumolo 2004, 26).

Knowledge workers are primarily motivated by job quality and content. They are driven by job satisfaction rather than remuneration. They seek personal achievement and responsibility and prefer to make their own decisions, as they know their highly specialised jobs and how to structure them for the best results, even better than their supervisors do (Drucker 2003). Increased decision-making responsibility therefore empowers them by increasing their job knowledge, which is the key to their performance (Leach, Wall, and Jackson 2003). The ability to think, process, and internalise information as knowledge, and the ability to create new concepts, solve problems, and make judgments are critical to their performance, so work processes and cultures should be designed to foster these outcomes (Burud and Tumolo 2004, 26). Work processes and cultures should act as an invisible support network that facilitates making connections and provides the required resources, rewarding outputs while refraining from constantly monitoring inputs. Getting the right people on the bus and in the right seats and getting them to want to get the bus to its destination makes overt authoritarian supervision superfluous and counter-productive (Davenport 2002). It is important to here to take note of the fact that such a hands-off flexible managerial approach insinuates work into life by transcending the traditional dichotomy between the professional and the personal. While this integration allows for self-management of the worker's time, which affords the knowledge worker increased flexibility to tend to the myriad other dimensions of life beyond work (Burud and

Tumolo 2004, 7–8, 35–54), it also orchestrates the internalization of stealth control in the form of self-responsibilization.

The idyllic picture that is held up for us is that of a sophisticated worker that does what s/he pleases, and what s/he loves to do, exempt from supervisory interference, with a large amount of freedom to self-manage work responsibilities and the execution of tasks. The reality of the neoliberal knowledge worker is far less utopian, however.

Ramifications

In this section, I attempt to plot the implications of the conditions of (self-) governance of the knowledge worker by employing Han's (2017) further specification of control as "smart power" that operates in a benevolent guise. Neoliberal knowledge workers often have a job that is meaningful, satisfying, and absorbing,[7] but that job—especially the knowledge-intensive, problem-solving aspects—requires razor-sharp focus and complete attention. These workers appear to enjoy almost complete freedom in terms of where and when the job is done—that is, as long as the work is done by the deadline. This flexibility regarding where and when the work is done has been made possible by advances in information technology and the internet revolution, which for better or worse, means that work is no longer bound to an office or office hours, and hence can be displaced into timeframes and spaces previously reserved for private commitments and leisure. This transposition of work into non-work timeframes and zones has been vastly accelerated by the 'COVID-19-rapid' and is probably here to stay in the post-pandemic world of knowledge work, in which flexible hybrid models will become the norm rather than an exception or supplement to traditional models.[8] Moreover, for all the freedom and flexibility neoliberal workers enjoy, they remain subject to an economic rationality in which efficiency dictates that the employer gets more for offering less. As a result, these workers work all the time.

Subject to neoliberal governmentality, managerial style and philosophy have been adjusted to the demands of the most precious investor in organisational success, the knowledge worker. The aggregate of governance on the macro-level (neoliberal), the meso-level (organisational), and the micro-level (self-governance) has spawned the flexible, placeless (or 'agile'), ever-connected, and hence also ever-working subject. Burud and Tumolo (2004) describe a 'dual-focus worker', but I contend that this is very much a single-focused worker who is ostensibly multitasking—a worker who is cognitively preoccupied with work while also tending to a kaleidoscope of everyday life tasks on the side. Multitasking has become the new routine. This worker is isolated—amid 'teamwork', family, and friends—task-oriented, and depoliticised. One might argue, to use Hannah Arendt's (1958) terminology, that in the form of the neoliberal knowledge worker, *homo faber* regresses to *animal laborans*.[9] Richard Sennett explains this distinction as follows in *The Craftsman* (2008, 7):

> *Animal laborans* is, as the name implies, the human being akin to a beast of burden, a drudge condemned to routine. Arendt enriched this image by imagining him or her absorbed in a task that shuts out the world, a state well exemplified by Oppenheimer's feeling that the atomic bomb was a 'sweet' problem, or Eichmann's obsession with making the gas chambers efficient. In the act of making it work, nothing else matters; *Animal laborans* takes the work as end in itself.
>
> By contrast, *Homo faber* is [Arendt's] image of men and women doing another kind of work, making a life in common. Again Arendt enriched an inherited idea. The Latin tag *Homo faber* means simply 'man as maker'. . . . *Homo faber* is the judge of material labor and practice, not *Animal laborans*'s colleague but his superior. Thus, in her view, we human beings live in two dimensions. In one we make things; in this condition we are amoral, absorbed in a task. We also harbor another, higher way of life in which we stop producing and start discussion and judging together. Whereas *Animal laborans* is fixated in the question 'How?' *Homo faber* asks 'Why?'

The neoliberal knowledge worker thus in fact works all the time in the heterotopia of every other daily activity. It is a heterotopia in that it encapsulates in a single space several incompatible spatial elements (Foucault 1967). The knowledge worker is displaced, yet always localisable. Armed with a cognitive apparatus that continues working on the complex problems of the day and armed with smart devices constantly at hand, working continues while life happens. As a result, this ever-increasing segment of the workforce ends up *living for the sake of work*, as opposed to working to live. This might be construed as an overinvestment in work with no direct correlation to any increase in quality of life.

Quality of life might be measured in vastly diverse ways. It may generally be postulated that these workers may earn more, but the additional earnings do not correlate proportionally with any perceptible or apparent increase in well-being. In fact, various authors, such as Wilkinson (2005) and Wilkinson and Pickett (2010), have documented and compellingly argued that there is a causal relation between the conditions typical of neoliberal society on the one hand, and the severe and noticeable rise in mental and physical disorders on the other. The rise in mental and physical disorders has been reported by

Verhaeghe (2012) and Han (2017). The corrosion of social bonds is noted by Sennett (1998, 2003, 2006).

At what point and for what reasons did knowledge workers start to live for the sake of work? How has knowledge work—construed as 'discretionary behaviour'—become compulsive? The short answer, I propose, is that neoliberal capitalism has found a way to turn 'wanting to work' into 'living to work'. Various factors play a role: the very *nature* of knowledge work, which is non-routine, engaging, and satisfying, and the shrewd neoliberal insight that economic success requires *investment in human capital*. This awareness, coupled with an *organisational culture* that makes available the necessary resources and the requisite freedom for entrepreneurial activity, enables neoliberalism to succeed in eliciting this kind of discretionary behaviour.

Considered more holistically, there appear to be three linked reasons for this development, as I already indicated briefly in the first chapter. Neoliberal knowledge workers *have to* work, overinvesting in work to respond to internalised coercion for self-responsible knowledge workers to be ever more efficient. They work all the time from anywhere, because it is *possible* to do so through connected smart technologies, giving the worker the capacity and management the control. Most intriguingly, neoliberal workers paradoxically *want* to work all the time, deriving satisfaction from the challenge posed by their work, which requires non-repetitive problem-solving and hence ingenuity and creativity.

Neoliberal governmentality capitalises on all three of these factors combined. Overinvested knowledge workers find themselves in fully fledged societies of control—chilling incarnations and perfections of Deleuze's (1992) prophecy. An important aspect of this society of 'free-floating' control, which has replaced the disciplinary society made up of environments of enclosure characteristic of every institution from the family to the school, is that what Deleuze (1992) calls the 'dividual' who is made to believe that s/he can 'to do whatever s/he wants' (as long as the job gets done). Control presents itself as a kind of freedom, in fact, an 'excess of freedom'. Herein the digital Panopticon differs in an important way from the Orwellian scenario of constant paranoia induced by Big Brother, as Han (2017, 69) explains. On the contrary, constant surveillance is supposedly not something to worry about, but something to welcome, knowing that it serves our best interests. It serves to monitor our behaviour in order to anticipate our needs. Above all, it serves to ensure our safety and security, be it in a time of global terror or a global epidemic. In Han's (2017, 69) words: 'Big Brother now wears a *friendly face*. His *friendliness* is what makes surveillance so efficient'. He wonders if the term 'surveillance state' is then not perhaps a misnomer, as today no one really *feels* watched or threatened.[10] And it is precisely this *feeling of freedom* that has become the problem (Han 2017, 71). The *feeling of freedom* that accompanies control blinds us to the fact that control disperses responsibility throughout life. In fact, a diffuse matrix or network of information-gathering algorithms track, code, and interpret everything into patterns that are constantly being interpreted and adjudicated. Mobile devices equipped with GPS and connected to the internet can track everything from our sleeping patterns to our internet surfing behaviour. If you have nothing to hide, the argument runs, you have nothing to fear; hence the compulsion in societies of control to police oneself through self-responsibilisation and to 'share'. We voluntarily 'share' the most intimate details about ourselves on social media platforms to collect 'friends', 'followers', 'reads', and 'likes'. Törnberg and Uitermark's (2020) social Synopticon emphasises the social dimension of this form of control that encapsulates a watching while being watched—more so than Han's (2017) digital Panopticon—but both recognise that this form of control mobilises the freedom of the (in)dividual subject. Han's (2017) notion of 'friendly Big Brother' stresses the apparent leniency and benevolence of this form of control. By contrast, Zuboff's (2018) notion of 'instrumentarian power' alerts us to the embedded algorithms in social/digital platforms, designed to anticipate users' behaviour and generate predictive data that do not depend only on *monitoring* online behaviour. These data are generated by actually *directing* online behaviour. Törnberg and Uitermark's (2020) social Synopticon sketches the isolated working screen-bound subject sending out echoes in cyberspace in her/his search for self-affirmation. From the perspective of this subject, constant surveillance has become vital because it is the source of social 'bonds', but also of safety, security, well-being, and health.

Importantly, coercion works differently from control, and the difference is instructive. Coercion (*you have to*) is an externally applied force that pushes or pulls, but does not incite. It may achieve the minimum amount of compliance, and only rarely conviction or whole-hearted buy-in.[11] Quite the opposite: more often than not, it evokes passive resistance in the form of the pervasive phenomenon of procrastination. Control (*I can*), as we have seen, is not seen as a limitation of freedom, but as empowering, benevolent, and beneficial. Once something is internalised as 'what is good for me', it becomes self-control, self-responsibilisation, and self-care. As noted, Han (2017) emphasises the *positivity* and *permissiveness* of power in the neoliberal regime, which makes it an exceptionally efficient technology of power, as it ensures that people subordinate themselves to power relations *on their own and of their own volition*: 'Such a dynamic seeks to activate, motivate and optimise—not to inhibit or repress. It proves so effective because it does not operate by means of forbidding and depriving, but by pleasing and fulfilling. Instead of making people *compliant*, it seeks to make them *dependent*' (Han 2017, 36). Complex control that appears open, informal, and non-linear operates to turn compliance into wholehearted conviction. Neoliberal working subjects do more than is required of them, and it feels good and right.

Han (2017, 37–38) identifies a few mechanisms of what he terms the 'smart power' employed by neoliberal governmentality, which to my mind helps to explain—at least in part—how it succeeds in producing working subjects that *like* doing more than is required, that is, working subjects that volunteer discretionary behaviour. It does not operate openly, but instead covertly guides the working subject's will to its own benefit. It does not rely on free choice (*Wahl*), but offers working subjects the opportunity of free selection (*Auswahl*). Because it constantly invites our opinions, needs, wishes, and preferences, it is able to read and assess our conscious and unconscious thoughts. Based on this, and combined with its own agenda of ever-increasing productivity and the maximisation of profit, it presents the worker with a 'menu'[12] from which s/he can 'freely' choose from a list of tailor-made options designed to engage voluntary self-organisation and self-optimisation. Hence, it manages to remain invisible. Power that remains invisible does not invoke any desire for resistance. Smart power therefore succeeds in getting workers to subjugate themselves by consuming and communicating as 'they click Like all the while' (Han 2017, 38).

The overinvestment in work appears to be disproportionate to necessity or correlative gain. On the face of things, the overinvested worker seems to enjoy no perceived increase in quality of life[13] even if s/he earns more. In 1905, Weber[14] wrote about modern humanity (*Menschentum*) and its loss of freedom and referred to people as mere 'cogs in a machine' (Owen 1994, 101).[15] The present incarnation of the subjectivity of knowledge workers would appear qualitatively different, as they are not bogged down by soul-destroying and mind-numbing routine work, but are challenged to be increasingly creative and innovative by every new work assignment. But like those cogs in the social machine, their entrepreneurial dedication betrays an almost vocational devotion. In the world of knowledge work, creativity appears to be the new conformity. This connected, creative cog might even be capitalism's most ingenious invention to date—content, self-controlled, self-motivated, and the perfect consumer.

Conclusion

Under the conditions of apparently greater autonomy and discretion that is so pervasive in the management literature discussing knowledge workers, governance takes the form of 'control'. Here 'control' should be conceived along the lines of Foucault's conception of government as the 'conduct of conduct' (Foucault 1982b, 203). Control involves the exercise of power that guides the possibility of conduct and pre-designs the possible outcome, while allowing subjects to act (behave) within an apparently open field of possibilities. This implies that control as a form of government connects techniques of subjection to techniques of self-formation or subjectivisation (what Foucault calls *subjectivation*). Techniques of subjection, as Foucault explains, are not entirely exempt from techniques of subjectivisation but are distinct from them in essential ways (Foucault 1982b, 203). Building on from Foucault's argument, I contend that the intricate process of subject-formation within the power constellations of neoliberal governmentality is made possible by what Törnberg and Uitermark (2020) call 'complex control'. Han (2017, 37) refers to it as 'smart power'—power that mobilises freedom itself to control the subject's conduct, to orchestrate the self-organisation of individuals themselves. Zuboff (2018) theorises this phenomenon as 'instrumentarian power' that monitors algorithmically directed 'spontaneous' online behaviour.

Control, then, operates below the radar, as an insidious, indirect elicitation of workers' buy-in. It orchestrates a guided and thus circumscribed set of possible actions below the veneer of limitless choices that pre-arrange the possible outcome. Knowledge workers are 'managed' by offering them a myriad (but in fact limited number) of possibilities for organising their 'work-life balance' in order to choreograph the desired outcome of optimal efficiency. This form of subjection is matched by unprecedented subjectivisation, which permits the working subject actively to enhance his/her own productive capacities. Subjectivisation—the government of the self by the self—holds the key to resisting subjection, but it now becomes a kingpin in the exhaustive execution of subjection. The wicked genius of the American brand of neoliberalism, or Anarcho-liberalism, associated with Milton Friedman and the Chicago School, as theorised by Foucault (2008), relies on the realisation that all labour, including wage labour, can be understood as a *voluntary* investment or entrepreneurial activity carried out in the individual pursuit of some sort of surplus value, future return, or wage (Foucault 2008, 224). This is the basis of the theory of human capital, which is different from other forms of capital in that it requires the human to be present if it is to be converted into surplus wealth. An in-depth consideration of the neoliberal theory of human capital goes beyond the scope of this chapter,[16] so suffice it to say that this theory recognises that the worker is fundamentally conjoined with her/his capacities as a kind of assemblage with a dynamic productive potential. This kind of labour—conceived as 'capital-ability' (Foucault 2008, 225)—is not merely a 'factor of production'. Rather, it has a qualitative and dynamic aspect. That is, in neoliberalism, the worker is in a very real sense 'an active economic subject', not just at work but in everything s/he does (Foucault 2008, 223). This working subject is not a partner in a 'process of exchange' as was traditionally conceived of, but a dynamic 'entrepreneur of himself', constantly balancing costs and benefits, and constantly mindful of the future impact of choices even in seemingly non-economic spheres. Han (2017) sees this subject as a 'project' that, in the hope of some return, pursues her/his own transformation by enhancing her/his basic physical capacities, mental skills, and attitude through the market (Foucault 2008, 226, 229).

To capitalise on this form of labour, the active economic subject requires an organisational logic that controls the worker's conduct *imperceptibly*, not just while that worker is at work, but in every aspect of the worker's existence. The control needs to be imperceptible because human capital depreciates in the face of overt coercive measures, because human capital in the form of knowledge work requires the worker's *voluntary devotion* in order to be optimally effective. The control needs to extend to every aspect of the worker's existence, because the worker's efficiency depends on his/her mental and physical well-being. This worker needs to buy into the neoliberal governance and accept the premise of the market, which in turn results in the constant development of her/his own human capital in order to survive and prosper. If s/he refuses to submit to the market rationality that inculcates an all-pervasive cost-benefit decision-making process, the worker will experience some measure of discomfort in the form of unemployability, job loss, or insufficient income, for example, thereby allowing the market to correct the worker's choice calculus. In this sense, the hegemony of neoliberal life appears to foreclose the possibility of any alternative mode of existence. It is this broad ontological power of neoliberalism that Foucault (2008) recognises. This power implies that

> by virtue of the way neoliberalism extracts surplus today—through the production of knowledge, desires and affects—the question of power is not simply a question of the production of subjectivity but, rather, a question of the real and intense ways in which the 'commanding heights' of the economy have become immanent through the hegemony of immaterial labour. (Kiersey 2011, 37)

In this way, neoliberalism succeeds in subsuming the volitional devotion of the hearts, minds, and hands of knowledge workers not only in neoliberal production, but in the very reproduction of social life.

Notes

1. A version of this chapter has been published as Hofmeyr 2022a.

2. To be sure, as Davis (2016) points out, in many parts of the world, aspects of the Second and Third Industrial Revolutions have yet to be experienced. This situation is complicated by the fact that new technologies are in some cases able to 'leapfrog' older ones. In 2013, the United Nations reported that more people in the world have access to a mobile phone than basic sanitation. In the same way, the Fourth Industrial Revolution is beginning to emerge at the same time that the Third (digital) Revolution is spreading and maturing across countries and organisations. As the novelist William Gibson is reported to have said: 'The future is already here—it's just not very evenly distributed' (quoted in Davis 2016, n.p.).

3. As a consequence of the Protection of Personal Information Act (South Africa's POPI Act)—the equivalent of the EU GDPR (General Data Protection Regulation), social/digital platforms such as Facebook are now required to ask users' permission to use the data generated by their online behaviour. However, when permission is not granted to accept cookies, for example, users are sanctioned by barring access to the online platform or to the full user experience.

4. According to the blurb, this book was awarded the 'Outstanding HRD Book of the Year by the Academy of Human Resource Development' and was hailed as 'essential reading for any manager today'. It served as a key reference in my attempt to understand knowledge work and how to leverage human capital.

5. Within this context it is important to acknowledge that knowledge workers are, in many respects, highly privileged relative to other workers and the pandemic has really brought this to the fore. Many knowledge workers did not face redundancy as they could continue their work unimpeded from home even under conditions of the strictest lockdown. Moreover, whereas the pandemic resulted in the loss of countless jobs and the bankruptcy of numerous businesses, it created a need for more specialised knowledge work on account of the large-scale online migration of many organisational activities.

6. It is worth qualifying this assertion because even for knowledge workers, the satisfaction, often rather abstract, may be too delayed, and there may well be a real sense of satisfaction in completing a clearly delimited concrete task. For example, the 'work' work of the knowledge worker is never ever done or completed, but the same knowledge worker may derive immense satisfaction from the completion of even a routine concrete task such as doing the dishes, or creative 'tasks' such as planting a bed of geraniums, baking a cake, quilting a runner, or building a scale model.

7. This is not to discount David Graeber's (2018) contention that many jobs that once involved meaningful and satisfying knowledge work have steadily deteriorated

to include aspects that are now mere box-ticking and bean-counting exercises, for example, formerly interesting work in the media and academia, where time is now increasingly taken up by completing compliance forms and time allocation surveys. More time is spent on reporting on work done than on doing the actual work. According to Graeber (2018), this accounts in part for why, instead of being enabled by technological advances to work a fifteen-hour week, as John Maynard Keynes predicted in 1930, many seem to be busier than ever. Graeber (2018) claims that real reason for keeping former knowledge workers employed in trivial jobs (or 'bullshit' jobs, as he calls them) is political—a population kept fully occupied with 'made-work' is less likely to revolt.

8. Trengrove (2021) reports that many companies in South Africa (and elsewhere) had to re-invent what they do and how they work on account of the lockdown measures during COVID-19, and predicts that the practice of working flexible hours remotely in many instances is here to stay. This will increasingly change the priorities of how much and what type of space an organisation needs—organisations will prioritise ubiquitous connectivity and secure information technology services. Organisations reportedly no longer consider presenteeism as a measure of an employee's value. In future, workspaces may well be designed to accommodate only 40 per cent to 50 per cent of employees simultaneously, Trengrove (2021) maintains.

9. Classical modernists such as Adam Smith, Locke, and Marx placed the notion of labour at the centre of their work. The resultant conflation of labour and work was famously challenged by Hannah Arendt in *The Human Condition* (1958).

10. This may change soon if privacy legislation fails to prevent employers from using the worker's computer camera for surveillance.

11. If force of a physical or psychological kind can result in a kind of Stockholm syndrome, then invisible complex control may have the same effect, especially in those workers that derive great satisfaction from complete compliance. Workers that are likely to fall into this category may colloquially be described as people-pleasers.

12. This is exactly what Foucault (1982b, 203) is referring to—and no doubt his discussion is the source informing Han's argument—when Foucault contends that the exercise of power consists in guiding the possibility of conduct and putting in order the possible outcome.

13. What 'an increase in quality of life' might mean to different individuals is obviously very different for each person. Here I refer to the fact that neoliberal knowledge workers work all the time, which results in less time for recreational activities and social interactions on the one hand, and a rise in stress-induced psychiatric disorders ranging from depression to burnout on the other. The obvious paradox is that they do this work anyway, even if it takes such a toll on their health and on their personal and social well-being, and the question remains—why?

14. Owen (1994) places Weber in a trajectory that runs from Nietzsche to Foucault on the grounds that his work can be read as a form of genealogical understanding and critique. He contends that '[f]or Weber, cultural science is concerned with how we have become what we are, that is to say, with articulating a history of the

present' (Owen 1994, 101). He adds that the 'purpose of Weber's accounts is the same as Nietzsche's, namely to provide a "context of meaning" within which the development of *Menschentum* may be understood and evaluated in terms of the fate of man in modernity' (Owen 1994, 101).

15. At the beginning of the twentieth century, Weber (1905/1992, 127–28) wrote:

> it is still more horrible to think that the world could one day be filled with nothing but those little cogs, little men clinging to little jobs and striving toward bigger ones—a state of affairs which is to be seen once more, as in the Egyptian records, playing an ever-increasing part in the spirit of our present administrative systems, and especially of its offspring, the students. This passion for bureaucracy . . . is enough to drive one to despair. It is as if in politics . . . we were to deliberately to become men who need 'order' and nothing but order, who become nervous and cowardly if for one moment this order wavers, and helpless if they are torn away from their total incorporation in it. That the world should know no men but these: it is in such an evolution that we are already caught up, and the great question is therefore not how we can promote and hasten it, but what can we oppose to this machinery in order to keep a portion of mankind free from this parceling-out of the soul, from this supreme mastery of the bureaucratic way of life.

16. The theory of human capital is discussed in Chapter 5.

CHAPTER FOUR

The Relation Between Work and Thumos

A Critical Interrogation of What Motivates the Knowledge Work Compulsion[1]

The question that confronts us now is what exactly lies behind the *volitional* devotion of the compulsively working knowledge worker. In other words, why do knowledge workers live to work, not only by choice, but even enthusiastically? There is, of course, the fact that knowledge workers are subject to pressure to meet deadlines, pressure that insinuates itself 'smartly', as we have seen in the previous chapter, and becomes internalised as self-responsibilisation to meet the demands of the job, which technology enables knowledge workers to do all the time, from anywhere. However, neither this pressure nor technological empowerment really explains the knowledge worker's quasi-religious *devotion* and commitment to work. This presents us with a paradox because what seems like a form of work addiction takes a heavy toll on the worker's health and private life. In fact, it would appear as if the overinvestment in knowledge work does not generate any proportionate gains for the working subject.

To arrive at some explication of the phenomenon of compulsive work, in this chapter I critically interrogate Fukuyama's (1992) contention that work has a thumotic origin. An attempt to grasp what thumos entails takes us back to the ancient roots of the construct, especially in the thought of Plato. Fukuyama (1992) claims that his argument is derived from Hegel's conceptualisation of the significance of labour, via Kojève's (1947) reading of Hegel, but is it evident that Hegel's theory has any relation to thumos as such? In this context we also have to interrogate whether the work compulsion of present-day knowledge workers might not merely be attributed to their work ethic. Briefly revisiting the history of the work ethic sheds some light on the extent to which this notion offers any answers to the question at hand.

The Problematics

In the information age, knowledge work has become the definitive form of labour that drives economic success. In the preceding chapters, I have reflected on what exactly knowledge work is and on what constitutes the optimal organisational culture in which knowledge workers might thrive, so as to be optimally effective and productive. I found that Kelloway and Barling's (2000) definition of knowledge work as '*discretionary* organizational behaviour' based on the use of knowledge is particularly useful, because it captures something both crucial and confounding about knowledge work that is not acknowledged in other definitions.

Obviously, eliciting this behaviour poses some challenges for management, because work is typically not conceived of as elective or optional, but rather as compulsory, based on the assumption that organisations pay their employees to produce certain deliverables within certain timeframes, creating a compulsion to work in employees who need to be paid. Today, a reconceived organisational culture has to manage the unique nature of knowledge work, which is no longer bound to a fixed office space or nine-to-five office hours. Knowledge work is wherever and whenever the knowledge worker is, creating an all-encompassing world of work, in which knowledge workers work all the time. The pressure of deadlines and ever increased efficiency does indeed compel knowledge workers to work continuously, but this compulsion has to be kept largely implicit because creative problem-solving work as discretionary behaviour cannot be forced without severely compromising its quality: a wise organisation can translate pressure into internalised coercion in self-responsible knowledge workers. The networked technological infrastructure and innovation that have enabled constant knowledge work anytime from anywhere are also widening the reach of management's more covert surveillance powers into the private time and life of the knowledge worker. Irrespective of the private demands of daily life, the worker is expected to be at the disposal of whatever and whenever the job demands.

One would expect knowledge workers to resent this takeover of their space and time, but instead, these workers do not merely work to live—they live to work, irrespective of the array of physical and mental illnesses and dysfunctions that have been documented (Verhaeghe 2012; Han 2017), and of potentially impaired social relationships (Sennett 1998, 2003, 2006). In many senses, then, volitional compulsive working has no readily discernible gains for these workers.

Given the nature of knowledge work as discretionary behaviour that depends on certain conditions of possibility, it cannot be demanded, merely encouraged. What then are the conditions of possibility that organisations have to meet to elicit knowledge work? At least three conditions have to be met. Organisations have to *empower* employees to be able to do it; they have to *motivate* them to want to do it, and finally, they have to provide employees with the *opportunity* to do it. Importantly, as Meyer and Allen (1997) point out, knowledge work, as a 'wanting to work', is an affective commitment that turns knowledge workers into *investors* in the organisation, rather than mere assets (Pfeffer and Sutton 2000). To evoke that commitment, these investors must feel free to invest their cognitive labour as their mood, feelings, and discretion dictate. The paradox is that the quintessential knowledge worker, who cannot be *forced* to work, is characterised by a seemingly devotional commitment to work—a commitment not to the organisation per se, but to the knowledge task at hand. Put differently, these workers seem to engage in *discretionary* behaviour compulsively and work all the time, unlike the material labourers of the pre-industrial and industrial eras. This calls for a critical investigation into the root of knowledge workers' motivation for *wanting to* work incessantly. As we shall see, this wanting to work flies in the face of how work has been theorised historically.

First and foremost, the knowledge worker typically is a supremely rational subject. Rationality under neoliberal governmentality consists in the imperative to subject every decision to a cost-benefit analysis: what course of action will render the greatest return? For such compulsive knowledge workers, unlike for the workers of the past, leisure and recreation only trump work when the leisure and recreation serve to optimise the workers' ability to render the work more efficiently. Given the nature of their highly specialised problem-solving jobs, even downtime is unconsciously at the service of creative problem-solving. The cognitive apparatus of the worker continues working to solve a complex puzzle even while the worker is supposedly *not* working.

Research has shown that employees' commitment to work is directly related to their level of motivation (Yusoff, Wan, and Idris 2013), but what precisely motivates employees has been found to differ markedly between different individuals (Burke 2007; Saraswathi 2011). If the motivation of knowledge workers is based on a cost-benefit analysis, then work compulsion should in theory be explained by the gains it generates, whatever form those gains take. Herzberg, Mausner, and Snyderman's (1959) well-known Two Factor Theory distinguishes between intrinsic and extrinsic factors of motivation. They postulated that extrinsic factors or hygiene factors are necessary to prevent employees' dissatisfaction, but are not sufficient to motivate workers. Instead, it is intrinsic motivation factors that increase employee's performance or productivity. This distinction between intrinsic or higher-level factors and extrinsic or lower-level factors is closely related to Maslow's hierarchy of needs, which places intrinsic factors such as recognition and self-actualisation above basic extrinsic needs such as (job) security, pay, benefits, and working conditions. Along similar lines as Herzberg et al. (2010), Drucker (2003) argues that knowledge workers are primarily motivated by job quality and content. They are, as already noted, driven by a sense of personal achievement and greater responsibility, which is seen as a sign of recognition. The complex, problem-solving nature of knowledge work does indeed lend itself to offering more work satisfaction. Something that adds to the (potentially enjoyable) challenge of knowledge work is the ever-accelerating pace of innovation. The necessity of reskilling, micro-credentialing, bespoke upskilling, and continuous learning means the core of what makes knowledge work knowledge-intensive is its dynamic, unpredictable nature. It fits the profile of the most competent and sought-after knowledge workers to hunger for more knowledge and expertise. Hence, they enthusiastically pursue continuous learning in the service of meeting ever-greater challenges, chasing job satisfaction, and self-actualisation. So even learning and self-development—which are not, strictly speaking, work—are in the service of work as a necessary condition for being able to do the work. Hence, it may justifiably be said that knowledge workers work *willingly* all the time despite the cost because of such intrinsic satisfaction.

What the existing theories fail to unearth, though, is the much more fundamental philosophical dimension that undergirds work motivation. There seems to be some mechanism at work that drives the irrational work-drivenness of the knowledge worker—an ambiguous ambition—a mechanism that neoliberal governmentality succeeds in capitalising on. It is this dimension that needs to be foregrounded if the subject-formation of the compulsively working contemporary knowledge worker is to be fully understood. What then should we call this mechanism—an ambition to self-actualise, a fervent work ethic, or a thumotic spiritedness?

Ambiguous Ambition?

Let us begin by exploring the possibility of a driving 'ambition' that may underlie knowledge workers' fixation. Throughout his work, Foucault's main concern was with 'the different modes by which, in our culture, human beings are made subjects' (Foucault 1982b, 208)—in the twin sense of the notion that encapsulates both empowering subject-formation and debilitating subjection. In his lectures presented at the Collège de France in the 1970s and early 1980s,[2] Foucault traces the genealogy of power through the last six centuries, from sovereign power through to disciplinary power, from policing (broadly conceived as policy, controls, and management techniques), to security and government (again, broadly conceived, and not reducible to the state). His preoccupation with power is not an end in itself, but a necessary tool for understanding subject-formation. Shortly before his untimely death in 1984, Foucault returned to antiquity—to the Greco-Roman practice of care of the self, as well as to *parrhesia* or truth-telling—in an attempt to engender a critical self-awareness of subjectivity as a contingent construction, rather than as a ready-made self that is simply to be discovered or deciphered by way of confessional or analytical practices. Moreover, he argues that this constructed subject identity has to be refused or rejected, since it is the very source of the self's subjection. For Foucault, subjectivisation, on the other hand, is the minimal freedom we retain to mould a different subject from this imposed subject identity. This is not an act of either overcoming or wholly destroying the imposed subject identity, for this would be to destroy the very subject itself. Transcending our limits is an erasure of the very limits that constitute the self, thereby wholly dismantling the self as subject. Rather, subjectivisation entails manoeuvring within that minimal margin of freedom and working on the limits of our subject identity to remould it into one that affords more room for being, acting, and thinking otherwise than that which is imposed.

Under neoliberalism, transcendence of existing limitations might be construed in terms of what the economist Joseph Schumpeter called 'creative destruction', which refers to a deliberate dismantling of established processes in order to make way for improved methods of production. This describes the mechanism employed by the market to clear the way for innovation in the manufacturing process to increase productivity. He describes it as the 'process of industrial mutation that incessantly revolutionises the economic structure from within, incessantly destroying the old one, incessantly creating a new one' (Schumpeter 1942, 83). Netflix would be a contemporary example of creative destruction to revolutionise entertainment—it has overthrown DVD rental and traditional media industries. In order to secure an increased measure of freedom for the subject, what is called for is *not* transcendence of the limits of the contours of the subject's identity, because this would effectively destroy the subject. Limits define and constitute as much as they might constrain and smother. Increased freedom is instead secured by way of a *transgression* of limits, not a transcendence of them. With the notion of transgression, Foucault (1963, 35) postulates a far more nuanced relationship to limits:

> Transgression, then, is not related to the limit as black to white, the prohibited to the lawful, the outside to the inside, or as an open area of a building to its enclosed spaces. Rather, their relationship takes the form of a spiral which no simple infraction can exhaust. Perhaps it is like a flash of lightning in the night which, from the beginning of time, gives a dense and black intensity to the night it denies, which lights up the night from the inside, from top to bottom, and yet owes to the dark the stark clarity of its manifestation.

So the limits of our identity serve to indicate who we are, what we have become, what we have been made into, but also what possibilities of being lie beyond them. In his later work, when Foucault was more explicitly concerned with subject-formation, with who we are in our present, he describes the 'philosophical ethos appropriate to the critical ontology of ourselves as a historico-practical test of the limits that we may go beyond, and thus as work carried out by ourselves upon ourselves as free beings' (Foucault 1983, 47). Transgression, then, involves working on the limits, as opposed to an erasure or overcoming of them. It is a painstaking historical as well as practical process of interrogating the relations of power/knowledge or governmentality that have made us what we are, and incrementally experimenting with ways of being otherwise.

Neoliberal governmentality prescribes and rewards a subject engaged in precisely such a process of 'creative destruction'—effectively destroying remnants of its less efficient self in the name of ever-increasing productivity. Han (2017, 15) dubs this a 'project' as opposed to a subject: 'As a project deeming itself free of external and alien limitations, the I is now subjugating itself to internal limitations and self-constraints, which are taking the form of compulsive achievement and optimization'. The model neoliberal subject, Han's 'project', is *Homo economicus*—not the classically conceived economic man as a partner in a process of exchange, but economic man as an entrepreneur of himself, 'being for himself his own capital, being for himself his own producer, being for himself the source of [his] earning' (Foucault 2008, 225–26). This is the norm of subject formation that neoliberalism dictates, that sustains neoliberalism, and which it incentivises in turn, since it enables the self not merely to survive but also to thrive under neoliberalism. It is a subject identity that is not merely externally imposed, but self-imposed and continuously remade to become ever more efficient through constant self-investment. Subjugation, then, is attended by a powerful sense of autonomy, and eventually becomes self-subjugation. Hence the neoliberal subject is caught in a double bind. The subject's identity is the very condition of possibility of the subject's being, but it is also the source of its subjection. That identity cannot simply be discarded without destroying the very self.

Transgression, as we have seen, is the continuous process of applying pressure to imposed limits so as to be able to be, do and think somewhat differently than is (self)prescribed. Foucault locates the means to achieve this in the ancient Greek injunction to 'take care of the self' (*heautou epimeleisthai*). To take care of the self is to make oneself the object of all of one's diligence. It is therefore not a rest cure, but painstaking, time-consuming labour. In fact, Foucault (1984b) finds here in the Greeks a response to the Kantian injunction: *Sapere aude!* 'Have the courage to use your own reason!' (Kant 1784, 7).

Present-day neoliberal governmentality has co-opted and perverted this injunction into a pervasive and lucrative self-help culture in which subjects have to accept responsibility themselves for the high toll taken on their mental and physical health by the constant optimal efficiency required by their jobs. Organisations have responded by way of corporate 'wellness' programmes to guide workers to self-manage their work-life balance, pre-emptively to create mental and physical health awareness. Along with constant work, and in order to work constantly, the subject also has to take responsibility for ensuring the mental and physical health and capability needed for sustained optimal efficiency.

Again, this raises the question of why knowledge workers are such zealous participants in the execution of their own working fate. What is at the heart—or rather soul—of this ambiguous ambition that propels knowledge workers' work-drivenness, despite its obvious costs, if the knowledge worker is not motivated by more money? Apart from the practice of care of the self, we find among the Ancients what Nietzsche might have called the *Entstehungsherd* (the originating hearth, the place of emergence) of the notion that along with reason and desire, there is something like an innate human spiritedness. It is this 'spiritedness' that may account for the irrational drive to live in order to work in the ambitious knowledge worker. Famously, Fukuyama (1992) has argued that labour has its origin in the ancient spiritedness that the Greeks called thumos (also commonly spelled 'thymos'; Greek: θυμός). In order to explicate more precisely what thumos might represent in human subjectivity today, what characteristics and types of actions and being it might account for, as indicated in the introductory chapter, it is worth revisiting how Plato theorised thumos.

Thumos in Plato

In his *Phaedrus*, Plato (c. 370 BCE) postulates that the soul has three component parts, which he explains by means of Socrates's allegory of the chariot. A chariot (representing the soul) is pulled by a rebellious dark horse, which symbolises man's appetites or desire, *himeros*,[3] and a high-spirited white horse, which symbolises thumos. (In Plato's *Phaedrus*, the noble white horse is described as 'a lover of honor and modesty and self-control; companion to true glory' (§253e), but no explicit mention is made of thumos, as in the *Republic*, which was probably written somewhat later.) The charioteer is Reason. Reason's challenge is to harness the energy of both horses, getting the divergent steeds that pull the chariot, or the soul, 'violently in different directions' (§248a) into sync to be able to drive the chariot successfully into the heavens for the soul to behold Truth and become like the gods. The soul's fate therefore depends on establishing a symbiotic cooperative relationship between the appetites and desires on the one hand, and thumos on the other.

In the *Republic*, thumos refers to the spiritedness with which we rise in defence of someone or something or even an idea that we hold dear and cherish; the willingness even to sacrifice ourselves in defence of a person, especially if that person cannot defend her-/himself. This desire is especially aroused in the face of injustice. In other words, thumos is the well-spring of righteous indignation, which leads to anger, which in turn gives rise to the desire for vengeance. It is what drives Achilles' constant struggle for glory, retribution, and vengeance in Homer's *Iliad* in the face of his ally Agamemnon's injustice and his friend Patroclus' death. It is what incites Antigone in Sophocles' tragedy to bury her brother Polynices and to defy what she sees as the intolerable injustice of Creon's refusal to grant him a proper ritual burial, leaving him unburied on the battlefield.

The *Republic* describes the guardians or gatekeepers of justice in the polis or city-state (§375a–356c). The guardians are naturally endowed with 'an invincible and unbeatable spirit' (§375b). To be able to perform their duty, they must be quick to anger, ready to fight, and victory-loving, so as to be willing to sacrifice their own good in defence of their polis and their fellow citizens. However, Plato, following Socrates, recognises that this spiritedness, left to its own devices, might lead to injustice—the chariot needs to be steered. Thus thumos must be balanced by gentleness acquired through philosophical education so as to acquire wisdom or the art of discernment and restraint when required. The dilemma, which Socrates already recognises, is that thumos is both a necessary condition for the possibility of justice and poses a fundamental challenge to it. Nature has to be augmented by nurture; in other words, only the education of the guardians can adequately restrain the thumotic element in the polis, and ensure that the guardians remain allied to the rationally calculating element in the polis, the rulers, and can thus be fierce toward enemies of the polis, but remain gentle to all the other citizens. Importantly, then, Plato believes that thumos is the source of a host of traits such as bravery, determination, and the need for justice. Therefore, Plato's idea of thumos is tempered by a need for civility and order, unlike the violent, self-destructive thumos of the Homeric epics or Euripides' and Sophocles' plays.

What Does Thumos Encompass?

Thumos as a notion has all but fallen into oblivion. Hence, there is no equivalent term in English that encompasses the scope of what it signified for the Greeks. Significantly, when no exact translation exists in a particular culture for an ideal, it can be argued that that ideal does not exist within that society. If that is in fact the case, can we say that our so-called civilized Western culture denies the existence of thumos, or worse, actively stifles it? I would contend that thumos is alive and active. For a start, the thumotic expression of rage has found its way into the waging of two world wars, and continues to this day in factional and gang wars,[4] religious conflicts, as well as violent protest action across the globe. In such forms, the thumotic expression of rage is condemned as non-rational excess, while it rages on unabated in politics, as Foucault's well-known inversion of Clausewitz's (1832, 87) dictum that '[w]ar is the continuation of politics by other means' avers. Foucault contends that politics is in fact war waged by other means (Foucault 1975, 168; 1977, 90; 1982b, 222). In popular forms, we see thumotic indignation at injustice on full display in spellbinding heroic or superhero movies, and it may always have accounted for our fascination with quest novels.

McKay and McKay (2011) explain that the concept covers a range of qualities such as indignation, courage, determination, spirit, enterprise, and ambition. It encompasses 'heart' as opposed to 'head'—a kind of self-regarding instinct that ranges from self-assertion, through self-respect, to our relations with others. It involves our concern for our reputation and good name. They cite Empedocles, for example, who calls thumos the 'seat of life'. It is the stimulus or drive to action (McKay and McKay 2013). Importantly, thumos is most closely associated with anger. In Greek writings, thumos 'seethes', 'rages', and 'boils'. It is a particular kind of anger that is sparked when our honour is violated, when our reputation is on the line, or our family or property is threatened. The anger of thumos can be directed outward toward others, but also inward toward the self when we fail to live up to our principles. Thumos not only produces anger, but also channels that anger into the impulse to fight. Once we are in a fight, thumos spurs us on to stay in the arena and to continue fearlessly to strive for victory. Such fearless indomitability is at the very heart of every great human achievement.

The rage of a mob of student protestors that sets libraries alight in an irrationally self-destructive attempt to speak out against injustice is the manifestation of their thumos. The rage of the brave women in Iran openly flouting the rule to wear the hijab in public might similarly be construed as a manifestation of their thumos, but a different—perfectly rational—form of it. For Plato, our thumos, when it is properly educated, is born of a rational type of courage—'the man who's going to be a fine and good guardian of the city for us will in his nature be philosophic, spirited, swift and strong' (*Republic* §376c). Thumos, then, also encompasses evaluation and discernment—the ability to judge whether the fight we are in is a worthy one. As Hobbs (2006, 22) puts it: '[C]ourage involves both emotional commitment and evaluative belief, an intellectual and emotional appreciation of what things are worth taking risks for, and in what circumstances'. Thumos, then, works in concert with reason and emotion, and therefore it is also related to gut feelings and intuition—what Barnouw (2004, 70) calls 'visceral thinking'. Along similar lines, McKay and McKay (2011) contend that you can know when a decision is right when both your mind and heart—your reason and thumos—align. And as Socrates recognised, it has to be subjected to the age-old principle, the golden mean, that stipulates that virtue lies between extremes; the thumotic drive needs to be guided to keep to the middle path of moderation or temperance, since an excess of thumos causes hubris and a deficiency results in shame.

Whereas the dark horse of desire runs toward pleasure and material wealth—evident in phenomena such as conspicuous consumption, for example—the ambition and drive for recognition and honour over security are where the noble white steed, thumos, wants to go. Thumos seeks not to be hamstrung by possessions and sensuality. Properly harnessed, the white horse of thumos can lead us toward *eudemonia* or full human flourishing.

It is important to remember in this context that reason, the passions, desires, or appetites, and thumos are independent 'agencies' in the human soul. This is explained by MacIntyre (1988, 16) in the example of Odysseus left alone on the battlefield in the *Iliad*. Overcome by fear in the face of the overwhelming numbers of the enemy, he is tempted to flee from the fight. He conducts a dialogue with his thumos: 'If I flee frightened of their numbers, that will be a great evil; but if I am taken alone, that is more terrible. . . . But why does my *thumos* say these things to me? For I know that the bad [*kakoi*] leave the battle, but that he who is excellent [*aristeuesi*] in fighting must stand his ground boldly' (Homer, XX, 404–10, quoted in MacIntyre 1988, 15). Odysseus himself, or rather his *thumos*, reminds him(self) that 'whoever is *agathos* as a warrior, rather than *kakos*, stands fast'. MacIntyre (1988, 17) contends that Homer does not ascribe to Odysseus a process of reasoning. Rather what he does is 'call to mind what he knows in order to counteract the effect upon his *thumos* of a disturbing passion, fear. What he says to himself stands [in relation] to the action that he then performs, not as a premise to a conclusion, but as a statement of what is required to a performance of that requirement' (MacIntyre 1988, 17). *Thumos* in this context may be defined as that which carries someone forward, the self as a kind of energy: 'Passions such as fear or anger or sexual longing swell the *thumos* and lead to action, often of a destructive kind' (McIntyre 1988, 16). Hence, MacIntyre (1988) argues that this conception of the relationship of the passions to the *thumos* precludes us from understanding the passions as affording reasons for a particular course of action. He maintains that this form of deliberation that precedes action is not a process of *rational* decision-making or practical reasoning. From a Platonic point of view, however, it might justifiably be countered that it is precisely the charioteer, Reason, that pulls the dark horse of passion (fear) back to align it with the course of the white horse of thumos, because it is the charioteer, Reason, that '*knows* that the bad [*kakoi*] leave the battle, but that he who is excellent [*aristeuesi*] in fighting must stand his ground boldly' (Homer, XX, 404–10, quoted in MacIntyre 1988, 15).

Interestingly, Fukuyama (1992) derives his argument from his reading of Hegel, via Kojève, claiming that Hegel postulates that work is motivated by this 'energy', thumos, which drives us forward and keeps us working even if our passions dictate otherwise. This is a contentious claim, but it is worth some critical consideration, given the significance accorded to labour in Hegel's philosophy.

Hegel: The Significance of Work

Hegel produced a historicist reformulation of Platonic political theory, offering us an innovative way to think about the importance of work. He argues that work is the most important activity in the development of self-conscious freedom. Writing on self-consciousness in the *Phenomenology of Spirit* (1807), he contends that work is of definitive significance to the bondsman who is a labourer: 'Through work, . . . the bondsman becomes conscious of what he truly is' (Hegel [1807] 1977, 118, §195).[5] He is not merely a human being who happens to labour for the sake of his overlord, as the following complex argument shows (I quote at length, because Hegel's idea unfolds across this entire paragraph):

> Through work and labour ['in fashioning the thing'], this consciousness of the bondsman comes to itself.
>
> [H]e becomes aware that being-for-itself belongs to *him*, that he himself exists essentially and actually in his own right. This shape [the object of his labour] does not become something other than himself through being made external to him; for it is precisely this shape that is his pure being-for-self, which in this externality is seen by him to be the truth. Through this rediscovery of himself by himself [the labourer], the bondsman realizes that it is precisely in his work wherein he seemed to have only alienated existence that he acquires a mind of his own. (Hegel 1977, 118–99, §196)

Work, conceived as a negative mediating agency, the activity giving shape and form, is at the same time the individual existence, the pure self-existence of the consciousness of the labourer or bondsman, which now in the work (as activity and mediating agency) it does is externalised and passes into the condition of permanence. The consciousness that toils and serves accordingly attains by this means the direct apprehension of that independent being as itself. By the fact that the form is objectified, it does not become something other than the consciousness moulding the thing through work; for just that form is his pure self-existence, which therein becomes truly realised. Thus precisely in labour where there seemed to be merely some outsider's mind and ideas involved, the bondsman becomes aware, through this re-discovery of himself by himself, of having and being a 'mind of his own' (Hegel 1977, 118–19, §195–96).

For Hegel, as Gare (1996, 351) explains, the ego is the result of development 'from immediate sensitivity to self-awareness, then to self-consciousness gained through a reciprocity of perspectives in interpersonal relationships, and finally to universality through participation in ethical and cultural life'. The dialectic of lordship and bondage[6] describes the narrative of how self-consciousness is gained through interpersonal relationships (Ashton 1999). The dialectic is premised on the fact that '[s]elf-consciousness exists in and of itself when, and by the fact that, it so exists for another; that is, it exists only by being acknowledged' (Hegel 1977, 111, §178). The two self-consciousnesses appear to one another as pure externality, which gives rise to a battle for recognition. At first, this battle is pursued as a battle to the death—the two competing self-consciousnesses must be willing to sacrifice everything concrete to gain infinite self-respect and similar respect from all others (Hegel 1977, 114, §187A). However, this leads to an obvious dilemma: neither can come to full self-consciousness without the other, hence the death of one will not only nullify the victory of the other, but spell the other's death. The outcome that should be pursued instead is the enslavement of the other, the reduction of the other's self-consciousness to a 'thing-like' status. In Hegel's dialectic this is the resolution of opposites into a higher unity or 'sublation'. Importantly, sublation in German signals both a 'doing away with' and a 'preservation'.

As Ashton (1999) explains, the battle between the two self-consciousnesses takes the form of the bondsman working to serve the lord. Work, then, is the kingpin that connects these two self-consciousnesses in their respective endeavours to gain recognition and therefore come to full self-consciousness. The bondsman becomes a mere object for the satisfaction of the lord's needs and wants. The bondsman, however, is not merely someone who happens to work for the sake of the lord; his labour is his being. His purpose is that of another—the fruits of his labour are not his own but those of his lord. Since the objects of his labour are his entire being, he is at the mercy of lord, the owner of these objects. Herein the being of the bondsman becomes a 'being-for-another', and this being exists only in the form and shape of thinghood—as objects of labour that are to be used. This poses an important obstacle to the lord's quest for recognition. If the self-consciousness of the bondsman is reduced to his being a mere instrument, the lord can no longer obtain reciprocal recognition. On account of this 'inequality', the bondsman is afforded the opportunity to come to full self-consciousness and to become the ideal that he contemplates in his lord, whereas the lord is not afforded the same opportunity. Work is the means through which the bondsman becomes 'self-actualized'—it empowers the enslaved worker through the discovery of his own boundless creativity.

For Hegel, then, the paradox of labour lies in the fact that it both enslaves the bondsman and sets him free. The objects of the bondsman's labour fill the social world and preserve the bondsman's action in them. The bondsman comes to realise that his labour is crucial in the creation and functioning of the world. His consciousness is externalised in his work and passes into a condition of permanence. Hence, the fruits of his labour are no longer mere dead things that shackle him to others, but the life-affirming definition of his very being. For Hegel, the 'pure self-existence' of the bondsman becomes 'truly realized' in the externalised object. Through the process of his labour and the objectification of its products, the bondsman creates a self-conscious existence (Ashton 1999).

For his part, the lord does not work for the objects of his desire and ends up lacking the self-consciousness acquired through work. The lord becomes dependent on the bondsman as the lord attains his satisfaction through the bondsman—through the objects that 'bear the hallmark of the subject who worked on them'. The lord, then, fails to become an independent 'being-for-himself'. Hegel contends that the only way in which the lord can realise his own self-consciousness is to relinquish his lordship over his bondsman, and to contribute to building his (the lord's) own world and to mutually recognise the labours of others as they recognise him (Ashton 1999).

Hegel caused a complete revolution in political philosophy with his conceptualisation of a civil society that separates the 'political' and the 'civil' for the first time. According to Pelczynski (1984, 3), Hegel's philosophy saw 'the rise of a depoliticized society through the centralization of politics in the princely or revolutionary state, and [the shift of the point of gravity to the economy, a change which . . . founds [its] expression in [the] political' or 'a national economy'. Hegel realised that the sphere of non-political existence was that of the majority, who 'earn their living through labour, production and exchange, and therefore belonged, for much of their lives, to a sort of national "domestic society" or state-wide "household"' (Pelczynski 1984, 4). Civil society is essentially the sphere where individuals leave the particularity and security of their families and engage in the 'strategic pursuit of 'selfish' interests', where 'each member is his own end, everything else is nothing to him' (Habermas 1985, 28, 37). Labour is the means through which we satisfy these 'selfish' ends, which in turn serve important purposes in civil society and in subject-formation. Through labour, a person develops philosophically and therefore personally as s/he 'overcomes the estrangement between the objective world and the subjective world; [s/]he transforms labour into an appropriate medium for [her/]his self-development' (Marcuse 1941, 77). In the shaping of natural objects by our labour we make these objects part of our own subjectivity as we are able to recognise our needs and desires in them.

These shaped objects are abstracted, become commodities, and are exchanged in the market. The commodities that the labourer produces and then sells become the means through which s/he is recognised by others. In this way, labour plays a pivotal role in the opening up of the subjective world of the individual to the intersubjective world shared with others. Importantly, however, this process of producing an object, which objectifies the labourer's subjectivity and then abstracting and therefore alienating what is effectively his/her own subjectivity from it, transforms the shaped object into a commodity-means. This process has both positive and negative consequences. Positively, this personal commodity abstraction implies that the individual can be recognised by others. In the *Phenomenology of Spirit* (1807), Hegel explains that labour's value resides in the fact that it is a 'universal activity':

> The labour of the individual for his own needs is just as much a satisfaction of the needs of others as of his own, and the satisfaction of his own needs he only obtains through the labour of others. As the individual in his individual work already unconsciously performs a universal work, so again he also performs the universal work as his conscious object; the whole becomes, as a whole, his own work, for which he sacrifices himself and precisely in doing receives back from it his own self. (Hegel 1977, 213, §351)

Of importance to my argument is Hegel's conceptualisation of labour as pivotal in the personal and social development of humankind, which for him is one and the same movement. Hegel offers an implicit critique of the liberal conception of work—as purely an economic activity—arguing that work is not merely something we do to survive, but is in fact the most important activity in the development of self-conscious freedom (Hegel 1977, 111–18, §178–96). Labour then is the means through which an individual, 'opposed to all other individuals', becomes a member of a community (Marcuse 1941, 77). Furthermore, the satisfaction of individual needs and 'wants' above subsistence level requires the universal labour of a community. The paradox that civil society presents to Hegel is that it elevates individuals from their particularity to the universal, generating social bonds, while engendering great inequality and poverty. In fact, Hegel recognises that civil society has several inherent problems. For the purposes of the present argument, however, only two are pertinent, as they concern his theory of labour and the labourer, namely alienation and poverty. These two problems are connected. The alienation caused by mechanical, machine, or factory labour operates by decreasing the value of labour in the same proportion as productivity increases, since it leaves the worker's own skill underutilised. In the process, the consciousness of the factory worker is diminished to a state of stupefaction. The spiritual element of labour as the source of self-conscious plenitude of life is lost in factory labour. For Hegel, the poverty associated with machine labour in capitalist economies is twofold: it casts bodies into a state of penury, but also results in the impoverishment of minds.

Let us start with the problem of machine labour causing *alienation*. For Hegel, 'all human history is a process whereby ideas objectify themselves in material reality' (Löwith 1991, 266). The idea of shelter, for example, is objectified into houses; the idea of the general interest of society is objectified into the institutions of the state. However, this objectification of ideas becomes a source of alienation because the mind fails to grasp the fact that these objectified things are in fact the mind's own products, not simply the embodiment of its own ideas. This alienation first takes place through the labour process when people begin to use tools in their construction of their world. Tools mediate human interaction with the natural world. Nature is only fully mediated by way of the machine, which is a 'self-sufficient' tool capable of deceiving nature into working for humankind. Hegel realised that the more humans subjugate nature, the lower they themselves sink, as the deception seeks revenge (Ashton 1999).

The use of machines removes work from nature and then work becomes more mechanical. According to Hegel, the use of machines reduces work for the whole of humanity, but not for the individual. Indeed, for the individual, work increases, for the more mechanical work becomes, the less value it has, and the more the individual must work. For '[t]he more man frees himself from the concretion of nature, the more he controls nature, the more he also becomes dependent upon nature; for the more an individual's knowledge becomes restricted to the production of one abstract article, the less capable he must be of satisfying all of his other needs' (Cullen 1979, 67). Referring to factory labour, Hegel contends that the value of labour decreases in the same proportion as productivity increases. Work thus becomes increasingly 'dead' as it is relegated to machines, and the individual's own skill is not required or used. The consciousness of the factory worker is reduced to the utmost level of deadened dullness. The connection between the particular sort of labour and the infinite mass of needs becomes wholly imperceptible, and soon turns into blind dependence. The spiritual element, the self-conscious plenitude of life, becomes an empty activity (Ashton 1999).

In *Elements of the Philosophy of Right*, Hegel (1820) emphasises the alienating effect of too much work: 'By alienating the *whole* of my time, as made concrete through my work, and the totality of my production, I would be making the substantial quality of the latter, i.e. my *universal* activity and actuality or my personality itself, into someone else's property' (Hegel 1820, 97, §67). As the individual abstracts his/her labour, s/he not only gains a sense of mutual recognition and the benefits of goods and services generated by others' work, but s/he also loses control over his/her own destiny as s/he finds himself 'totally at the mercy of a system of exchange over which [s/he] has absolutely no control' (Plant 1993, 100). The stupefying and dehumanising effects of labour outlined here have indeed been perpetuated by the capitalist system, and even more so by the unconstrained market of American neoliberalism.

The other problem with civil society, the one which poses an even greater threat to the working classes, is *penury*, the impoverishment of the body. Hegel understands the rise of poverty within the discourse of economics and specifically as a result of overproduction due to the use of machine labour and competition, especially from abroad. It is precisely when civil society is in a state of unimpeded activity that the labourer is likely to be thrown into a state of poverty. For Hegel, it causes not only the destitution of the human as a body, but also the impoverishment of the mind (Ashton 1999).

Hegel sees physical poverty as a condition relative to a particular society. Poverty of the spirit is about the way we are conceived in our community and occurs when an individual's need to identify with both her/his central life-activity, work, and with the broader society of which s/he is a member, goes unfulfilled. Hegel recognises that poverty has a spiralling effect, in that when individuals fall into poverty, they are also cut off from other areas of society such as 'the acquisition of skill, education, access to justice and even organized labour' which are the very institutions that connect individuals to their community (Plant 1984, 230). Hegel recognises the double-bind that poverty presents to civil society:

> If the direct burden [of support] were to fall on the wealthier class, or if direct means were available in other public institutions . . . to maintain the increasingly impoverished mass, the livelihood of the needy would be ensured without the mediation of work; this would be contrary to the principle of civil society and the feeling of self-sufficiency and honour among its members. Alternatively, their livelihood might be mediated by work (i.e. by the opportunity to work) which would increase the volume of production; but it is precisely in overproduction and the lack of a proportionate number of consumers who are themselves productive that the evil [Übel] consists [*besteht*]. (Hegel 1820, 267, §246)

Here Hegel recognises that the cycle of poverty only leads to further alienation, which manifests itself in resentment and rancour against society in general.

Kojève's influential interpretation of Hegel in his 1933–1939 lecture series,[7] in which he takes the lord and bondsman to be the central trope, was taken up in Fukuyama's *The End of History and the Last Man* (1992). In his reading of Kojève's Hegel, Fukuyama contends, as I have mentioned, that labour has a thumotic origin. Fukuyama (1992) reminds us that according to traditional liberal economic theorists, desire and reason are adequate to account for the differing propensities to work. They maintain that the degree to which individuals are willing to work is essentially the result of a rational calculation in which workers weigh the unpleasantness of work against the utility of the material benefits arising out of work. The notion of a 'work ethic', on the other hand, calls for a different explanation of the motivation to work, and it is worth considering whether and to what extent an individual's or a society's work ethic might explain the contemporary knowledge worker's work compulsion. If we accept that thumos might be said to be an inherent psychic dimension that manifests to a greater or lesser extent throughout the history of human endeavour, might it also be conjectured that a work ethic is not so much an inherent human ethos but rather conditioned by an array of social, cultural, and historically specific and varying factors? To answer this question, in the next section I revisit Hill (1992), who provides instructive insight into the historical context of the work ethic.

A Brief History of the Notion of a Work Ethic[8]

A particular 'work ethic is a cultural norm that places a positive moral value on doing a good job and is based on a belief that work has intrinsic value for its own sake' (Cherrington 1980; Quinn 1983; Yankelovich and Immerwahr 1984, cited by Hill 1992). From a historical perspective, this cultural norm is a relatively recent development (Lipset 1990). For much of the ancient history of the human race, work has been hard and degrading. Working hard, in the absence of compulsion, was not the norm for the Hebrew, Greek, Roman, or medieval cultures (Rose 1985). The Hebrew belief system viewed work as a 'curse devised by God explicitly to punish the disobedience and ingratitude of Adam and Eve' (Rose 1985, 28). The Greeks likewise regarded hard physical labour as a curse (Maywood 1982), as can be deduced from the meaning of the Greek word for work, *panos*, taken from the Latin *poena*, meaning sorrow (Tilgher 1930). Manual labour was for slaves, while cultural norms sanctioned free men to pursue warfare, large-scale commerce, and the arts, especially architecture and sculpture (Rose 1985). In Plato and Aristotle, one finds clear evidence that the purpose for which the majority of men laboured was 'in order that the minority, the élite, might engage in pure exercises of the mind—art, philosophy, and politics' (Tilgher 1930, 5, cited by Hill 1992, n.p.). Braude (1975) describes the Greek belief that a person's prudence, morality, and wisdom is directly proportional to the amount of leisure time that person has. The Romans adopted much of their belief system from the Greeks, and they also held manual labour in low regard (Lipset 1990, cited by Hill 1992, n.p.). The low status of work in the great Roman Empire (which first began to develop in 625 BCE, was founded in 27 BCE after the fall of the Roman Republic, and was dissolved in 476

CE)[9] that spanned most of Europe, the Middle East, Egypt, and North Africa, can be explained by the fact that manual work was done by slaves; only two non-military occupations were suitable for a free man—agriculture and business enterprise (Maywood 1982). Philosophically, both the Greeks and the Romans viewed the work that slaves performed and the wealth that free men possessed as a means to achieve the supreme ideal of life, namely humans' independence from external things, self-sufficiency, and satisfaction with themselves (Tilgher 1930, cited by Hill 1992, n.p.).

The fall of the Roman Empire marked the beginning of the Middle Ages during which work still held no intrinsic value. Work served the purpose of meeting the physical needs of one's family and community, and to avoid idleness, which leads to sin (Tilgher 1930). It was not until the Protestant Reformation that physical labour became culturally acceptable for all, even the wealthy. With the Reformation, that period of religious and political upheaval in Western Europe during the sixteenth century, came a new perspective on work. According to Weber (1905), John Calvin introduced the theological doctrines which, together with those of Martin Luther, conceived of work in an entirely novel way. Calvin's revolutionary concept of predestination identified the Elect as those chosen by God to inherit eternal life. Not knowing whether a person was one of the chosen ones led to deep-seated existential insecurity, which could only be mitigated by way of an austere and industrious life, the success of which was taken as a sign that one was indeed a member of the Elect, since—as Calvin preached—to work was God's will. The new norms regarding work which developed out of the Protestant Reformation encouraged work in a chosen occupation, which was considered a calling. No greater spiritual dignity was bestowed on one job over another, and diligent work was aimed at maximising profits for the purpose of reinvestment in one's business. There was no proscription on changing from the craft or profession of one's father if it secured the greatest earnings possible. Key elements of this 'Protestant work ethic', as Weber dubs it, were diligence, punctuality, deferment of gratification, and the primacy of the work domain (Rose 1985, cited by Hill 1992, n.p.). According to Marx's materialist viewpoint, the Protestant work ethic followed on from changes in the economic structure. It provided a religious legitimation for the long working hours required by the new industrial system, and the poor working conditions that typified that system (Anthony 1977; Bernstein 1988). Weber (1905), on the other hand, maintains that the rapid expansion in commerce and the rise of industrialism that coincided with the Protestant Reformation was a direct result of shifts in theological beliefs (Rose 1985, cited by Hill 1992, n.p.). Hard work coupled to a frugal lifestyle was considered an indication of being chosen; work was now not a means to but a *sign* of God's recognition. Hence work could be elevated to the status of a 'calling' coupled to a 'this-worldly asceticism', which stood as testimony to one's status of having been 'elected'. The Protestant Reformation and the spread of a theology, which ordained the divine dignity of *all* occupations, as well as the right to *choose* one's work, established the underpinnings of an emerging capitalist economic system (Hill 1992). This work ethic, which gave 'moral sanction to profit making through hard work, organization, and rational calculation' (Yankelovich 1981, 247), spread throughout Europe and to America through the Protestant movement (Hill 1992).

With the coming of the Industrial Revolution in the mid-nineteenth century, work was radically transformed. The work ethic became secularised, and the idea of work as a calling was replaced by the concept of public usefulness. In industrial America, to work hard was advocated as a social duty to prevent the country from falling into economic ruin (Rodgers 1978). Contrary to the spirit of the work ethic, according to which an individual could be master of her/his own fate through hard work, machine manufacture and the intensive division of labour that came with industrialisation stripped the individual of control over the quantity and methods of personal production. In the factories, skill and craftsmanship were replaced by discipline and anonymity. The division of labour in factories doomed the semi-skilled labour force to operate one machine or the worker to the assembly line repeatedly to perform only one miniscule part of a manufacturing process. Work was not only stripped of the promise of salvation, but devoid of any intellectual stimulation and economic reward, which posed a serious threat to the work ethic (Gilbert 1977, cited by Hill 1992, n.p.).

Industrial management responded by adopting an authoritarian style that considered workers incapable of autonomous or self-directed work. As a result, the *scientific management* concept was developed, predicated on specialisation and the division of jobs into simple tasks. This model was premised on the belief that monetary gain was the primary motivating factor for workers: increased productivity, after all, theoretically should result in increased pay for the workers. However, even though this model became increasingly widespread in the early 1900s, it became apparent that other factors than pay were significant in worker motivation (Draft and Steers 1986).

By the end of World War II, the 'scientific' model was considered inadequate and outdated to deal with the needs of industry. The behaviourist school of thought then in vogue maintained that workers were not intrinsically lazy, but adaptive. If the working environment failed to provide a challenge, workers became lethargic. But if it offered appropriately challenging opportunities, workers in turn became animated and creative. In response, managers attempted to find ways to make work more fulfilling, but generally, an adversarial relationship between employees and employers persisted (Jaggi 1988).

In the late 1950s, job enrichment theories began to provide the basis for fundamental changes in employer-employee relationships. Herzberg, Mausner, and Snyderman (1959) identified factors such as achievement, recognition, responsibility, advancement, and personal growth, which, when they were provided as an intrinsic component of a job, tended to motivate workers to perform better. Importantly, Herzberg et al. (1959) found that factors such as salary, company policies, supervisory style, working conditions, and relations with fellow workers impaired worker performance if these were not adequately provided for, but they did not particularly improve worker motivation when they were present. In 1960, McGregor introduced a participatory management style as a means to provide workers with job enrichment. Unlike authoritarian styles of management, which operated by way of top-down directive control over workers who were assumed to be unmotivated and in need of guidance, the principles of participatory management assert that worker involvement in decision-making provides valuable input and enhances employee satisfaction and morale (Jaggi 1988). Importantly, Yankelovich and Immerwahr (1984, cited in Hill 1992, n.p.) recognised participatory management as a way 'to put the work ethic to work'.

The second half of the twentieth century saw a rise in jobs primarily dealing with the production of information, especially in the United States (Porat 1977; Naisbitt 1984). Contrary to industrial age jobs, information age jobs were high-discretion jobs and required considerable thinking and decision-making skills on the part of the workers (Yankelovich and Immerwahr 1984; Miller 1986). In a workplace characterised by high discretion work, the work ethic became a much more important construct than it was during the manipulative era of machine work. Such jobs provide workers with greater self-expression and self-fulfilment in their work. Yankelovich and Harman (1988) reported that this shift resulted in a significant transformation in the meaning of the work ethic. As we have seen, throughout much of history, work was associated with pain, sacrifice, and drudgery. With the information age, however, came a new kind of work that was perceived as good and rewarding in itself. Wattenberg (1984) reported that most (knowledge) workers were satisfied with their work and wanted to be successful in it. According to Yankelovich and Harman (1988), the work ethic of the 1980s stressed skill, challenges, autonomy, recognition, and the quality of the work produced. Autonomy was identified as a particularly important fact in workers' satisfaction with their jobs. Motivation to work involved trust, caring, meaning, self-knowledge, addressing challenges, opportunities for personal growth, and dignity (Walton 1974; Maccoby 1988). Information age jobs were ideally suited to provide the control over their work and sense of empowerment that workers sought.

As a result of the rapid changes associated with the information age workplace, codified and systematised knowledge that was not limited to a specific organisational context became important in the 1980s and 1990s (Maccoby 1988). This necessitated higher levels of education and skills at solving problems, managing people, and applying the latest information to the tasks at hand. The information age also saw changes in the extent to which people were given control or empowerment in their work. For workers who acquired positions of supervision or ownership, their motivation to accomplish personal goals through success in the organisation enhanced the expression of work ethic attributes (Barnard 1938). Importantly, Yankelovich (1981) found that economic reward had lost its ability to motivate many workers. In the absence of some reason other than high remuneration for working hard, productivity could be expected to decline. Hence, within this context, the work ethic and a management style that unfettered that ethic are considered significant factors for maintaining and increasing performance (Hill 1992).

Thus a work ethic is a cultural norm that places a positive moral value on doing a good job, and it is based on the belief that work has intrinsic value for its own sake. Like all cultural norms, a person's adherence to or belief in a work ethic is principally influenced by socialisation. Hence, adherence is individual- and culture-specific—the given historical overview of the work ethic, for example, has shown it to be a relatively recent phenomenon, born with the Protestant Reformation, and then, Weber contends, the spiritual impulse to work hard, live frugally, and accumulate ever more profit for its own sake that originally buttressed capitalism became unmoored from its religious underpinnings, but has remained a definitive factor in the continuous rise of capitalism in a more secularised form.

The nature of work has also been shown to play a key role in workers' motivation to work. It has been shown, for example, that even an individual with a strong work ethic can become disinclined to work at mind-numbing repetitive factory work, whereas the challenging knowledge-based work of the information age appears to bolster workers' motivation. Hence the work ethic has waxed and waned as the pre-industrial age morphed into the industrial age, and the post-industrial age arrived (Bell 1973).

However, even if the work ethic is a contingent aspect of the motivation to work, it cannot account fully for the pervasive phenomenon of overinvestment in work evident in contemporary knowledge workers. This brings us back to Fukuyama's contention that work has a thumotic origin. Fukuyama (1992) derives this contention from his reading of Kojève's (1947) interpretation of Hegel, but authors such as Blunden (2003) have convincingly argued that for Hegel the struggle for recognition and honour are phenomena characterising the denial of basic rights in modernity—specifically property rights. For Hegel, he contends, there is no mysterious 'drive for recognition'. Rather, recognition is a real material need. My own interrogation of Hegel's conceptualisation of the significance of labour by way of Ashton's (1999) explication has likewise unearthed no reference in Hegel to any irrational drive that might be attributed to thumos. Nevertheless, I find Fukuyama's (1992) contention of the thumotic origin of workers' drivenness worth further consideration.

The Thumotic Origin of Work?

Fukuyama (1992, 225) reminds us that traditional liberal economic theory, spearheaded by Adam Smith, posits that work is an essentially unpleasant activity undertaken for the sake of the utilities of the things created by work. That utility can be enjoyed primarily in leisure. In a certain sense, then, what motivates people to work is the prospect of the opportunities work creates for *not* working, in other words, for leisure. The motivation to work, so it is theorised, is determined by a rational cost-benefit analysis: the utility of the material benefit arising out of work and the leisure it affords must exceed the disutility of work, such as long working hours, the sacrifice of family time, etc. According to traditional liberal economic theory, then, reason and desire suffice to account for the differing propensities to work. When it comes to compulsively working knowledge workers, as we have seen, this explanation falls short, because their motivation to work does not correlate with their consumption patterns in non-existent leisure time. For his part, Fukuyama (1992) argues that the notion of work ethic implies that the degree to which people work is related to culture and custom, and hence is related to thumos (Fukuyama 1992, 225). Here he connects the motivation to work to a work ethic, which, as a culturally conditioned phenomenon, he then ascribes to thumos. From a Platonic point of view, thumos might indeed come into play when it comes to a person's work ethic. But precisely because a work ethic is culturally conditioned, the motivation to work cannot be ascribed to the work ethic as a cause, because the work ethic is a relatively recent historical phenomenon. Thumos, on the other hand, may be argued to be an innate component of the soul that has manifested in more or less preeminent ways throughout various epochs in history. The brief historical overview of the work ethic, offered in the previous section, does indeed testify to the fact that an overinvestment in work is not exclusively or definitively related to compensation, and hence is irrational from a strictly utilitarian point of view. Fukuyama cites the examples of the contemporary 'type-A' personality—the hard-charging lawyer or corporate executive—or the Japanese 'salaryman' employed by a competitive Japanese multinational corporation that easily works seventy or eighty hours per week, with few or only short holidays: 'They work so hard that they are never able to make use of their money; they can't enjoy their leisure because they have none; and in the process they ruin their health and their prospects for a comfortable retirement, because they are likely to die sooner' (Fukuyama 1992, 225).

While I agree with Fukuyama that workaholics clearly derive satisfaction from the work itself, or the status and recognition that it provides (Fukuyama 1992, 226), in critically assessing the hypothesis of the thumotic origin of work, I am not so much interested in the fraction of the working population that has a certain personality type or belongs to a culture in which a strong work ethic is instilled, that fraction of the workforce that operates at the pinnacle of a capitalist economy in high-flying, high-pressure, high-earning jobs. What I am interested in is what motivates the much more common knowledge worker in the information age ceaselessly to plough attention and time into work. In the previous chapter, I have argued that the neoliberal knowledge worker has a meaningful and fulfilling job, and that, given its challenging and problem-solving nature, it is all-absorbing. Connected mobile smart technologies have situated work *within* the life and times of the personal and private spheres. A case in point is the fact that the notion of a 'working holiday', which is a contradiction in terms, has become common parlance and practice. Instead of recognising and resenting the invasion of work into leisure time, the neoliberal knowledge worker may instead embrace the introduction of leisure into working time. For all the freedom the knowledge worker enjoys, s/he remains subject to an economic rationality that dictates ever-increasing efficiency. The neoliberal knowledge worker may, as a result, be typified as single-focused—even while multitasking, which is the direct result of the (self-)colonisation of private life by work obligations. In other words, amid the array of everyday life responsibilities and activities, the knowledge worker is in fact cognitively preoccupied with the problem-solving task of the day and armed with smart connected devices that either 'zoom' the worker to work, or insinuate work and managerial control into the home, the car, the supermarket, or wherever the private routines of the day take the worker. As the new game-changing resources that give successful organisations a competitive edge in the fast-paced informational economy, knowledge workers need to stay one step ahead of the game by living for the sake of work.

This overinvestment in work fails to correlate with increased quality of life (which admittedly means different things to different individuals), in other words with a proportionate increase in utility or well-being. These knowledge workers are not daunted by the potential negative outcomes of compulsive working on their mental and physical health (Verhaeghe 2012; Han 2017). Nor do they appear to be deterred by the disintegration of collective bonds documented by social theorists such as Bourdieu (1998), Boltanski and Chiapello (2007), and Sennett (2006) as a result of the rise of a kind of narcissistic self-aggrandisement in the face of the neoliberal governmentality that prizes competition even in cooperation, and individualisation even in the context of teamwork. Boltanski and Chiapello (2007) specifically emphasise the new capitalism's network-based form of organisation founded on employee initiative and autonomy in the workplace, which they describe as a putative freedom bought at the cost of material and psychological security, and resulting in a more successful, pernicious, and subtle form of exploitation.

The question remains: Why, then, does the neoliberal worker *want to work* all the time? Does Fukuyama's (1992) contention that the motivation to work is rooted deep in the human psyche as a fundamental ontological drive of sorts that work together—although not necessarily in concert—with reason and desire, hold compelling explanatory power? For Plato, to be sure, it is indeed the white horse of thumos that compels us to pursue honour and justice, but he calls for modesty and self-control as opposed to blind ambition or self-aggrandisement. He conceives of thumos as the seat of righteous indignation in the face of injustice that causes harm to those we hold dear, and hence the *guardian* of collective bonds, not as the source of the death knell for those bonds. The quick temper and readiness to fight of the guardians of the polis, seated in their thumos, were always in the service of maintaining justice in the polis. To prevent the excess to which the powerful spiritedness is naturally prone, Socrates, so Plato tells it, recommends that thumos be balanced by gentleness acquired through philosophical education so as to instil wisdom, that is, the art of discernment, and he calls for restraint when required. Plato's notion of thumos is not the brutal rage that leads to the self-destruction of the majority of the heroes of Homeric epics, but the wellspring of bravery, tenacity, and the need for justice. From a Platonic perspective, it thus seems at least plausible that thumos accounts for the irrational work-drivenness of neoliberal knowledge workers. It is a work-drivenness that is not in the service of merely satisfying the desires and appetites, which, if left unbridled, atrophy into deplorable vices such as the blind ambition to do whatever it takes, at anyone's expense, to get ahead. However, does it also explain why the *average* neoliberal knowledge worker *inadvertently* lives for the sake of work?

Admittedly, knowledge workers work all the time because they are subject to immense pressure to perform and deliver, but as Han (2017, 34) points out, power that functions through coercion does not represent power of the highest order: 'The greater power is, the *more quietly* it works. It just *happens*: it has no need to draw attention to itself'. In fact, today, 'power is assuming increasingly *permissive* forms. In its permissivity—indeed, in its *friendliness*—power is shedding its negativity and presenting itself as freedom' (Han 2017, 35). This is a crucial insight, since it means that the apparently *free* working subject has internalised the injunction to work. As this injunction is now something that emanates from within the working subject, the worker does not feel pushed and pulled to work through compulsion, but is driven by conviction. However, the unquestioned wholesale conviction displayed by the ever-working subject, even in the face of the evident toll that constantly working takes, cannot be entirely accounted for by the clever charade of other-induced coercion, masquerading as self-motivated conviction. The inherent contradictions of a *de facto* irrational, obsessive, and self-destructive work-drivenness are bound, inevitably, to result in severely detrimental side effects for the working subject. And they do. At both the rational and the emotional levels, the working subject is bound eventually to become disenchanted by the clever ploy of 'smart power'. Nevertheless, despite the havoc it wreaks on the working subject's mental and physical health, on collegial and familial relationships, the knowledge work addict displays an almost devotional commitment to the task at hand. To be sure, the neoliberal workplace lends a hand by way of extensive wellness programmes to mitigate the destructive effects of an overinvestment in work. However, even 'managing the side effects' cannot wholly account for the worker's steadfastness, while the argument of a thumotic origin for this work-drivenness goes a long way toward explaining it.

Conclusion

The argument that no equivalent term exists in English for what thumos signified for the Greeks—that if there is no exact translation for an ideal, it might be taken to mean that this ideal does not exist within a particular society—does not entirely hold water. If one accepts the Platonic postulation of thumos as a fundamental ontological drive, that, along with reason and desire, constitutes the third component part of the soul, how can it not exist in a society? One could instead speculate that the values, characteristics, and actions that spring from thumos are either wrongfully attributed to reason or desire, or actively suppressed so as to go unrecognised or unaccounted for. Given that the model neoliberal citizen who thrives in the information age is marked by characteristics such as fierce ambition, industriousness, entrepreneurial ingenuity, and steadfastness even in the face of impossible odds, it seems implausible to suggest that thumos does not exist or is actively suppressed in contemporary society.

As we have seen, classical economists have ascribed motivation to work primarily to the wages that people can earn. More generally, it is often taken for granted that increased earnings serve to satisfy our desires and appetites. We work, in other words, to appease the dark horse, and then the charioteer Reason is tethered to its insatiable appetite.

The salient role of an economic rationality and the persistence of materialism among consumers under neoliberalism unquestionably still apply. We can well ask whether reason and desire have supplanted thumos as the motor force of work. As I have shown, there is no mention of an irrational thumotic drive in Hegel's theorisation of labour, but the significance he attributes to labour may justifiably be attributed to a thumotic origin when one reads Hegel's arguments through a Platonic lens. If the ego attains full self-consciousness through the reciprocity of perspectives in self-consciousness, and finally universality through participation in ethical and cultural life, and labour is the vehicle for that participation, then labour is not merely a means, but the very being of the labourer. Labourers come to realise that it is their labour that creates the world and enables it to function. Work, for Hegel, is a central life activity. Work is the means through which labourers become 'self-actualized'. The fruits of workers' labour are the life-affirming definition of their very being. In Hegel, it is the labourer that transforms labour into the appropriate medium for her/his own self-development, but these shaped objects that become commodities exchanged on the market are also the means through which the labourer is recognised by others. In her/his work, the labourer sacrifices her-/himself, but importantly, in doing so—precisely by doing so—s/he receives back from it her/his own self.

Hegel's conception of civil society, which separates the political from the civil, brought the centrality of 'the economy' or state-wide 'household'—the sphere of the majority working to earn a living—to his attention. Concerning labour and the labourer Hegel's conception of civil society brings with it two problems. The first, as we have seen, concerns alienation. Labourers find themselves in their work, as well as a sense of mutual recognition, but they also find themselves at the mercy of a system of exchange over which they have no control. Hence, the shadow side of labour entails alienating and dehumanising effects that have been greatly amplified by the capitalist system's unfettered markets. The second problem related to labour that Hegel foregrounds, is poverty—poverty not only of the body but also of the mind. Hegel recognises the rise of poverty on account of overproduction, enabled by the use of machine labour, and competition. Even more fundamentally, the very human spirit becomes impoverished when the need to identify with work as a central life-activity and with the broader community, goes unfulfilled.

Hegel, then, maintains that work is not merely an economic activity or something we do to survive. For him, work is the most important activity in the development of self-conscious freedom. This implies that it is an entirely tenable argument that work is rooted in thumos—that which drives the self forward in its quest for recognition and flourishing. It is from the thumotic component of the soul that qualities such as determination, enterprise, and ambition emanate. Thumos is perhaps best understood as an independent self-regarding instinct of sorts that ranges from self-assertion, through self-respect, to our relations with others. All of these dimensions are encapsulated in Hegel's conceptualisation of labour.

We may conclude, then, that read through a Platonic lens, it is thumos—not primarily reason or desire—that fuels the worker to work. Knowledge work in particular—as challenging, entrepreneurial, creative, and problem-solving—ignites the thumotic dimension of the soul. It is what spurs the worker to rise to the occasion and persevere until the job is done. It is then not so surprising that the neoliberal knowledge worker's work-drivenness is irrational from a utilitarian point of view, in other words, that the surplus gains for the workaholic are not necessarily evident in conspicuous consumption or increased health or well-being. Work, it would seem, appeases not the dark horse of desire, but the white stallion of thumos, what Empedocles called the 'seat of life' (McKay and McKay 2011)—that part of the soul that seeks recognition, and which, when appeased, generates an immense and addictive form of gratification or well-being.

Notes

1. A version of this chapter has been published in a truncated format as Hofmeyr 2021b.

2. Cf. Foucault's lecture courses published in English as *Society Must Be Defended* (1975/1976), *Security, Territory, Population* (1977/1978), *The Birth of Biopolitics* (1978/1979), *The Hermeneutics of the Subject* (1981/1982); *The Government of Self and Others* (1982/1983), and *The Courage of Truth* (1983/1984).

3. Desire is *himeros*: the derivation is from *merē* (particles), *ienai* ('go'), and *rhein* ('flow').

4. At the time of writing, the Russian invasion of Ukraine dominated headlines.

5. This version is Arnold V. Miller's 1977 translation from the fifth edition of *Phänomenologie des Geistes*, edited by Johannes Hoffmeister, Philosophische Bibliothek Band 114, published in Hamburg by the Felix Meiner Verlag in 1952.

6. For this explication of the lord-bondsman dialectic I am indebted to Paul Ashton's 1999 talk, 'Hegel and Labour' presented at the 'Legacy of Hegel' seminar held at the University of Melbourne on February 5, 1999. In his account of labour in Hegel, Ashton draws extensively on Marcuse's *Reason and Revolution: Hegel and the Rise of Social Theory*.

7. Kojève's lectures were published in 1947 as *Introduction to the Reading of Hegel: Lectures on the Phenomenology of Spirit*. While Kojève also commented on many other sections, he took the eight paragraphs in the *Phenomenology of Spirit* on lordship and bondage (§IV A.3: 189–96) as his starting point and developed it into a whole philosophy of his own focusing on a 'drive towards universal mutual recognition'. The significance of Kojève cannot be as an interpreter of Hegel, but rather, in the aftermath of World War II, to have given philosophical expression to the demand for recognition from those who were being denied recognition in bourgeois society (Blunden 2003).

8. This section is largely indebted to Hill's (1992) 'Historical Context of the Work Ethic'.

9. The source of these dates is Milwaukee Public Museum's article, 'The Roman Empire: A Brief History'.

CHAPTER FIVE

The Hinge Connecting Work Compulsion and Neoliberal Governmentality[1]

The living-to-work phenomenon among certain working populations—specifically knowledge workers in neoliberal economies—that I have been referring to has been documented and theorised by several authors, including Hunnicut (1988), Robin and Dominquez (2008), and Schulte (2014). This development stands in stark contrast to economist John Maynard Keynes's prediction in his 1930 essay, "Economic Possibilities for Our Grandchildren"[2] that in the span of two generations people might be working just fifteen hours a week. His argument for a 15-hour week was that with the efficiency of new technology and new ideas, people would get more productive. As our labouring efforts became increasingly more efficient, fewer hours were to render the same results and people would work less. Reality testifies to the opposite. Harvard economist, Richard Freeman theorizes that one of the things that Keynes underestimated was the human desire to compete.[3] The Gallup Poll of 2014 reported that even then, many 'adults employed full time in the United States already indicated working an average of 47 hours per week, almost a full working day longer than the supposedly standard five-day' working week implied by a nine-to-five schedule (Saad 2014, n.p.). 'In fact, half of all full-time workers indicated that they typically worked more than 40 hours; nearly four in ten said they worked at least 50 hours' (Saad 2014, n.p.). Interestingly, the poll further reported that '[h]ighly engaged workers who log well over 40 hours still have better overall well-being than actively disengaged workers who clock out at 40 hours' (Saad 2014, n.p.). With the advent of the COVID-19 pandemic, the Gig Economy, and teleworking, reports have been flooding the internet over the past two years of the alarming increase in overworking in advanced societies across the globe (see, for example, Maurer 2020; Guy 2021; Kost 2020; and Hart 2021). In the Nobel Prize Dialogue on the Future of Work hosted by the University of Pretoria on May 18, 2021, the panelists stressed the importance of work as a source of both income and meaning in life. Panelists predicted that flexible teleworking, hybrid models of working, and working from home will be an increasingly important part of how we will work in the post-pandemic world. The Gig Economy is also predicted to play an increasingly prominent role in the future of work, which foregrounds the need for continuous upskilling of the workforce, micro-credentialing, and bespoke reskilling. One persistent concern is that this development signals an increase in precarious contract and temporary employment for many, and there was a call to dignify the 'side hustle' as an important form of entrepreneurialism. These developments do not signal shorter working weeks, but longer, more intensive, and informally structured working hours. Rather than hours of work, the emphasis is on deliverables, irrespective of how long it takes to complete the work. My focus in this chapter is therefore on more answers regarding the neoliberal knowledge worker's '*have to-can-want to*' triad, the Golden Triangle of the living-to-work phenomenon, where the 'opium of the working masses' resides.[4]

It would appear that the rationale for the knowledge worker's voluntary work compulsion might reside in a possible connection between neoliberal governmentality and this wanting-to-work-constantly phenomenon. The inquiry is set against the backdrop of an overarching diagnostics of the present, focusing on the subject formation of an increasingly decisive part of the workforce in fully fledged neoliberal economies, if not the definitive part: the knowledge worker. Following Foucault's theorisation of neoliberalism as a form of governmentality that entails exhaustive biopolitical controls, I seek to make sense of the culture, ethos, or spiritedness of work under these conditions of control, and specifically as it pertains to knowledge work.

In neoliberal economies, competition is lauded as a necessary condition for optimal efficiency and ever-increasing profit generation. It is thus logical that there is an imperative for self-responsible neoliberal workers to work all the time simply because they *have to*, in order to meet the demands of knowledge work, which by its very nature is driven by the rapidly accelerating rate of technological and informational innovation. This represents one side of the triangle.

The second side of the golden triangle is the fact that these workers *can* work all the time because they are enabled to do so by their being continuously connected as part of deterritorialised network, as we have already seen in chapter 3. Ever-increasing technological innovation and accessible infrastructure have been a decisive facilitator of the increasing globalisation of neoliberalism. The internet, the vehicle for this network, was created and developed in the last three decades of the twentieth century, and has grown exponentially, propelled by the ongoing expansion of the increasingly sophisticated technological infrastructure. It has now been widely adopted and is used in all areas of human activity. According to datareportal.com, a total of 5 billion people around the world use the internet today—equivalent to 63 percent of the world's total poplulation. The latest data indicate that world's connected population grew by almost 200 million in the 12 months to April 2022.[5] It is further reported that the number of people worldwide with access to a smartphone with internet access surpasses six billion and is forecast to grow by several million in the next few years. China, India, and the United States are the countries with the highest number of smartphone users (O'Dea 2021). The internet has created a *global* economy, 'an economy whose core components have the institutional, organisational, and technological capacity to work as a unit in real time, or in a chosen time, on a planetary scale' (Castells 1996, 102). Thus,

> [w]hile capitalism is characterized by its relentless expansion, always trying to overcome limits of time and space, it was only in the late twentieth century that the world economy was able to become truly global on the basis of the new infrastructure provided by information and communication technologies, and with the decisive help of deregulation and liberalization policies implemented by governments and international institutions. (Castells 1996, 101)

As mentioned in the introductory chapter, what Castells calls the 'new economy' has three distinctive and intertwined features. First, it is *networked*. This has made possible the second feature: it is *global*. Third, it is what he terms *informational*, 'because the productivity and competitiveness of units or agents in this economy (be it firms, regions, or nations) fundamentally depend upon their capacity to efficiently generate, process, and apply knowledge-based information' (Castells 1996, 77). These features of the 'new economy' explain the central role of the knowledge worker as the creator and user of these technologies, and the fact that knowledge work has become inextricably tethered to information technologies. In a networked, global economy, not hampered by different locations and time zones, these networked technologies are one of the key enabling features of the living-to-work phenomenon, creating what Castells (1996, 36) calls a 'space of flows' and 'timeless time' to overcome traditional geographical and temporal boundaries. The term 'space of flows' refers to 'the technological and organizational possibility of practicing simultaneity (or chosen time in time-sharing) without contiguity'

(Castells 1996, 36). 'Timeless time' refers to the fact that it is now possible to 'compress time (as in split-second global financial transactions) and to scramble the sequence of social practices, including past, present, and future, in a random order' (Castells 1996, 37). In short, if knowledge work is situated in the network society, and the network society has obliterated the limitations imposed by time and space, knowledge work *can* indeed be performed at any time, irrespective of place.

Against the backdrop of these two sides of the golden triangle, we may now go back to the third side, the curious phenomenon among knowledge workers that they appear to *want to* work all the time, despite the physical, emotional, and psychological toll of such practices. In an attempt to interrogate this paradoxical living-to-work phenomenon of highly engaged knowledge workers critically, in the previous chapter I revisited Fukuyama's contention in *The End of History and the Last Man* (1992) that work has a thumotic origin. I concluded that he is right in arguing for the persistence of 'irrational' forms of thumos that influence economic behaviour to contribute to the wealth of the nation (Fukuyama 1992, 234). Thumos, which lies at the heart of the human need for recognition and thus drives the ambition to ever increasing self-improvement and success, must be appeased. If it *is* appeased, then thumos generates an immense—indeed addictive—sense of gratification. This thrilling sense of fulfilment may help to account for the paradox of engaged compulsive workers' *wanting to* work all the time, even at the expense of their physical and mental health. The increase in 'overall well-being' of engaged workers, then, is less a reflection of the state of their physical or mental health than of a fundamental form of psychic satisfaction. In this chapter, I flesh out my earlier suggestion that the neoliberal economic theory of human capital harnesses thumos to the profit incentive, exploiting the innate thumotic spiritedness that is the very energy or drive that fuels work compulsion among compulsive knowledge workers.

It would appear that neoliberal economic theory has found a way to tap into this gratifying spiritedness to generate the competitive entrepreneurial spirit, which is the very fuel that sustains neoliberal politico-economic expansion. In what follows, I draw on Foucault's lecture course at the Collège de France of 1978–1979, *The Birth of Biopolitics* (2008), to unearth the hinge that connects neoliberal governmentality to the innate human spiritedness, thumos, which fuels work addiction.

Foucault on the Chicago School of Neoliberalism

In his lecture course, Foucault shows a particular interest in the American brand of neoliberalism, or Anarcho-liberalism, associated with Milton Friedman and the Chicago School. They found it odd that although classical political economy maintained that the production of goods depends on three factors—land, capital, and labour—it left the third, labour as human capital, almost completely unexplored (Foucault 2008, 219). Indeed, the classical economists sought to neutralise labour by reducing it exclusively to the factor of time. In other words, they argued that an increase in the labour factor would simply mean the presence of an additional number of workers in the market—the possibility of employing more hours of labour. This reduces labour theory to a mere quantitative analysis devoid of any qualitative dimension (Foucault 2008, 220). Foucault (2008, 221) points out that even Marx, who made labour the linchpin of his analysis, conceived of labour not as concrete, but as entirely abstract; he considered labour divorced from all its qualitative variables and transformed it into labour power, measured by time, deployed in the market and paid for by wages. Here labour is nothing but a commodity that is reduced to the effects of any value produced. By the neoliberals' account, this abstraction is not the product of capitalism itself, but of the way in which economic theory has conceptualised capitalist production. The challenge for the neoliberals, then, was how to introduce labour—understood qualitatively as a concrete variable—into the field of economic analysis, which, since Adam Smith, focused exclusively on the interconnections between three mechanisms: the mechanisms of production, exchange, and consumption in a given social structure.

The neoliberals discovered that the key to the science of economics is something that cannot be neatly quantified and accounted for, namely human behaviour or the internal 'rationality' or 'strategic' programming of individuals' activities. If economics 'is the science of human behaviour as a relationship between ends and scarce means, which have mutually exclusive [or alternative] ends' (Foucault 2008, 222), then the focus of economic science, according to the neoliberals, is the analysis of a form of human behaviour. What takes centre stage now is the nature and consequences of 'substitutable choices', in other words, the study of the way in which and the reasons for which scarce resources (labour as human capital) are allocated to competing ends (Foucault 2008, 222). Why does the worker choose to invest labour in one particular job, rather than in another? Why does the worker spend so much time on this particular task, as opposed to other component tasks of the job, or as opposed to other demands of daily life? What makes the worker more invested, committed, and motivated to work? The neoliberals realised that to bring labour into the field of economic analysis, one has to put oneself into the position of the person who works. In short, '*[w]hat . . . does working mean for the person who works?*' (Foucault 2008, 223, my emphasis).

Here Foucault turns to the theory of human capital, whose most famous exponents are the US economists Theodore Schultz and Gary Becker. Their key insight was to remove the worker from economic analysis as a mere object—the object of supply and demand in the form of labour power—and to insert the worker as an active economic subject. Human capitalist theorists Schultz (1961) and Jacob Mincer (1958) maintain that individual competences and the knowledge of workers expanded during the post-war period, which meant that productivity increased, and as a consequence, the value of working time and of salaries increased as well. This in turn stimulated increased consumption. The theory of human capital relies on self-regulation through the market, modelling individuals as entrepreneurs, and conceiving of their actions as investments or disinvestments in their own lifespans and quality of life. Schultz (1961) and Mincer (1958) hoped that this virtuous circle would usher in the society of knowledge. It is specifically on the basis of Becker's work that Foucault in his lectures deciphers the rationale of neoliberal governmentality in its clearest form, distilling its nucleus as the figure of the enterprising self. Foucault points out that the neoliberals realised that the optimisation of the self's entrepreneurial or enterprising capacities requires *investment*. Hence the now familiar economic injunction: invest in human capital.

For Schultz and Becker, people simply work to earn a wage, an income. From the workers' perspective, a wage is not the price at which their labour power is sold, but an income for them. Income is the product or return on capital. Inversely, capital is everything that can, in one way or another, be seen as a source of future income. This capital—*human* capital—is therefore 'all those physical and psychological factors which make someone able to earn this or that wage' (Foucault 2008, 224). For workers, their labour is capital, 'an income stream', as Schultz (1971, 75) calls it. According to Foucault, this is not a conception of labour power, but a conception of 'capital-ability', which turns workers into a sort of enterprise for themselves. The individual worker thus becomes an enterprise unit (Schultz 1971, 225).

The protagonist of American neoliberalism takes the form of a reconceived notion of *Homo economicus*, namely *Homo economicus* as an entrepreneur of her-/himself. The classical conception of *Homo economicus* is the partner of exchange, the person who assesses needs (demand) based on which utilities might be supplied for that exchange. In neoliberalism, the worker as an enterprise unit is an entrepreneur of her-/himself—

being her/her own capital, her/his own producer, and her/his own source of earnings. Referring to Becker's postulates in 'A Theory of the Allocation of Time' (1965), Foucault explains that the man of consumption, insofar as he consumes, is also a *producer*. What does he produce? He produces his own satisfaction, understood as utility or use-value; *he produces the satisfaction that he consumes* (Foucault 2008, 226). What intrigues Foucault here is Becker's analysis of the production functions of consumption activities.[6]

Becker (1976, 134) contends that workers as consumers consume commodities from which utility is obtained. In economics, utility refers to the advantage, pleasure, or fulfilment a person gains from obtaining or consuming a good or service. 'These commodities are produced by the consumer unit itself through the productive activity of combining purchased market goods and services with some of the household's own time' (Becker 1976, 134). For Becker, the consumer produces satisfactions, and these satisfactions are equated with utilities or that which have use-value for the consumer. My own contention, which I would like to critically assess here by way of Becker's own theory and Foucault's engagement with it, is that the 'satisfaction' produced and consumed by knowledge workers is the use-value derived from *thumotic* satisfaction.

Michael and Becker (1973) point out that consumption should not be interpreted to mean the exchange of money for market goods and services, as well as the acquisition of utility (or satisfaction) from these goods and services. Such an interpretation sheds no light on whether the utility is derived from acquiring, possessing, or using the purchased item. In fact, 'the demand for a product might be derived from a desire for some more basic aims that are produced using characteristics of the product' (Michael and Becker 1973, 385). Goods are usually desired not for their own sake, but for some specific service which they perform. By 'consuming' tertiary education, for instance, the utility of higher erudition is produced. This utility, the expertise gained, in turn, might then be consumed to produce higher income. Higher income, in its turn, can be consumed to finance a more lavish lifestyle or leisure time. This argument is persuasive as far as it goes, but in the case of a compulsive knowledge worker, compulsive work and the higher income it produces do *not* appear to be consumed for most of the usual utilities or satisfactions, as constant work does not allow for leisure time to consume these utilities or satisfactions. However, the perseverance of the preference for work, what Becker and George Stigler call the 'stability of this preference' (Becker and Stigler 1995) and the ability to sustain it in the form of a stabilised 'way of life', suggests the production of another more basic, invisible satisfaction. This satisfaction, as I have suggested, in line with Fukuyama (1992), is *thumotic* in origin, and hence it compensates for other utilities such as the satisfactions derived from our relations with others, which include a sense of belonging, of being acknowledged and loved.

It can therefore be postulated that knowledge workers 'consume' their creative problem-solving work itself and in the process they directly produce their own thumotic satisfaction. The ever-working knowledge worker is an enterprise unit whose compulsive entrepreneurial activity is *fuelled* by thumos, while it also *produces* thumotic satisfaction. How then can knowledge work produce something that is an inherent part of the human psyche? Production, here, should be understood as igniting and putting to work that which can just as easily go underutilised and hence atrophy—wither away—because it is not used, much like a muscle.

What do I mean here by the thumotic satisfaction produced by the knowledge worker? Knowledge work in our network society is nothing like the plodding, soul-destroying kind of work that fuelled preceding incarnations of capitalist economies. Bell (1973) depicts pre-industrial labour as a game against nature, in which men wrest their living from the soil, waters, and forests, and industrial labour as a game against fabricated nature, in which men are reduced to mechanical machine operators. What sets the creative problem-solving work of the knowledge economy apart from previous forms of work is its exemplary ability to engage the worker, who, in the process, willingly foregoes other traditional sources of satisfaction. As an existential form of satisfaction, thumotic satisfaction cannot be reduced to mere economic use-value, because it is essential to the well-being of the soul. Nor should this 'satisfaction' be understood as mere 'job satisfaction', which is commonly attributed to a personality-job 'fit' or empirical facts about the nature of the job, the workplace, and relationships with colleagues and management. To be sure, all these factors can potentially have a negative impact on the production of thumos if they are not conducive to worker welfare, such as a toxic workplace culture, a lack of collaborative collegiality, or an overly top-down autocratic management style. Nevertheless, knowledge work is engaging not merely because it is challenging and creative, but because it produces its own thumotic satisfaction. The aforementioned factors may be necessary conditions, but they serve as means to the end, which is the production of that thumotic satisfaction. Much like the desire for happiness, for example, thumotic satisfaction cannot be pursued as an end in itself: it is produced as the side effect of a host of other contributing factors. The desire for this addictive satisfaction is insatiable when it is the object of consumption. This voracious desire propels further consumption, in the form of work. It is therefore an endless and self-generating cycle of work consumption and satisfaction production that fuels compulsive work—a *perpetuum mobile* of sorts, unless the absence of one of the necessary conditions breaks the cycle. In order to assess the credibility of this line of argumentation, we have to interrogate more closely Foucault's engagement with Gary Becker. Foucault's argument in this regard sheds light on the underlying economic rationale of this cycle of consumption and production by knowledge workers.

Biopolitical Control

A critical and persistent dimension of Foucault's philosophical project as a whole may be described as a 'diagnostics of the present' (Foucault 1984, 43). He sought to undertake 'a historical investigation into the events that have led us to constitute ourselves and to recognize ourselves as subjects of what we are doing, thinking, saying' (Foucault 1984, 43). His consideration of neoliberal governmentality, too, may be conceived as a 'historical and critical ontology of ourselves' (Foucault 1984, 44) that endeavours to come to a critical understanding of the limits imposed upon us as subjects historically in order to interrogate our contemporary reality and to grasp the points where change is possible and desirable (Foucault 1984, 44). The present site of subject-formation (subjection) of knowledge workers, as I have argued, is one in which their existence is reduced to incessant working in the context of the globalising neoliberal governmentality that operates by installing exhaustive controls. The extent to which this site might be probed for possible fissures where resistance to imposed limits might be possible will be taken up in the next chapter. First, however, we have to interrogate the nature of these conditions of comprehensive control, as applied in a neoliberal economy.

Exhaustive control, applied as inconspicuously as possible, is a salient feature of neoliberal governmentality. Becker's approach exemplifies what Foucault theorises in terms of biopolitical control—power is exercised not over individuals, but over entire populations through the normalising use of statistics. 'Becker's preference for indirect intervention might seem to preserve the independence [and freedom] of individuals, [but] under biopolitics, individual liberty is itself the means by which populations are governed indirectly' (Newheiser 2016, 3). Neoliberal economics mobilises individual liberty while manipulating the range of choices at the individual's disposal. This is encapsulated in Becker's definition of *Homo economicus*, which Foucault (2008, 270–71) outlines as follows: '[T]he person who must be let alone . . . he is the subject or object of *laissez-faire*'. According to Becker, *Homo economicus* must and can be let alone, because he 'responds systematically to . . . systematic modifications artificially introduced in the environment'

(Foucault 2008, 270). Because of that, '*Homo* œconomicus is someone who is eminently governable' (Foucault 2008, 270), and hence is the very subject that has made possible 'the restriction, self-limitation, and frugality of government' (Foucault 2008, 271). Becker makes this claim on the basis of his contention that practically all social phenomena which include rational and non-rational conduct operate according to market processes, and this makes them calculable, predictable, and hence pliable to indirect manipulation (cf. Becker and Stiegler 1995, 7). According to Foucault (2008, 259), Becker displaces an 'exhaustively disciplinary society' in favour of 'a society in which the mechanism of general normalization and the exclusion of the non-normalizable' are no longer needed. Becker's approach relies on a normalising power that operates precisely by means of *inclusion*. What counts as the norm here is determined through a statistical analysis of a given population, 'a plotting of the normal and the abnormal, of different curves of normality' (Foucault 2007, 63). This economic approach can tolerate the non-normalisable precisely because it absorbs deviation. Becker's claim that every aspect of human behaviour is rational concerns patterns of behaviour across a population, rather than every individual case (cf. Becker and Stiegler 1995, 650). Eccentricity is irrelevant at the level of generality. Importantly, however, the certainties produced by statistical normalisation hold profound implications for individuals. While Becker 'tolerates' the existence of irrational individuals (the outliers who do not fall within the range of the extrapolated norm), 'he argues that changes to the environment would constrain the possibilities for impulsive behaviour to the extent that even the irrational would act as if they were rational' (Newheiser 2016, 8). For example, expenditure on non-essential goods decreases when the price of essential goods is increased. Becker (1993, 400) realises that this form of indirect control is the most effective way to obtain commitment.

Becker's theorisation of economic normalisation corresponds to Foucault's theorisation of biopolitics in the first volume of the *The History of Sexuality* (1976). In that volume, Foucault (1976) explains that biopolitics positively fosters and sustains the life of a population through the application of technical expertise. This expertise relies on 'the action of the norm. . . . Such a power has to qualify, measure, appraise, and hierarchize, rather than display itself in its murderous splendour . . . it effects distributions around the norm' (Foucault 1976, 144). Foucault points out, however, that 'a power whose task it is to take charge of life needs continuous regulatory and corrective mechanisms' (Foucault 1976, 144). The purpose of such controls is to distribute 'the living in the domain of value and utility' (Foucault 1976, 144). This historical outcome of a technology of power centred on life, that is, *biopower*, is a 'normalizing society' (Foucault 1976, 144). Power as control in a normalising society operates by subjecting every facet of life to 'infinitesimal surveillances, permanent controls . . . to an entire micro-power concerned with the [individual] body' (Foucault 1976, 144). In addition to the individual body, the object of control is the entire social body, which is subjected to a range of interventions, comprehensive measures, and statistical assessments (Foucault 1976, 145–46).

This form of power, which establishes its dominion over life throughout its unfolding, then, is a bi(o)polar technology of power. The two poles work in consort. The one pole centres on the body as machine, 'its disciplining, the optimization of its capabilities, the extortion of its forces, the parallel increase of its usefulness and its docility, its integration into systems of efficient and economic controls' (Foucault 1976, 139). Foucault (1976, 139) calls this '*an anatomo-politics of the human body*'. The other pole of the biopower coin is a '*biopolitics of the population*' (Foucault 1976, 139), which takes the species' body as its object. We glimpse here in Foucault's thinking a departure from the disciplinary power that he theorised in *Discipline and Punish* (1975), where he is not yet concerned with the ethics of the self and processes of subjectivisation that he develops in the subsequent volumes of *The History of Sexuality*.

It is in this period that Foucault's thinking reveals remarkable similarities with Becker's. Both theorise a technology of power that is focused on the individual body without being concerned with the individual as such. The real objective of this technology of power is the normalisation of the population as a whole in order to distribute the living in the domain of value and utility. Statistics 'tolerates' individual outliers, but statistical normalisation has far-reaching consequences for the individual in that it mobilises sophisticated controls either to condone or to penalise forms of being and behaviour that do not conform to the presiding economic rationality, which dictates the application of a cost-benefit calculus even to the smallest details in life.

In *Society Must be Defended*, his Collège de France lectures from the same year (1976) in which the first volume of *The History of Sexuality* was published, Foucault (2003, 245) explains that biopolitics deals with the population as a scientific, political, and biological problem, which makes it a power problem. When power has to deal with the 'population', it has to deal with collective phenomena that have economic and political effects that only become pertinent at the mass level. 'They are phenomena that are aleatory and unpredictable when taken in themselves or individually, but, which at the collective level, display constants that are easy, or at least possible, to establish' (Foucault 2003, 246). Here Foucault is arguing that, as a technology of power, biopolitics is different from disciplinary mechanisms. It works through scientific techniques ('forecasts, statistical estimates') in order to affect and effect collective behaviour at the general level, in other words, at the level of the population. The purpose of these techniques is not to modify any given individual insofar as s/he is an individual, but to intervene at the level at which these general phenomena are determined, at the level of their generality (Foucault 2003, 246). He adds that regulatory mechanisms must be deployed 'to establish an equilibrium, maintain an average, establish a sort of homeostasis, and compensate for variations within the general population and its aleatory field' (Foucault 2003, 246). In the context of these lectures, he uses the term 'security mechanisms' for the controls that have to be installed around the random element inherent in a population of living beings so as to optimise a state of life. Like disciplinary mechanisms, they are designed to maximise and extract forces. However, security mechanisms do not work at the level of the body itself, but act in such a way that they achieve overall states of equilibration or regularity. In short, it is a matter of 'taking control of life and the biological processes of man-as-species and of ensuring that they are not disciplined, but regularized' (Foucault 2003, 246–47). Foucault takes up these problematics in greater detail in the subsequent lecture course, *Security, Territory, Population* (1977–1978), in which he traces the emergence of the political problem of the population, which is conceived as 'a variable dependent on a number of factors', which are 'by no means all natural (the tax system, the activity of circulation, and the distribution of profit are essential determinants of the population rate)' (Foucault 2007, 366). Hence, the population is the object of and provides 'a hold for concerted interventions' (Foucault 2007, 366). Although the term 'biopolitics' is mentioned only twice in his lecture course of the following year, titled *The Birth of Biopolitics*, Becker's theory enables him to understand how biopolitics functions in the context of neoliberal governmentality. At the start of these lectures, Foucault explains that the necessary condition of possibility for a thoroughgoing analysis of biopolitics is understanding the economic truth informing (neo)liberal governmental reason.

Liberalism, of which neoliberalism is a species, is a governmental practice that is not satisfied with respecting or guaranteeing this or that freedom; rather, it is a consumer of freedom. It can only function when a number of freedoms actually exist: freedom of the market, freedom to buy and sell, the freedom to exercise property rights, freedom of discussion, etc. This implies that if liberalism needs or consumes freedom, it must also produce it: liberalism must produce freedom, and it must organise freedom. This art of government, Foucault avers, appears as the 'management of freedom', producing what its subjects need to be free to act rationally and freely, and according to a cost-benefit rationale that is rewarded by the market. Foucault (2008, 33) explains that the market constitutes 'a site of veridiction', which he posits not as 'a law (*loi*) of truth, [but as] the set of rules enabling one to establish which statements in a given discourse can be described as true or false' (Foucault 2008, 35). Liberalism is intent on ensuring the freedom necessary for freedom: the management and organisation of the conditions in which one can be free, which necessarily requires the imposition of limitations. Because individual and collective interests can potentially threaten each other, liberalism cannot simply let freedom operate freely; it must actively manage the subjectivity of its subjects. At the heart of this liberal practice then is the tension between the imperative to produce freedoms and the fact that this very act entails establishing limitations, controls, forms of coercion, and obligations relying on threats. In this context, the very act of producing freedom risks limiting and destroying that same freedom. Here Foucault cites the example of 'a free labour market' that relies on 'a large enough number of sufficiently competent, qualified, and politically disarmed workers to prevent them exerting pressure on the labor market' (Foucault 2008, 63, 68). The 'free' labour market, then, necessitates controls to ensure the adequate training of workers, while imposing visible limits on the scope of political actions available to them by regulating the operation of unions in organisations, for example, as well as invisible limits that effectively depoliticise workers. One of the ways in which such depoliticisation is achieved is by generalising or 'democratizing' an artificially imposed economic rationality of competition to every aspect of human existence. In this process of generalisation, economic rationality becomes normalised to the point where it is mistaken as the natural order of things, which dissolves resistance to it and actively engenders compliance.

Another tactic of depoliticisation is self-responsibilisation. If a worker is responsible for itself as entrepreneurial 'project' (Han 2017, 15), s/he is no longer subject to an externally imposed system of constraints, which may invoke opposition. On the contrary, as Han (2017, 15) explains, '[a] sense of freedom attends passing from the state of subject to that of project'. This masks the accompanying constraints: 'As a project deeming itself free of external and alien limitations, the *I* is now subjugating itself to internal limitations and self-constraints, which are taking the form of compulsive achievement and optimization' (Han 2017, 15).

This logic is extended in Becker's neoliberal conception of the subject, who, as we have seen, is entirely governable. Foucault accordingly suggests that Becker's subject is nothing but the correlate of governmental power. In terms of Foucault's account, biopolitics offers liberty, but only to subjects whose freedom it has formed in advance. It 'freely' offers employment opportunities, but only to those who are sufficiently qualified, competent, and especially politically disarmed, so as to play according to the rules of the game of freedom without questioning the impingements of freedom and injustices which it gives rise to. Neoliberalism accommodates opposition or recalcitrance in the form of diversity or deviations from the norm, but it comes at the cost of a sophisticated normalisation. Because 'neoliberal biopolitics forms the very freedom it claims to protect, it allows for the extension of power' (Newheiser 2016, 14–16).

Foucault's critical consideration of Becker's neoliberalism is informed by a notion of critique akin to Kant's. This critique does not condemn or derive its power from hyperbole, but seeks to unmask the contingency of systems of power that are taken for granted. Foucault, then, exposes how biopolitics works from the inside, and as a result we may feel ourselves to be free, but the conditions of possibility of freedom are pre-determined by the very order to which 'free' subjects are subjected.

Becker on 'Stable Preferences'

Vatter (2018) seeks to come to a more precise understanding of the structure of the neoliberal, economic conception of freedom, which would explain the connection between neoliberal economic theory and biopower. A closer interrogation of Becker's microeconomic analysis leads Vatter (2018, 67) to contend that the neoliberal economic conception of freedom is crystallised around Becker's approach to the notion of 'revealed preference'. This refers to the argument that choices reveal preferences. This implies that Becker goes further and insists on the 'stability of preferences'. Preferences, understood as subjective freedom, here function as the medium for a process of subjectivation that is internally related to the exercise of biopower, the power to conduct or govern populations or aggregates of individuals (Vatter 2018, 67).

Becker himself generally does not establish the conditions of possibility of a comprehensive economic approach applicable to all human behaviour, but when he does, he tends to think about it as the application of a rational choice methodology (Becker and Stigler 1995, 7). Rather than a comprehensive approach applicable to all human behaviour, Becker's economic approach is the application of a 'methodological individualism' (Vatter 2018, 66). Therefore his economic approach functions, as I have mentioned, along the lines of 'the conduct of conduct'—as Foucault defines power relations—by orchestrating the way in which individuals conduct themselves. Vatter (2018, 67) points out that this implies that Becker's microeconomics is much more than merely an 'economic' theory. Rather, it is inherently instrumental to the constitution of neoliberal governmentality.

Becker's approach hinges on three determinants, namely 'assumptions of maximizing behaviour, market equilibrium, and stable preference' (Becker 1976, 5). Economists of the Austrian School have questioned these assumptions as purely 'theoretical' or 'abstract', because they have no real purchase on how human beings 'really' act. Vatter (2018, 68) suggests that, taken from a purely economic point of view, it may or may not be true that these assumptions do not relate to real actions, but that from a biopolitical perspective, which focuses on how human conduct is actively governed, this objection misses the point entirely. In Foucault's two lectures dedicated to the Chicago School of neoliberalism on March 14, 1979 (Foucault 2008, 216–33), and on March 21, 1979 (Foucault 2008, 239–65), his treatment of Becker focuses mainly on the revolutionary consequences for the traditional idea of *Homo economicus* when s/he is conceived of as an enterprising human being who is characterised by a desire to maximise the utilities derived from her/his human capital.

As we have seen in the preceding section, Foucault's analysis of neoliberal governmentality conceives of it as operating in exactly the opposite way as the disciplinary systems of the preceding era (Foucault 2007, 63; 2008, 259). Neoliberal governmentality plots both the normal and the abnormal, that is, 'different curves of normality, and the operation of normalisation consists in establishing an interplay between these different distributions of normality and [in] acting to bring the most unfavourable in line with the more favourable' (Foucault 2007, 63). Disciplinary societies extended external laws internally by way of normative mechanisms (Foucault 2008, 259). Neoliberal governmentality does not operate by way of 'a mechanism of general normalization and [one in which] the exclusion of those who cannot be normalized is needed' (Foucault 2008, 259). Rather, neoliberal governmentality leads Foucault toward an image of society in which minorities and deviation from the norm are tolerated, 'in which the action is brought to bear on the rules of the game rather than on the players, and finally in which there is an environmental type of intervention instead of the internal subjugation of individuals' (Foucault 2008, 259–60). The technology of power that is applied to the rules of the *game* rather than the *players* is biopolitics, a style of government that regulates populations through biopower. Biopolitics, as Foucault sees it, is exemplified in Becker's (1964) concept of human capital.

Based on a biopolitical understanding, human capital is oriented toward making the individual's *life and labour* into an enterprise that generates utilities. To encapsulate the entire scope of *life*, provision also has to be made for minoritarian forms of life to generate a surplus of utility. To achieve this, the 'environmental' factors open to the opportunities and to the liberties in supply and demand have to be regulated. Becker (1976) postulates that what prevented certain territories and behaviours from becoming objects of rational utility calculus was the belief that changes in behaviour are due to arbitrary changes in the preferences or tastes of economic actors. If one assumes instead that preferences are 'stable over time' and relatively similar across cultures, genders, and classes, then it is possible, in principle, to analyse changes in behaviour as a function of changes in costs and benefits, in other words, as changes in restrictions rather than in preferences. Preferences, then, can be 'optimized' by properly regulating incentives (Vatter 2018, 75). To clarify, 'Becker is not making a substantial or empirical claim about tastes, but rather a methodological one' (Newheiser 2016, 16). He argues that changes in the observed behaviour of an agent can be explained in terms of changes in the factors determining her/his expectations of utility—information, stocks of personal and social capital, time, prices, etc.—relative to fixed tastes or preferences. The advantage of the methodological assumption of fixed preferences affects the manner in which expected utility theory is applied to the explanation of behaviour (Bradley 2008, 2).

Becker's concept of human capital thus allows neoclassical, neoliberal economics to depart from the priority assigned by Smith, Ricardo, and Marx to production and exchange in the economic cycle, and shifts the emphasis to labour and consumption. As Vatter (2018, 76) explains, 'Becker's concept of "human capital" attempts to account for what happens in markets as a function of what has happened outside markets and before the economic actor enters into the market'. This brings us to Foucault's discussion of Becker's notion of human capital, which opens with the question of why individuals work at all: 'What does working mean for the person which works?' (Foucault 2008, 223). Here Foucault explains that Becker maintains that one works to produce a good that is to be exchanged on a market, rather than because one wants to.

Importantly, for Becker, labour is not 'work', just as consumption is not 'production'. Here Arendt's (1958) analytical distinction between labour and work allows us to be more conceptually specific, although in the literature, generally, the terms work and labour are used interchangeably, as I have done for the most part. For Arendt, labour is associated with consumption, and work is associated with production. Arendt (1958) argues that people labour as part of a 'cycle' of consumption (not of production), whose desired end result is the increase of pleasure (utility) and the decrease of pain. Labour for Arendt (1958) includes any activity aimed toward maintaining or reproducing life. The products of our labour are used up in consumption and thus our labours leave nothing permanent behind—labour 'never "produces" anything but life' (Arendt 1958, 88). As animals we are subject to biological necessity and the natural processes of an earthbound biological life. The constraint of necessity on human life, for Arendt, is directly opposed to freedom; insofar as we are embodied creatures tethered to our biological needs, we cannot be free. Thus, for Arendt, 'the cycle of consumption has a negative connotation because it keeps the subject tied to the sphere of animal life, *zoe*' (Vatter 2018, 76). Human lives require a world to inhabit that labour alone cannot produce, because labour only 'feeds' consumption and, as a result, it leaves nothing behind. Arendt suggests that '[t]his destructive, devouring aspect of the laboring activity . . . is visible only from the standpoint of the world and in distinction from work, which does not prepare matter for incorporation but changes it into material in order to work upon it and use the finished product' (Arendt 1958, 100). 'Work then elevates us beyond the repetitious and mute cycle of nature and gathers us into a common reality and shared objective space' (Hayden 2014, 37). Arendt thus implies that work creates a world in common, one in which the subject is able to distinguish itself only through a proper or autonomous *bios* (Hayden 2014, 37–40). For Arendt, then, labour is associated with consumption, and work is associated with production.

Becker is concerned with labour/consumption, not work/production, because, according to him,

> the cycle of labour and consumption reaches an equilibrium and stabilizes into a 'form of life'—what Foucault calls an 'enterprise'—that maximizes utility. In turn, it is this 'form of life' that actually explains the preferences of the individual, and not the 'existential choices' that are traditionally associated with the idea of a free and autonomous *bios*. (Vatter 2018, 76)

From the perspectives of Arendt and Becker, classical economics wrongfully conceives of labour in a teleological fashion, starting from what it takes the end product to be, namely the commodity that is produced. As a result, classical economics confuses labour with production, collapsing labour into work. For classical economics, 'work' (the labour force in Marx) is exchanged ('alienated' in Marx, the Latin sense of *alienare*, to estrange, make another person's) for a salary, but for neoclassical economics, this is not the case for labour as a biopolitical capacity or capability, as the output of human capital.

Becker suspects that one cannot 'live' merely for a salary. He conceives of labour starting from the consumption of goods that (re)produces 'living' labour in a certain 'form' (which reveals the real preferences of the labourers). For him, 'animal-like' consumption is in reality 'productive' of utility at the species-life level. My *bios* (the kinds of roles that I 'choose') may create the impression that I am 'alienated' from my labour, but if I persevere in my labour preferences, as expressed in my form of life (*zoe*) that is because I am making a profit that may be invisible to others. From the perspective of human capital theory, for example, the gender wage gap is not a consequence of wage discrimination between men and women in the marketplace. Rather, it is a function of the different 'life-choices' made by women and men before they have even entered the market, as Vatter (2018, 76) has realised. For example, women are said to choose professions with lower risk/reward disparity. Their jobs are often part-time jobs or pay less, but these occupational choices are based on women's utility calculus, which factors in having and caring for children (Becker 1993, 394).

In contradiction of this position, feminist critiques of human capital point out that the asymmetry in procreative and care duties between women and men is not something that is 'chosen' but rather expresses a relation of domination (Vatter 2018, 78). Brown (2015, 105) explains this as follows:

> As provisioners of care for others in households . . . women disproportionately remain the invisible infrastructure for all developing, mature, and worn-out human capital—children, adults, disabled, and elderly. Generally uncoerced, yet essential, this provision and responsibility get theoretically and ideologically tucked into what are assumed as preferences issuing naturally from sexual difference. . . . It is formulated, in short, as an effect of nature, not of power.

If it is a relation of domination that 'conducts' or orchestrates the 'free' rational choices of the members of the family enterprise, then, as Vatter (2018, 78) suggests, 'the concept of human capital, although it factors species-life into its economics, . . . remains an 'alienated' conception of species-life'.

For Becker, Vatter (2018, 78) explains, labour-power does not 'flow' from the living and labouring subject to the product where it 'dies' as it is transformed into 'dead' capital, as Marx would have it. Becker contends that the choice for this or that product, and so its consumption, is a function of labour-power, 'producing' itself as one form of life that is preferred over another (Vatter 2018, 78). For him, consumption always already contains production. In its consumption, living labour 'flows back' from the products into living labour as an 'income stream' generated by human capital.

Foucault explains that the breakdown of labour into capital has some important consequences. If capital is that which makes possible a future income, in the form of a wage, capital is inseparable from the person who possesses it. The worker is 'a machine that produces an earnings stream' (Foucault 2008, 224). This earnings stream is not an income, precisely because the machine constituted by the worker's ability is not sold from time to time on the labour market against a certain wage. As a result, the worker is not alienated in the process.

This human 'machine' is the aggregate of innate abilities and capabilities acquired by way of investment or nurture, for example, in the form of education or training. By definition, the worker has no disposable capital. Hence, this machine needs to be bolstered. It is bolstered by operating as an enterprise unit engaging in entrepreneurial economic activity consisting of investments, which optimises its ability to consume its labour capability, which, in turn, produces satisfaction. According to Foucault (2008), for Becker, income streams are generated from a cycle of consumption that begins and ends with the form of life that lies outside the market. This living-labour, while it has a lifespan, an ageing, and an obsolescence (Foucault 2008, 224–25), is practically always at the disposal of the labourer. Human capital can be 'put to work' all the time and in every place. For Becker, living-labour as a consumption cycle has to secure itself as a stable self-reinforcing cycle, otherwise the individual will not sustain labour activity for very long, as the life process of the labouring activity has not yet established itself as an enduring or sustainable process or attained a 'form of life' (Vatter 2018, 80).

If we take these insights from Becker's theories of human capital and the allocation of time, and apply them to knowledge workers, the working subject appears to be an enterprise unit, which is a stabilised 'form of life' comprised of the cycle of labour and consumption in equilibrium. Understandably, this cycle of production of utilities or satisfactions and its consumption *has to* reach an equilibrium to be sustainable. What the 'form of life' reveals are the worker's preferences. Compulsively working workers' preference, then, is work as opposed to competing satisfactions or utilities such as leisure or family time. If these workers persevere in this preference for compulsive work, it is because they are indeed making a profit that may be invisible to others, namely the thumotic satisfaction produced and consumed by way of creative, problem-solving knowledge work. It should be remembered that this 'form of life' of the worker is situated in the context of neoliberal control that pre-organises the free choices at the disposal of workers, conducting the conduct of the enterprise unit according to a cost-benefit calculus that serves the objective of a pervasive neoliberal political-economic programme or governmentality. This implies that this form of control actively harnesses not mere productive output, but the very thumotic satisfaction that propels it. To return to Plato's allegory of the soul with the charioteer, Reason, steering the dark horse of Desire and the noble white steed, Thumos, toward the heavens, it appears that the neoliberal knowledge worker's Reason is subject to an economic rationality that is only rational insofar as its choices are made based on a cost-benefit calculus that renders optimal returns regarding their work addiction. The steed that serves this objective is thumos, associated with 'the fire in the belly', a courageous spiritedness. The dark horse of Desire usually associated with conspicuous consumption is not the definitive force here, as the satisfactions or utilities produced by knowledge workers are not conspicuous or visible (hard work for them does not, first and foremost, serve the purpose of making and spending money and enjoying leisure).

The next question is how this 'form of life' can be sustainable over time, because it is bound to have a negative impact on the worker's mental and physical health, as well as on family ties and social bonds. One finds the answer in the last aspect of Foucault's reading of human capital, which is the requirement not only of investment in human capital itself, but in the 'environment' of the enterprise unit. Here Foucault employs the idea of *Vitalpolitik*, which entails 'the application of the economic grid' to that which was formerly defined in opposition to the economy: social phenomena (Foucault 2008, 240). This approach directly connects neoliberal economy to biopolitics: 'The enterprise schema involves acting so that the individual . . . is not alienated from his work environment, from the time of his life, from his household, his family, and from his natural environment' (Foucault 2008, 242). This entails 'the economization of the entire social field'. At the same time, this *Vitalpolitik* has to compensate for the detrimental effects of the market in the realm of values and existence.

In American neoliberalism, the application of this German Ordoliberal principle becomes absolute and generalised, without limit. The production of a 'healthy' environment in which labourers can conduct their enterprise entails access to wellness programmes, the regulation of work/life balance, etc., that is, the entire scope of issues known as 'human resources' (Vatter 2018, 81). Becker recognises that these kinds of environmental regulation that generate the maximum return of human capital can all be reduced to a logic of addiction (cf. Becker and Stigler 1995). From the perspective of classical economics, addicts exemplify irrational behaviour because they are (often literally) willing to pay any price for the satisfaction they derive from the addictive substance of their choice. For Becker, addictions are not 'positive' or 'negative' based on the qualities of the commodities that are consumed, but solely based on whether the consumption patterns stabilise into a form of life that generates a surplus. As Vatter (2018, 80) puts it, 'Becker's economic theory reveals neoliberal or biopolitical society as one ruled by the "addictive personality"'.

From Becker's perspective, control, the conduct of the labourer's conduct, starts before and outside the market to ensure that populations enter into the market with sufficient human capital to start off their self-enterprise. Neoliberal economic rationality is concerned with '[w]hat type of stimuli, form of life, and relationship with parents, adults, and others can be crystallised into human capital'. In the same way, Foucault explains, all activities that concern the health of individuals serve to improve human capital, and to preserve and employ it for as long as possible (Foucault 2008, 230).

Foucault (2008) concludes his analysis of Becker's (1964) work by situating the theory of human capital in relation to Schumpeter's (1942) explanation of why Marx's fundamental 'law of capital', which postulates the diminishing rate of profit, is wrong. According to Foucault (2008, 231), Schumpeter maintains that 'the tendency of the rate of profit to fall actually turned out to be continually corrected' on account of 'innovation, that is to say, the discovery of new techniques, sources, and forms of productivity, and also the discovery of new markets or new resources of manpower'. The neoliberals are not content to trust 'the permanent stimulation of competition to explain the phenomenon of innovation'. If there is innovation, they believe it is on account of 'the income of a certain capital, of human capital, that is to say, of the set of [privatized] investments we have made on the level of man himself' (Foucault 2008, 230). The rate of profit decreases in the production of market goods, but it does not decrease in the creation of utilities or satisfactions, of that 'surplus' of life due to the consumption of 'invisible' non-market commodities such as love, friendship, personal empowerment, or a healthy lifestyle (Vatter 2018, 82)—or the preferred substance of addiction, in this case feeding the knowledge worker's thumos. It is this imperceptible surplus that accounts for the equilibrium reached in the cycle of labour and consumption that crystallises as a 'form of life', in other words, as an 'enterprise' that is sustainable, at least for some time. So the consumption of these 'invisible' non-market commodities serves as the imperceptible support network that helps to sustain the entrepreneurial life that keeps the knowledge worker captivated because of the thumotic satisfaction it generates.

Conclusion

The Chicago School of neoliberalism of the 1970s defined human capital as the knowledge and set of competences that individuals can turn into objects of deliberate investment, such as education and training. In the network society today, the human has come to be understood as a sustainable resource, one able to (re)generate itself continuously. Innovation has become the product of investment in the human, or in human capital. This approach has fundamentally transformed organisational and managerial cultures and ushered in an era of the ever-expanding field of human resources. Beyond the workplace, as Foucault points outs out, neoliberal governmentality generalises or 'democratizes' this economic rationality by turning the self into an entrepreneur of her-/himself. This generalisation of the economic rationality delegates the responsibility to improve the self to individuals themselves in the form of ostensibly free and rational choice. The more rational the choice, the more the economic reward in the playing field of biopolitical control. As a result, the theory of human capital has succeeded in reducing the economic game to the pursuit of purely individual and atomistic interests that are subject to normalisation and the continuous regulatory and corrective mechanisms that it entails.

In addition, as Paltrinieri (2019, 160) points out, because the notion of human capital concerns the 'quality' of the population, it implicitly extends the eugenicist logic into political economy and into the scientific measurement of human differences, contradicting the egalitarian principles allegedly at the basis of our democratic societies. Neoliberal control, then, operates both on a micro and macro level. Apart from the biopolitics of the population or the 'species body', the delegation of the responsibility of self-improvement to the individual self now results in a kind of private eugenics, Paltrinieri (2019, 160) adds, which Foucault touches on in passing by suggesting that when the problem of the improvement of its human capital becomes paramount in a society, the implications at the level of actuality include the deliberate choice of a spouse or 'co-producer of . . . future human capital'—a co-producer that should be endowed with significant human capital (Foucault 2008, 229). Historically, as the 'quality' of the active population improved, in other words, its stock of competences and knowledge, productivity increased and, in consequence, the value of working time and of salaries also increased, which stimulated increased consumption. As early as the mid-twentieth century, Schultz (1971) and Mincer (1958) predicted that this virtuous circle would usher in the society of knowledge (Paltrinieri 2019, 158–60).

Today the knowledge worker is unequivocally the definitive propellant of the economy. These workers are valuable for their expertise in a particular field, and their seemingly vocational devotion to their work. The overarching argument that I have pursued here is that the theory of human capital at the heart of the neoliberal governmentality of control actively engenders an irrational work-drivenness among knowledge workers by tapping—not primarily into their rational or desiring selves—but into their *thumotic* selves.

The line of argumentation may be recapitulated as follows: according to the neoliberals, the central focus of economic science is the analysis of human behaviour, that is, the study of the way in which and reasons for which scarce resources (labour as human capital) are allocated to competing ends. What is the rationale and motivation for work if the worker is conceived as an active economic subject rather than as a mere object in economic analysis? Foucault (2008, 224) explains human capital as the array of physical and psychological factors that qualify a worker to earn a certain wage. That 'ability machine' or 'income stream' cannot be separated from the human individual who is its bearer and embodiment. As enterprise units, workers are entrepreneurs of themselves, their own capital, their own producers, investing in continuous learning or upskilling to produce their own human capital. These workers' stable preference for constant work is after all an expression of their perceived subjective freedom.

Of particular interest to Foucault in Becker's theory of human capital are the production functions of consumption activities: insofar as the 'labourer' consumes, s/he is also a producer of precisely the satisfaction that s/he consumes. For Becker, these satisfactions are equated with utilities, the use-value to the consumer. I contend that this 'satisfaction' both produced and consumed by the knowledge worker is the use-value derived from thumotic satisfaction. The ever-working knowledge worker is an enterprise unit whose compulsive entrepreneurial activity is fuelled by thumos, while it also produces the thumotic satisfaction, which is reinvested as 'invisible profit' to sustain perseverance in the preference for compulsive 'labour'. This cycle settles into a state of homeostasis or a 'form of life' sustainable for a certain period.

How does thumotic satisfaction factor into the satisfactions or utilities produced by the consumer? For most workers, goods, according to Becker's theory, are desired not for their own sake, but for some specific service that they perform. So the 'goods' of continuous learning offer the utility of up-to-date expertise regarding the latest developments. The utility of expertise becomes the 'goods' consumed to secure a better job, whose utility is higher prestige and a higher income, which becomes the 'goods' consumed to finance a more lavish lifestyle or leisure time, spent with family and friends. This cycle, which includes the utility of enhanced social bonds, does not apply to compulsive knowledge workers, whose compulsive work appears to leave no room for the proportionate enjoyment of the usual fruits that workers' labours afford. Hence, there has to be another explanation for the 'stability of this preference' for work (Becker 1976) and the ability to sustain it in the form of a stabilised 'way of life'. Again I suggest that this preference is *thumotic* in origin.

Apart from the primary or first order circuit of consumption of commodities and production of utilities, there are secondary, tertiary, and more orders or circuits of production and consumption. What these surplus orders succeed in accessing is the circuit of thumotic satisfaction. It is this soul-seated, foundational circuit that sustains the primary circuit. For the knowledge worker, it is work itself that directly produces thumotic satisfaction. In Becker's parlance, in its consumption, living labour 'flows back' from the product—thumotic satisfaction in the case of the knowledge worker—as an 'income stream' generated by human capital. This has allowed neoliberal governmentality to harness a source of labour in the form of the knowledge worker that wastes no time on the production of thumotic satisfactions such as recreational activities that take the worker away from the job itself: it has engineered the most 'productive machine' to date.

Notes

1. A version of this chapter has been published as Hofmeyr 2022b.
2. Available online: http://www.econ.yale.edu/smith/econ116a/keynes1.pdf]
3. Source: https://www.npr.org/2015/08/13/432122637/keynes-predicted-we-would-be-working-15-hour-weeks-why-was-he-so-wrong]
4. The so-called Golden Triangle is a region in Southeast Asia notorious as a global hub of narcotics production; see Arora (2019).
5. Source: https://datareportal.com/global-digital-overview#:~:text=A%20total%20of%205%20billion,12%20months%20to%20April%202022.]
6. Foucault refers to Michael and Becker's article, 'On the New Theory of Consumer Behavior' (1973), in which they argue for a reformulation of the theory of consumer behavior based on the household production function suggested in Gary Becker's earlier article, 'A Theory of the Allocation of Time' (1965).

CHAPTER SIX

The Feasibility of Resistance in the Workplace[1]

In this concluding reflection, I return to my original question of what knowledge workers are today in relation to a globalising neoliberal governmentality in which their lives are reduced to constant work under conditions of stealth control. Here I conclude my investigation by revisiting Foucault's theorisation of biopolitics and a critical attitude as virtue, as well as his theorisation of resistance to plot the risks to which the knowledge worker is exposed. I also explore the conditions of possibility, as well as the probability of the success, of productive resistance in workplace.

The typical neoliberal knowledge worker is characterised, as I have maintained, by her/his paradoxical addiction or compulsion to work. For a compulsive knowledge worker, beyond the world of work, there may be some escapist consumption and guilt-ridden procrastination, but the worker will return again and again to work in an attempt to fulfil a soul-seated craving for a kind of satisfaction of an existential and/or ontological kind, driven by thumos. In other words, for the constantly self-controlled, self-responsible, neoliberal knowledge worker, work addiction, as I have shown in chapter 4, defies reason and desire because it is fuelled by the thumotic satisfaction it produces. It is therefore *not* the appetites that are associated with contemporary capitalist profit-seeking and consumption, as is generally assumed—not the dark horse of desire—*but the spirited white stallion of thumos* that draws the chariot.

In respect of resistance, importantly, Plato contends that practical wisdom is needed to know when one should harness thumotic anger and when one should display gentleness. This wisdom is instilled by a philosophical education to learn restraint and forbearance. Thumos is both a necessary condition for the possibility of justice (which implies resistance to injustice) and poses a fundamental challenge to justice, if thumos is incorrectly applied. The dilemma can be resolved through education. The ingenuity of the neoliberal theory of human capital is, as I have shown, that it harnesses this spiritedness of the soul *against* its original role of anger against injustice. Hence, the neoliberal foregrounding of human capital as most decisive for optimising productivity and increasing profit provides the answer to how neoliberal capitalism succeeds in drawing on the soul-seated spiritedness to generate the requisite competitive entrepreneurial spirit as a driving force. This harnessing of thumos to achieve the aims of neoliberal governmentality implies that resistance becomes nearly impossible, because thumos as the very source of indignation in the face of injustice, and the readiness to stand up and oppose it, has already been neutralised as an addictive object of consumption.

So is resistance possible? The case studies and their analysis by Courpasson, Dany, and Clegg (2012) offer a heuristic toward providing a method for producing practicable avenues of productive collective resistance in the workplace. Nevertheless, I critically interrogate their analyses by contextualising them against the backdrop of the 'complex' mechanisms of control that operate in the contemporary neoliberal organisations in which knowledge workers find themselves, which, I contend, makes the success of the method of resistance proposed by Courpasson, Dany, and Clegg (2012) highly improbable. In line with the spirit of Foucault's analyses, I prefer to offer not solutions, but rather problematisations, because solutions are themselves prone to being co-opted by prevailing relations of power and put to work to further the very agendas they seek to resist. One example of such co-option is precisely the way in which neoliberal governmentality has succeeded in putting the thumos of knowledge workers to work by applying the theory of human capital that informs the latest management theories pertaining to knowledge workers.

Biopolitical Control Again

The subject as an entrepreneurial project in the making is inscribed in a process of continuous self-improvement. Here self-improvement takes the form of a normalised internalised injunction. This is the means through which power insinuates and inscribes itself 'smartly' (Han 2017, 34) into every minute aspect of life through self-learning, smart-connected devices that track our flows of physical movement and the rhythms of our biological processes. Smart watches count our steps and remind us to take our daily exercise in the name of our health; they track our sleeping patterns, calling on us to get more hours of deep sleep to ensure optimal efficiency and focus during our working or waking hours (which have become one and the same, in the case of neoliberal knowledge workers). The consumption patterns of knowledge workers are traced in minute detail, whether these patterns relate to online resources and research consumption, or online shopping through digital platforms that redirect the clicking subject's conduct through highly seductive clickbait that nudges the web surfer to craft a path of online activity that renders the maximum profit returns. The online working life of every knowledge worker is traceable, directable, and, as such, controllable. It has become possible to know when we are where, with whom, and what we are doing. It has even become possible to trace *how* we are doing with the help of Woebots or mental health chatbots or digital therapists.

In chapter 3, we saw that the unprecedented pace of technological innovation is catapulting us into a future that Törnberg and Uitermark (2020, 1) term 'complex control'. They contend that 'control is increasingly moving to lower-level strata, operating by setting the context and conditions for self-organisation. Thus, the order of things emerges naturally from the rules of the game' (Törnberg and Uitermark 2020, 1). The era of digital platforms has been welcomed as the era of unprecedented freedom that puts the self in the driver's seat against the static, linear, and top-down configurations of former regimes of governmentality. The digital platforms through which neoliberal governmentality wields biopolitical control over the life of the individual and the population is 'open, informal and non-linear' (Törnberg and Uitermark 2020, 2). Importantly for our topic in this chapter, Törnberg and Uitermark (2020, 2) ask: 'To what extent does self-organization actually imply *empowerment* or *freedom?* Who is the "self" in "self-organization"?'.

Digital platforms are an integral part of enabling remote and even global work, but also an integral part of control. Unthinkable little over three decades ago, digital platforms are now essential social and economic infrastructure. User-generated content is such a standard part of new technologies that 'digital' and social' have almost become synonymous. Admittedly, whereas in ever more contexts the digital/social conflation does apply, in the knowledge work context, digital often means complex software for specialist purposes, which is not social, even though it may enable remote access and sharing within the company or between companies. Here proprietary restrictions may constrain sharing. That said, the knowledge worker as individual is firmly imbedded in the digital/social world as a result of the conflation of work and life, or the invasion of work into private life.

Törnberg and Uitermark (2020, 1) points out that social/digital platforms are deceptively claimed to be spaces for personal liberation where every voice can be heard, every form of individuality can be expressed, and everyone's intellectual and democratic potential can be realised (Zuckerberg 2019). This is claimed to be the benefit of the 'sharing economy' (Puschmann and Alt 2016). Benkler (2002) hails these platforms as representing 'commons-based peer production', drawing on the positive connotations of the 'commons' as our shared product of the power of the people, not of top-down governance. Such apparent self-organisation implies the utopian political ideal in which private actors act autonomously for the common good and pursue collective objectives (Mattijssen et al. 2018), not intermediated by prosumption, and free from central control. This principle underlies the sharing economy and social platforms—for example, Wikipedia, Airbnb, or Uber, as well as Twitter or Facebook (Benkler 2006; Srnicek 2017). It also underpins self-organised systems whose components are partly autonomous, although they interact with the whole (Heylighen et al. 2006, 125 cited by Törnberg and Uitermark (2020, 3)). For the neoliberal economy, this allows a kind of 'swarm' behaviour (Mitchell 2009; Ball 2012; see chapter 3), which offers resilience, given the inherent redundancy of each individual part of the same class—each and every part's role can just as easily be performed by any other similar part of the same class. This allows a shift away from bureaucratic structures, and a shift to apparently organic or informal social relations. Such adaptability and resilience are vital in the face of rapid changes, including global social and ecological crises (Gunderson and Light 2006), and is particularly useful because it does not require hands-on central intervention but can be created through 'self-organization, self-regulation, and self-governance' (Helbing 2015, 2 cited by Törnberg and Uitermark (2020, 3)).

Bauman (2000) theorises that the concomitant acquisition of consumption freedom signals the depoliticisation of the citizen, who, reduced to a mere consumer, loses her/his capacity for political action. This contention is based on Bauman's conviction that freedom has a collective basis. Importantly, he draws our attention to the fact that just because something is individualised and 'bottom-up' that does not necessarily mean that it serves the interests of its constituents or constitutes an expression of their will. Bauman's (2000) contention regarding the depoliticisation of the citizen is supported by my own argument that suggests that the neoliberal knowledge worker who lives to work is not interested in opposing the injustice to which s/he is subjected, because s/he is incapable of recognising the injustice of the neoliberal working existence and the radically unequal world it contributes to. The worker is incapable of this recognition, because her/his thumos has already been harnessed by neoliberal capitalism by way of a governmentality that funnels this self-regarding energy and spirit into the self's individual entrepreneurial projects.

The paradoxical individualisation of the social/digital platforms of the post-disciplinary society signals fundamental disempowerment. Digital technology affords unparalleled flexibility in the construction of the subjectivities of its users while separating them from others—they socialise with a screen, offering curated *visions* of the world and even of the Facebook, Twitter, and Instagram 'selves' of others, and not with the visceral suffering or rejoicing of another *in* the world. Halpern (2015) and Kitchin, Lauriault, and Wilson (2017, cited by Törnberg and Uitermark (2020, 4), point out that the digital interface comprises an encoding of an epistemology, representing what is important and orchestrating how the user can navigate the world by what it includes, how it is included, and what it omits. Such representational logics structure the agency and subjectivity of the user, not merely by defining the user's role, but also by determining in an inconspicuous but decisive way how the user conceives of, relates to, and inhabits her/his social world. The digital platform interface embodies an ontology that defines what the world is, and what it is not:

> How the user will act is a function of what affordances and view of the world . . . the platform provides. . . . While the user is free in the sense that [s/he] gets to choose from a menu of options, what is on the menu, the order of the options, or the subtle designs that shape how it is perceived, is provided by the platform. (Törnberg and Uitermark 2020, 4)

A useful example of this operational logic is Netflix. Halliman and Striphas (2016) report that the system 'in total influences choice for about 80% of hours streamed at Netflix'. This ontology draws on the insights of social psychology to optimise engagement, such as the fact that negativity rather than positivity captures attention (Rozin and Royzman 2001). Fear-inducing bad news, reports of trauma and violence, conspiracy theories, disasters, crime, micro-aggressions, hate speech, etc., are examples of the content of cyber feeds and prompts that engage users much more than good news or happy thoughts, locking each user in her/his own individualised bubble, an ever-diminishing self-fulfilling prophecy of how the world is perceived to be and the user's place in it. As Törnberg and Uitermark (2020, 5) remark, in truly Foucauldian vein, '[t]hrough platform design, the platform citizens' agency can be reconfigured as easily as the platform can itself, making the "conducting of the conduct" of subjects precise and efficient'.

As I have shown in chapter 3, drawing on Bauman's (2013) notion of the 'Synopticon', Törnberg and Uitermark (2020) describe the contemporary form of control and surveillance as the 'social Synopticon', using digital platforms, in which the many watch the many, unlike in the age of disciplinary power, as theorised by Foucault (1975), when, in the Panopticon, the few watched the many to exercise control, or in Bauman's Synopticon, where mass media allowed the many to watch and admire the few. The social Synopticon of digital/social platforms allows us to *think* that 'we write ourselves into being' (Sundén 2002) and constitute social indicators of reputation and standing (Ert, Fleischer, and Magen 2016 referred to by Törnberg and Uitermark (2020, 5)). The human need for recognition and our insecurities are exploited for corporate profits, as these platforms employ typical elements of game playing (for example, point scoring, competition, game rules) to encourage engagement with a product or service.

Similar to Törnberg and Uitermark (2020), Han (2017) uses terms such as the 'digital Panopticon', 'smart power', and 'friendly Big Brother'. He also considers relations of power as control and surveillance, arguing that the model neoliberal working subject does not resist but willingly welcomes constant surveillance as benevolent, because surveillance implies recognition. Such surveillance can take the form of audits, indicators, grading and rankings. The *quid pro quo* for remaining competitive is religious self-discipline and self-surveillance. This is the biopolitical control of neoliberal governmentality in action, curating competition, using market-based forms of control, hiding the mechanisms, and depoliticising the working subject. The illusion of *spontaneity* is a vital component of this control. I repeat Törnberg and Uitermark's (2020, 6) warning that phenomena that emanate from mass-interactive systems are hard to trace back to specific causal roots, making them appear to have arisen spontaneously, 'as if micro-level causes were not just as much a function of external constraints and conditions' (Törnberg and Uitermark 2020, 6). In the light of this warning then, I find rather unconvincing and naïve Rose's (1999, 244) denial that this may be interpreted as 'a super-Panopticon at work' and his argument that '[j]ust because a technology has a potential use, such as that of surveillance, does not imply that this is the use to which it will be put' (Rose 1999, 244). He is quite right in suggesting that '[t]he productive subject is to be governed as a citizen, as an individual striving for meaning in work, seeking identity in work, whose subjective desires for self-actualization are to be harnessed to the firm's aspirations for productivity, efficiency and the like' (Rose 1999, 244), but this *surface* form of governance does not mean that he is right in claiming that 'advanced liberal strategies for the government of the productive self do not understand and regulate the worker as a psycho-physiological machine whose output is to be optimized by surveillance, discipline and sanction' (Rose 1999, 244)—the 'surveillance, discipline and sanction' are just applied in a far more covert and subtle manner.

Foucault's analyses of neoliberal governmentality already showed, more than forty years ago, that the supposedly free market is anything but free: it is carefully constructed and maintained. Nor are the digital/social platforms on which knowledge workers constantly work disintermediated: they recast modes of interaction into quantified and datafied forms that permit control through intervention and manipulation of social reality and ideological choices (Feenberg 2002; Van Dijck and Poell 2013). Politically designed 'choice architectures' of digital platforms 'nudge' users toward particular behaviours by curating the contexts in which people make decisions to ensure predictability (altering how/which information is offered, the options available and default choices, or creating implicit/explicit awards, scores or rankings) (Törnberg and Uitermark 2020). The illusion of choice and spontaneity makes all that the users encounter seem 'natural' or 'inherent' as an outcome of digital technology. The wealth, power, and recognition enjoyed by only a few in this complex power system is hidden by the apparent self-organisation of these systems, exonerating them from any political, conflictual, or power dimensions (Törnberg and Uitermark 2020, 8). Self-organisation is perceived as inherently good, and as inevitable, because it is purported to arise from some mysterious synergy of the commons. The question I asked in the introductory chapter still stands: if 'the new instrument of control is horizontal, decentralized, networked communication' (Törnberg and Uitermark 2020, 9), in which actors not only voluntarily but enthusiastically engage in constantly, to what extent is resistance possible—especially if resistance is not sought because control is intangible?

Foucault and the Possibility of Resistance

If we are to draw on Foucault in our attempt to answer the question, we need to call to mind the evolution of the notion of resistance in Foucault's later works, starting with *The History of Sexuality. Volume I* (1976), from reaction to creation through to normalisation, which I have traced in Hofmeyr (2008). To what extent is resistance possible, given that the power relations at work in neoliberal governmentality have successfully tethered the noble white stallion of thumos to the unquenchable aspirations of the self as a project: the entrepreneurial self? Bearing this 'project' in mind, it is instructive to remember that Foucault revisited the Greco-Roman notion of care of the self as a site of potential resistance in the form of creative self-formation. Specifically in the second and third volumes of the *History of Sexuality*, Foucault returns to antiquity to develop a contemporary 'post-moral(ity)' ethics of self-transformation. To be clear, Foucault's conception of ethics, which is realised as a practice of 'care of the self', entails the self's relation to itself and not some subscription to a rigid moral code. 'Care of the self' conceives of the subject as individual agency characterised by its capacity for self-formation *amid* power relations, as we shall see. In other words, being situated amid the forces that constitute subjectivity does not mean that we cannot counter them through self-creation—unless these forces amount to a physical determination. Given the present neoliberal configuration of complex power that has insinuated itself precisely within the site of individual agency, it seems implausible that care of the self could still be capable of subverting the 'government of individuation' (Foucault 1982b, 212) through the invention of new forms of *self*-government.

In Foucault's later work, resistance undergoes a certain evolution (Hartmann 2003; Thompson 2003; Hofmeyr 2008), and it is instructive to revisit this evolution with a view to the possibility of resistance under the present conditions of complex power relations. In the chapter titled 'Method' in volume I of *The History of Sexuality* (1976), Foucault understands resistance as a *tactical reversal*: resistance can be pinpointed where local clashes are assimilated or re-inscribed into the existing order. This re-appropriation entails a mutual conditioning in which both active and reactive forces are strategically altered. In other words, although power bears the inherent threat of domination, the threat is countered by the constitutive potential of reversal—the possibility of overturning subjugating relations of force. Here, Foucault theorises 'mobile and transitory points of resistance, producing cleavages in a society that shift about, fracturing unities and effecting regroupings, furrowing across individuals themselves, cutting them up and remolding them, marking off irreducible regions in them, in their bodies and minds' (Foucault 1976, 96).

I find this conceptualisation far more realistic and convincing than the likelihood of some great revolutionary liberation once and for all, or 'radical ruptures' or 'massive binary divisions' (Foucault 1976, 96). The possibility afforded by reversal to overturn subjugating relations of force confines resistance to a reactive stance. In other words, it is confined to the ability to seize the power to *react to* constraining governmental regulations, institutionalised normalisations, and societal intolerance. The question that emerges, however, is if resistance is a mere *re*-action or negation, what is inherently *creative* about it? Care of the self as creative resistance—as fashioning oneself as a work of art, as Nietzsche and Foucault suggest—is after all a positive action on its own terms.

Between the publication of volume I in 1976 and the subsequent second and third volumes of Foucault's *History of Sexuality* in 1984, there is certainly evidence of a shift of emphasis regarding power and resistance, if not a fundamental rethinking of the analysis of power and knowledge. According to Miller (1993), Foucault's turn toward governmentality and the technologies of the self can be understood as an implicit concession on Foucault's part, an admission that his depiction of power and resistance in volume I was too constrictive. Miller (1993) portrays the period of Foucault's 1977–1978 Collège de France lectures as 'a time of crisis for him'. In his 1978 lectures, Foucault (2008) turned abruptly to what was then a completely new topic, that of governmentality:

> There is nevertheless a certain irony about this work in these months. Despite the deployment of fresh historical evidence and the marshalling of a new battery of concepts, the disposition of forces described . . . is essentially the same as that described in . . . *Discipline and Punish*. His approach changed but he still didn't know where he was going. (*cf*. Miller 1993, 298–301, cited in Hofmeyr 2008)

Notwithstanding Miller's reservations, I have postulated in Hofmeyr (2008) that there is a readily discernible modification in Foucault's consideration of power and resistance in this period, culminating in his 1982 essay, 'The Subject and Power'. Here, and in the second and third volumes of his *History of Sexuality*, the self is radically reconceived: the self is now no longer considered as the passive product of an external system of constraint and prescription, but as the active agent of its own formation. Foucault consequently articulates a more positive means of resistance, that is, resistance as autonomy through heteronomy. There is, however, also a continuity in Foucault's thinking between the first and later two volumes of *The History of Sexuality*. In the well-known 1984 interview titled 'The Ethic of Care for the Self as a Practice of Freedom', it becomes apparent that resistance as creative force cannot do away with the necessity of resistance as a reactive force. Here Foucault (1984c) introduces the self as conceived by the Greeks, as *individual agency* that is self-sufficient and self-transformative. He theorises 'care of the self' as a site of resistance opposed to all those material, historical, economic, discursive, and linguistic structures, practices, and drives that are constitutive of subjectivity. He is not proposing that the subject can ever entirely rid itself from relations of power, but rather that the self's embeddedness in power '*does not* entail the necessity of accepting an inescapable form of domination' (Foucault 1977, 141, my emphasis). The struggle against the submission of subjectivity (Foucault 1982b, 212) is possible precisely because it occurs in the same place as power. If we understand the exercise of power as a mode of action upon the action of others, the freedom to act and to react is implicit to power. That is why resistance to power can only occur amid relations of power (Foucault 1977, 221; 1980b, 142). The subject seizes autonomy not only despite of, but also through, heteronomous power relations. The disempowering forces which it resists are also the very forces that enable self-creation. Greenblatt (1980) explains that the freedom of the art of the self does not consist in self-creation, but in the experience of self-formation in the face of all the other forces that fashion us (Hofmeyr 2008).

Foucault's conception of power therefore leads, as I have argued (Hofmeyr 2005; 2008), to the conclusion, that 'the conditions of existence which are to be transformed are woven from the same cloth as the practice of transformation itself' (Balibar 2002, 15)—they are both of the order of 'an action upon an action' (Foucault 1982b, 221). While the relations of power are indeed *constituent*, the more or less stabilised social norms, the norms of behaviour, are *constituted*. What this means is that liberty might just be within our grasp, but not attainable once and for all. Liberty is not a state, but entails continuous *practices* or exercises of freedom. While the ubiquity of power dissipates the fantasy of autonomous self-creation, it enables heteronomous practices of freedom—a hard-earned freedom that is not freedom *from* power, but freedom *through* power, despite power and because of power (Hofmeyr 2005, 115). Power in Foucault is the common domain of both liberty and subjugation, the place where freedom is both realised and diminished or annihilated. Power cannot be resisted from outside. Being situated *in* the relational network of power (that makes resistance necessary) is the condition of possibility of resistance. Precisely because of this situatedness, every act of resistance calls into being new relationships of power that in turn have to be resisted (Foucault 1984c, 4). Balibar (2002, 19) warns that this signals the danger of the self being caught in 'an infinite regress'. 'Regress' here may be understood as a series of actions (practices or technologies of the self) in which resistance is continually reapplied to its own result without approaching a conclusive state of absolute liberation (Hofmeyr 2005, 115). The subject, then, is caught in an infinite regress of cycles of repetition of liberation and domination. Every newly created self-indentity is co-opted by the power relations in which it is entangled, and hence necessitates self-refusal if it is not to succumb to domination. 'The trajectory leading from resistance to liberation, from liberation to domination, and back again (via resistance) has to be inscribed *in* the very fabric of individual subject-formation as a constant practice or exercise of liberty' (Hofmeyr 2005, 115).

Accordingly, to avoid normalisation, every new formation of resistance has to dismantle itself in an effort to resist more effectively. Put differently, every newly created subject identity has to constantly recreate itself if it is not to risk being incorporated in the prevailing regime. Think, for example, how capitalism mobilises countercultural subject identities to promote products as 'cool', 'hip and happening', thereby taking into its fold those that are 'alternative' or counter-cultural, those that wish to diverge from the mainstream. The hoped-for effectiveness of countless relays of reimaginings of the self is situated in the fact that it presents the powers that be, not with one force of resistance, but with countless small individual acts of self-(re)formation (Hofmeyr 2008).

However, in the context of neoliberal governmentality with its complex network of biopolitical controls and powers of omnipotent surveillance that seek not to normalise, but to capitalise on difference and variations from the norm, the prevailing order has succeeded more effectively than ever in defusing whatever subversive potential these relays might have by putting them to work. It has latched onto our thumotic drive toward creative self-actualisation through the invention of the entrepreneurial subject—a project invested in constant self-improvement and reinvention. Instead of constituting a more effective provocation of inhibiting governmental rationalities, these forms of self-actualisation and self-empowerment turn out to be sanctioned and actively encouraged by biopolitical control—their seditious potential is sublimated through incorporation in schemes orchestrated by precisely those powers they seek to contest. In other words, instead of effectively promoting new forms of subjectivity through the refusal of the kind of subjectivity coupled to biopolitical control, as Foucault (1982b, 216) urges, the self's transformative labours are forging exactly the kind of ambitious individuality that furthers the agenda of efficiency and ever-increasing profit generation. The latest governing techniques posit 'intelligent' limits—limits sensitive to our every creative, entrepreneurial ambition, which means that being 'different' has itself become a part of subjugation (Hofmeyr 2008, 110). But before we conclude that Foucault's notion of care of the self no longer has any chance of success as a means of resistance in the context of the forms of biopolitical control operative in the information age, it is worth revisiting his understanding of the critical attitude as virtue, which I discussed in chapter 2.

The Critical Attitude[2]

Critique, Foucault insists, 'only exists in relation to something other than itself' (Foucault 1978, 25). It is a certain way of relating to existing reality, to knowledge, action, society, culture, and also to others, that despite this dependency and heteronomy remains *other*. In other words, as critique it only exists when it succeeds in remaining outside, when it resists being assimilated into its object. As 'a means for a future or a truth that it will not know nor happen to be' (Foucault 1978, 25), it is aimed at exposing the limits of its object and this exposure of the limit, in turn, is associated with the practice of virtue—as if virtue is to be found in the very opposition to the established 'order of things' (Hofmeyr 2008, 111).

Virtue is usually understood as uprightness or righteousness. Foucault contends that it is associated with an ethics, that is, with the way in which the self relates to itself, which in turn conditions its conduct toward others. Critique as virtue is associated with an ethics that resists blind subjection to objectively formulated moral codes. 'True to its Latin root *virtus*, it should be conceived in terms of force or strength, the strength not to merely submit to, but to critically engage with, those norms' (Hofmeyr 2008, 111). In the second volume of *The History of Sexuality*, *The Use of Pleasure*, Foucault explains that classical moral reflection addressed men concerning precisely those forms of conduct in which they were called upon *to exercise their rights, their power, their authority, and their liberty*. The moral demands made on men did not inhibit their conduct by way of prohibitions, but incited them to exercise and affirm their privilege, potential, and autonomy. The themes of austerity did not express essential interdictions but may be conceived as the elaboration and stylisation of an activity in the exercise of its power and the practice of its liberty (Foucault 1984c, 23; Hofmeyr 2008).

Critique, as we have seen, is not something that can be defined independently of the various objects by which it is itself defined. In this lecture, Foucault situates it in terms of government, in 'how *not* to be governed' (Foucault 1978, 28). Here he is not proposing the transcendence of all imposed limits, opting for anarchy or asking how to become wholly ungovernable. He is not therefore simply returning to his earlier notion of 'tactical reversal', of resistance understood as negation or opposition. It is a specific question that emerges in relation to a specific form of government, already cited in chapter 2, namely 'how not to be governed *like that*, by that, in the name of those principles, with such and such an objective in mind and by means of such procedure, not like that, not for that, not by them' (Foucault 1978, 28).

Accordingly, critique consists in challenging the demand for complete compliance by subjecting every governmental obligation imposed on individuals to a rational and reflective assessment. We have to face these imposed principles head on, not in a gesture of rejection, but as an act of defiance that challenges and displaces them in order to *develop* the arts of governing (Foucault 1978, 28–29). Moreover, to be distrustful of governmentally imposed absolutes, in the way Foucault intended, implies a critical practice that fundamentally transforms us in the process. Foucault's notion of an aesthetics of existence entails 'those actions by which men not only seek to set themselves rules of conduct, but also seek to transform themselves in their singular being . . . to make their lives into an *oeuvre* that carries certain aesthetic values and meets certain stylistic criteria' (Foucault 1984c, 10–11). Butler (2000, 218, cited in Hofmeyr 2008, 112) explains this as follows:

> Such lives do not simply conform to moral precepts or norms in such a way that selves, considered pre-formed or ready-made, fit themselves into a mold that is set forth by the precept. On the contrary, the self fashions itself in terms of the norm, comes to inhabit or incorporate the norm, but *the norm is not in this sense external to the principle by which the self is formed.*

As I have explained in Hofmeyr (2008, 112), what Foucault terms 'the politics of truth' (1978, 32) pertains to those structures of power that predetermine what will and will not count as truth, that delineate a given field of knowledge, and that consequently organise the world in a certain controlled and controllable fashion. Critique takes effect as soon as the subject gives her-/himself the right to question the politics of truth, as soon as the individual starts challenging the confines of her/his power/knowledge-determined world. According to Foucault (1978, 32), this activity of questioning pre-established subject identities and trajectories will be 'the art of voluntary insubordination, that of reflected intractability' that would 'ensure the desubjugation of the subject'.

Foucault further postulates that 'critique means putting forth universal and indefeasible rights' (Foucault 1978, 30). As a result, the emphasis shifts away from prohibitions to rights, away from subjection to freedom. However, it does not state these rights as positive rights. By 'putting forth' these rights, one is claiming the flexibility and manoeuvrability of identity and action to which one is entitled. It is the act of recuperating agency that necessarily challenges pre-given power/knowledge structures. It implies the positing of limitation itself, the positing of the *right* to limit imposed force relations. In Foucault's words, to '"not want to be governed" is . . . not accepting as true . . . what an authority tells you is true, or at least not accepting it because an authority tells you that it is true, but rather accepting it only if one considers valid the reasons for doing so' (Foucault, 1978, 31, cited in Hofmeyr 2008, 112).

Here it is important to realise that the reasons provided for a governmental injunction always operate in two different registers that are difficult to disentangle, which makes for the cunning of this technique of power. If the governmental rationality instructs you to 'transform yourself', the explicit reasons might not be objectionable at all. Why not create your life as a work of art or 'project' if you can thereby fully actualise your potential, which, in the end, will cultivate a strong community supported by capable and enterprising individuals? At the same time, however, one should be vigilant of the *underlying order* or implicit 'rationality', which supports a certain governmental imperative—the politics of truth, in other words (Hofmeyr 2008, 112). Enterprising self-improvement and self-transformation might be encouraged not because the presiding governmentality has any vested interest in the uniqueness of its citizens, but rather in their entrepreneurial ingenuity as human capital. Individuals will then be urged to pursue their enterprising aspirations within the governmentally regulated framework provided, so that these desires can be sublimated and channelled toward the greater objective of ever-increasing efficiency and profit generation.

The critical act of discernment required is by no means easy, for, as Butler points out, what will constitute a ground of validity for accepting authority? If accepting authority merely depends on consent, Foucault's position risks being reduced to a form of voluntarism. However, the critical practice does not stem from innate human freedom, but 'is formed instead in the crucible of a particular exchange between a set of rules or precepts (which are already there) and a stylisation of acts (which extends and reformulates that prior set of rules and precepts)' (Butler 2000, 222, cited in Hofmeyr 2008, 113).

So when Foucault talks about self-stylisation, he is referring to a certain ethical labour (*travail éthique*), which the self performs on itself in relation to the rules and values that s/he is supposed to adhere to (Foucault 1984b, 27). However, morality must be defined, not by the conformity of the action with the code, but in reference to the intention and the freedom of the subject, and thus, ultimately, to the way in which the will determines itself. Thus, in clear opposition to the subject's subjection to the law characteristic of codified pre-/proscriptive moralities, Foucault advocates an ethics that can be derived from the 'conduct' of the individual—the way in which s/he gives 'deliberate form' to her/his liberty (Foucault 1984c, 4). Self-transformation is therefore concerned with the way in which one ought to 'conduct oneself'—'that is, the manner in which one ought to form oneself as an ethical subject acting in reference to the prescriptive elements that make up the code' (Foucault 1984b, 26). Given the code of conduct and various ways in which individuals conduct themselves, which can be defined by their degree of conformity with or divergence from the code, there are different ways to 'conduct oneself' morally. '[F]or what is morality', asks Foucault (1984c, 4, cited in Hofmeyr 2008, 113), 'if not the practice of liberty, the deliberate practice of liberty?' The practice of freedom is therefore not synonymous with respect for the law. In the second and third volumes of his *History*, Foucault repeatedly stresses that the Greeks had very few codes and prohibitions. Strict adherence to these was never an object of great moral concern. What was important was the necessity for the subject to determine and express not only his will, but also his *way of being* through action. How I ought to act then also becomes a matter of how *I choose* to act—whether I choose to conform to or diverge from the code (Foucault 1984b, 26). It is a choice that cannot be reduced to voluntarism, for it reflects an entire mode of being (Hofmeyr 2008, 113).

Foucauldian self-stylisation then refers to forms of ethical subjectivisation; that is, the way in which we constitute ourselves as ethical subjects of our own actions. And if ethical subjectivisation is always directly tied to the moral code, self-stylisation will change as the rules change, as it constitutes a critical attitude toward those rules. So even if present-day governmental rationalities prescribe or incorporate self-transformation and constant self-investment to defuse its subversive potential, the process of self-creation proposed by Foucault cannot be reduced to this. As a critical response to the rule, it will always be 'in excess of' the rule. For such a critical response does not simply entail objecting to this or that governmental demand, but uncovering the order in which such a demand is inscribed. It is at this point that the real risk involved in the critical attitude surfaces. If it is not just a specific law that one questions, but its very epistemological underpinning, which legitimates the rules of governmental validity, then questioning the law entails renouncing the established grounds of its validity. This is something different from and far more dangerous to the status quo than the simple rejection of a given law (Butler 2000, 222, cited in Hofmeyr 2008, 114). The practice of critique, if it is practised consistently, should then not only be able to keep track of changing governmentally imposed limits, but also of the politics of truth that supports it. Resistance effectively posed to one limit by extension also questions the entire order that supports it (Hofmeyr 2008, 113–14).

What Foucault is referring to here is clearly personal individual resistance that requires us to question the politics of truth that underlies the field of force relations that the self finds him-/herself in. How would such personal individual resistance that entails the use of critique relate to collective resistance, the kind that one would associate with organisational or political change? If personal resistance based on the attitude of critique threatens to uncover the illegitimacy and injustice of the grounds that give the rule of governance its validity, and claims the right and obligation to insist on *not* being governed like *that*, is there a place for it in collective organisational resistance? At this preliminary point, I might venture to suggest that personal individual resistance is a necessary condition for collective resistance. I would further posit that it is a necessary condition, but perhaps not a sufficient one in the context of contemporary organisational governance, which entails complex mechanisms of controls. As a form of resistance that questions the very grounds of validity that underpin governance structures, it might prove too dangerous to be taken into account seriously by those in organisational positions of power. In other words, it might merely be confined to the margins, recouped by the norm, or snuffed out before it can have any concrete effect. As a result, individuals that pose such resistance in an unqualified and unilateral manner might simply find themselves out of a job.

It is worth remembering here that for Foucault the critical attitude is not about becoming wholly ungovernable or a gesture of wholesale rejection of the rule of governance, and this at least suggests that individual resistance might serve as the trigger of productive collective resistance and constructive organisational change. It is fair to assume that within the context of organisations, effective bottom-up resistance would require a certain decisive measure of collective resistance to be effective. However, we should be careful to make too sharp a distinction between the individual and the collective. For Foucault, the individual is one node in a network of power relations. This network implies that each node is fundamentally connected to every other point. The action, or 'counter-conduct', of one node necessarily affects all the others. Whether the relation between individual resistance (as a trigger) and collective resistance holds, and how it might function in the context of the workplace, is the subject of the next section.

Resistance as a Critical Attitude

How, then, does the critical attitude as a virtue take shape as resistance—not blind rebellion, but constructive or productive resistance—in the workplace? I repeat, with Foucault (1978), that productive resistance is not about becoming ungovernable, but about how not to be governed *like that*, in the name of *those principles* exclusively driven by profit generation *at the expense of ideas*. Examples of 'productive resistance' in the workplace that did produce change that significantly challenged top management decisions have been instructively documented by Courpasson, Dany, and Clegg (2012), who identify four steps in the process of productive resistance that they plotted, based on two case studies. What they call 'enclave insurgency' in two different companies started with (1) a trigger, which led to (2) the formation of an enclave. Next, (3) the enclave made its concerns public within the context of the company, which then (4) resulted in a temporary realignment of power relations. Importantly, this kind of outcome requires resistance to be based on principles that supported the core business of the company, to be initiated by powerful and successful stakeholders in the company, and to be directed at a *receptive* management that is equally driven by the *core* business of the company. Such dissent might be met with initial indignation, but it is eventually accommodated and new roles emerge. What is evident about this documented 'productive' resistance is that it depended on a number of decisive preconditions. It was initiated by the *right* people in the name of the *right* principles and met by the *right* management, and this allowed the resistance to succeed. The *right* management in this context is management motivated not exclusively by profit generation at whatever cost, but by the core business of *knowledge generation* of the company. A striking aspect of both case studies is that the conflict that arose was between two camps: researchers (knowledge workers) and their need for autonomy and power over decisions in key projects on the one hand, and those involved in the bringing to market and marketing of the products and their concern to expedite the delivery of products to market and to recognise the constraints of competition on the other hand (Courpasson, Dany, and Clegg 2012, 810). The resisters cast competing values into relief—'the durability of science and how quickly a scientific endeavour becomes a marketable product' (Courpasson, Dany, and Clegg 2012, 810). A crucial ingredient in the success of dissent as productive resistance is management's acknowledgement of the researchers' expertise and their legitimate participation in decisions as a condition for the company's success. Courpasson, Dany, and Clegg (2012) claim that they have proved that successful or productive resistance is within the capability of the workers, as opposed to being at the discretion of management. However, their entire argument hinges on two case studies that featured management that, although initially displeased, was willing to consider the case put before it by the dissenters, because management was itself driven by ideas rather than primarily by profit. In both cases, the respective chief executive officers recognised that the core business of their companies was the innovative ideas of their employees, and that it is these very ideas that are wholly responsible for whatever profit followed.

Numerous other case studies show the converse: that neoliberal governmentality prioritises profit regardless of the cost. One example that comes to mind is Ford South Africa's failure to recall the Kuga SUV after being alerted to a manufacturer's defect that caused forty-seven vehicles to catch alight and led to the death of one person as a result. Insurance companies confirmed that they had alerted the company to issues related to the Kuga, going back as far as 2014. A crucial point about this case is that it was one company's (the insurer's) profit incentive that suffered to the benefit of another's

(Ford's). In the end, it was profit generation that decided the battle and drove the resistance (Hosken and Knowles 2017). The reason why we now see recalls of defective products on a scale not seen before is not usually that companies acknowledge that the products pose a serious safety risk to the public but that companies realise that not recalling them 'cause[s] significant financial and reputational damage to the companies concerned' (Burrows 2018). The automotive industry has experienced the biggest product recalls in history by cost, resulting in more than 70 per cent of the value of recall-related insurance losses in a given year. This is followed by the pharmaceutical industry. Johnson & Johnson's Tylenol recall is known as 'the recall that started them all', and it set the precedent for the way in which corporations are supposed to handle such cases. The company spent one hundred million dollars to recall thirty-one million bottles of its best-selling product after seven people died in the Chicago area after ingesting Extra-Strength Tylenol laced with cyanide, on account of product tampering. The company's swift and decisive action is credited with saving the Tylenol brand, which at the time accounted for 17 per cent of the company's profits. The stock price recovered within two months after taking an initial dive (Burrows 2018).

Kiplinger lists another nine of the biggest product recalls of all time for products that caused thousands of deaths, resulting in civil and criminal charges on account of defects and fraud, and billions of dollars of cost in profit loss, product recalls and repairs, and the settlement of legal cases or payment of fines incurred, and even bankruptcy of some of the companies in question (Burrows 2018). The list features examples such as the 2014 recall of General Motors vehicles with faulty ignition switches what could shut down the engine without warning, thus disabling power steering, brakes, and air bags. These faulty switches were linked to 124 deaths and more than twice as many injuries in 2014. The cost to the company of the recall amounted to $4.1 billion. Merck's 2004 recall of Vioxx, a painkiller targeting arthritis pain, cost the company $8.9 billion. Vioxx was responsible for an estimated 140,000 heart attacks resulting in 88,000 deaths in America. Then, in 2015, Volkswagen cheated on diesel emission costs by using software to cut their emissions to meet regulatory standards when the vehicles were tested. It was found that the engines emitted pollutants up to forty times the levels permitted in the United States. This lapse of business ethics cost the company $18.3 billion. At the top of the list of recalls is the Takata air bag recall, which started in 2008. Faulty air bag inflators made by the now-bankrupt Takata were used by almost every major vehicle manufacturer on the planet. It has been estimated that the recall will amount to more than thirty-seven million vehicles in the United States alone, and globally one hundred million inflators are under recall. It was further estimated that it could take until 2023 to recall and fix every vehicle fitted with a faulty Takata air bag (that was before COVID-19 delayed the process). In 2016, Takata estimated that total recall costs would amount to at least twenty-four billion dollars (Burrows 2018). While the first precedent for faulty product recall set by the Tylenol incident certainly involved contestation of the organisational lapse of business ethics by a collective, this was ultimately a form of resistance driven by the mitigation of reputational damage and the greatest profit generation over the long term for the company, without questioning the politics of truth that underlies the organisational governance structure. The many examples of companies' initial reluctance to recall faulty products may arguably be attributed to management's incipient deafness to critical voices alerting them to the faults. As we shall see, one of the key conditions of possibility of productive resistance in an organisation is a receptive management that is driven by the integrity of the design of their products first as opposed to short-term profit generation.

To return to the two case studies cited by Courpasson, Dany, and Clegg (2012), both feature situations in which opposition arose between the organisation's knowledge workers and its 'market guys': the knowledge workers wanted to advance fundamental research, the market-focused faction were exclusively interested in advancing the profit incentive at the expense of such research, which they did not consider to be rendering marketable products quickly enough. They were interested in products, rather than concepts (Courpasson, Dany, and Clegg 2012, 810). While Courpasson, Dany, and Clegg's dissenters did not wholly succeed in circumventing the decisive decision-making power of management at the outset of the process of dissent, the cases do show that the 'success' of dissent hinges on whether it is posed by the right people, and in the right way. In other words, of critical importance in both cases is *how* and by *who* dissent is carried out: the dissenters need to mobilise ideas ingeniously to show the dissenters' commitment to ideas in the interest of the organisation, and they should not be seen to dissent to further their own interests or because they are 'ungovernable'. In both cases, dissent started with a trigger, then dissent was voiced to test the waters for support within the organisation and specifically among influential employees. The next step was to identify the vested stakeholders that were committed to the cause and willing to take it on. The success of dissent thus hinges on being posed by a pool of highly successful, influential employees in senior positions, employees who enjoy management's respect and are considered team players rather than rebels. Another important step is to identify the positions of the various players on the playing field—not only who is in favour, but also who opposes the issue at stake—and where they are located in the organisational hierarchy. The issue is then posed to management in a constructive and informed manner that compels management to take it seriously. Decisive for the success of productive resistance is management's initial recognition that it is the mobilisation of concepts in the interest of ideas that trump the marketers' insistence on products.

How to pose resistance that produces change that significantly challenges top management's decisions is therefore far from evident. Courpasson, Dany, and Clegg (2012) themselves recognise that the potential positive effects of productive resistance are not enough to guarantee its accommodation by top management. The first obstacle to accommodation, they note, is 'the risk that top management will fail to grasp the relevance of resisters' claims, especially in contexts where it does not trust lay employees and presumes them to be reluctant to change and to make extra effort' (Courpasson, Dany, and Clegg 2012, 803). Fox (1974) refers to this familiar scenario as the low trust/high control syndrome, a scenario that resonates with conditions in the workplace under biopolitical control, although in that case the 'low trust' and 'high control' are both veiled, since being constantly watched, monitored, tracked, and traced is self-imposed and the 'controlled' worker experiences her-/himself as free. Resistance also risks being met with opposition by top management, as it could potentially delegitimise management's past actions and decisions (Courpasson, Dany, and Clegg 2012, 803) and/or question the very 'politics of truth' upon which techniques of power rest. I would wager that this fear of losing face accounts for much of top management's obstinacy and intolerance in the face of constructive critique. Shifting from contention to cooperation to achieve settlements (O'Mahony and Bechky 2008) is not only far from evident, but highly unlikely in workplaces where command and control have been the norm. As Courpasson, Dany, and Clegg (2012, 804) contend, the dissenters have to 'give powerful proof of their superior understanding of a given situation . . . craft their concerns and proposals in a skilful way that makes obvious that they can be productive for the organisation even while opposing present policies'. They suggest, in other words, that resisters should be able to 'create temporary realignments of normal power relations in which the commanded achieve control of an agenda that is presumed to govern them' (Courpasson, Dany, and Clegg 2012, 804). What makes this manoeuvre so unlikely is the fact that this should all be done without bringing top management or any of their previous actions into disrepute, or making them look incompetent.

An additional dimension, which I cannot explore in the present context in any great detail, but which is too critical a factor to omit, is the fact that 'the modern, open, more flexible corporate world' has been found to be the perfect breeding ground for psychopaths (Babiak and Hare 2007). Although the prevalence of psychopathy in the general population is relatively small—only about 1 per cent—they are far more prevalent in the corporate environment, because the business world incentivises ruthless behaviour, regardless of the cost to others, to further its agenda. These personalities may appear articulate, intelligent, and charismatic to outsiders, but their general behaviour is 'controlling, aggressive, threatening, and abusive'. Their aggression tends to be 'predatory in nature', devoid of the emotional upheaval that typically accompanies violent or aggressive behaviour in other perpetrators. Moreover, their aggression is *instrumental*, simply a means to an end, and is seldom followed by any normal concern for the suffering or harm inflicted on others (Babiak and Hare 2007, 17–18). If Babiak and Hare's (2007) research is taken seriously, and we accept that psychopathic personalities are more prevalent in contemporary corporate environments that attract these personalities because these environments provide power and control, and that actively incentivise these personalities' ruthless, unconscionable behaviour, then productive resistance becomes even more improbable.

This argument becomes even more compelling when we consider Paulhus and Williams' (2002) characterisation of Machiavellianism, understood as the manipulative personality; subclinical or 'normal' narcissism characterised by grandiosity, entitlement, dominance, and superiority; and subclinical psychopathy, which means that these socially aversive personalities are not considered clinically pathological. If it is indeed these Machiavellian, narcissistic, and psychopathic personality types that populate the top management structure of the average contemporary organisation, it is doubtful that they would be receptive to any 'realignments of normal power relations in which the commanded achieve control of an agenda that is presumed to govern them' (Courpasson, Dany, and Clegg 2012, 804). Indeed, these personality types are known to actively undermine cooperative and positive power practices in underhanded and self-serving ways; they are thus unlikely to '"listen to" challenges from below and coproduce a process to accommodate resistance' (Courpasson, Dany, and Clegg 2012, 806). The resisters in Courpasson, Dany, and Clegg's (2012) cases opposed authoritarianism in a decisive manner that, while cooperative, did not call for a truce. In fact, they confronted top management with an ultimatum insisting that if no discussion of the issues in question were possible, they would not proceed with the annual performance evaluations of their local collaborators. It is precisely such acts of backing top management into a corner that incur the merciless wrath of the typical narcissist or psychopath, which results in severely detrimental effects for the resisters.

What I nevertheless find highly compelling about Courpasson, Dany, and Clegg's (2012) research is the Foucauldian rationale they provide for drawing on the 'stories of resistance' as their data collection strategy. They provide two reasons:

> (1) Stories of resistance show how resisters politicize contested categories. They help supersede purely formal accounts that can mask contested definitions. (2) Stories of resistance clarify how opportunities for resistance derive from regular power relations. More specifically, we consider that it is 'through everyday practical engagements [that] individuals identify the cracks and vulnerabilities of institutionalized power' and stories of resistance shed light on how individuals actually 'make a diagnosis of social contexts' (Ewick & Silbey 2003, p. 1331), because stories of resistance reveal 'conscious attempts to shift the dynamics or openly challenge the givenness of situational power relations. (Courpasson, Dany, and Clegg 2012, 806)

For Foucault, the possibility of resistance is always centred around 'the most immediate, the most local power relations at work' (Foucault 1976, 97). It is within the context of the local, the concrete, specific, and contiguous that Foucault asks how the human subject fits into certain games of truth, such as those one might encounter in practices of control (Foucault 1984c, 1). It is within the enmeshment of power/knowledge or governmentality as truth/control that he emphasises 'practices of liberty over processes of liberation' (Foucault 1984c, 3). What is the practical form that liberty or freedom takes? Here Foucault makes a crucial distinction between power and domination. The all-pervasive field of power relations is always mobile and agonistic in the Greek sense of combat in which the opponents retain the power of acting and reacting. By contrast, domination is a congealment of power relations into a state in which one opponent makes it impossible for the other(s) to react and the relation solidifies into one of complete subjugation. This implies that relations of power necessarily entail and require relations of resistance. Where there is power, there is resistance. When and to what extent do these relations or acts of resistance become practices of liberty? Resistance becomes a practice of liberty when it succeeds in realising more manoeuvring space than was previously possible, when the subject assumes her/his right to question relations of power on their potential or imminent effects of domination and to counter them in such a way so as to modify the relation between action and reaction.

Against this strategic backdrop, the individual subject, as noted earlier, takes the form of a node in a network of power/knowledge. Being constituted in and through power, this 'individual' is something other, or something more, than a distinct singularity. This is not to say that Foucault is personifying power and depersonifying or dehumanising persons by making them into effects of power. The individual is still vulnerable to subordinating forces but is also invested with the possibility of resistance through subjectivisation (*subjectivation*). As Butler (2002, 19) points out, the 'effect' in Foucault 'is not the simple and unilateral consequence of a prior cause. "Effects" do not stop being affected: they are incessant activities, in the Spinozistic sense. They do not, in this sense, presuppose power as a "cause"; on the contrary, they recast power as an activity of effectuation with no origin and no end'.

The all-pervasiveness of power relations, then, should not push us into defeatism. 'Individual' action, understood as an acting or reacting relation of force, cannot simply remain localised (or be conceived as individualistic), because it has the potential to cause a chain reaction or ripple effect through the social (or organisational) fabric—as Courpasson, Dany, and Clegg's (2012) case studies illustrate. Certainly, force relations can either mutually support each other like links in a chain, or be isolated from one another due to disjunctions and contradictions (Foucault 1976, 92). Foucault's insistence that power is never subjective, that it cannot be reduced to an individual subject's decision or action, can also be understood in this light. There might be an initial instigating agent of resistance, as was the case in the cited case studies, but the possibility of resistance is itself inextricably linked to pre-existing relations of power. Moreover, because it is neither localised nor isolated, the individual's 'practices of liberty' would then also have the potential of effecting larger-scale political changes. In fact, if we are to accept Foucault's claim that power is all-pervasive, the individual's practices of liberty become a necessary condition for political action (Hofmeyr 2005, 117). However, liberation in turn installs new relations of power, which again have to be controlled by practices of liberty. The practices of liberty then appear as a *necessity* emerging after liberation—to maintain freedom (Hofmeyr 2005, 112).

Conclusion: A Call to Constant Critical Vigilance

I recognise and appreciate that the real-life case studies cited by Courpasson, Dany, and Clegg (2012, 814) provide concrete and practicable ways and means to articulate and formalise claims about issues that were hitherto not recognised by top management, as well as possible ways to solve the tensions.

Nevertheless, I am plagued by a persistent worry about the actual feasibility of productive resistance in contemporary organisations. Is productive or collaborative resistance a realistic option in the average neoliberal organisation, which is, after all, characterised by complex relations of control? What complicates the possibility of resistance even further is the inextricable entanglement of our own interests with those of power. The financial success of the organisation also serves our own interests.

But when does profit generation come at too high a cost? It comes at too high a cost when expediting the process of delivering marketable products comes at the expense of the fundamental research and knowledge generation that informs the design of those very products. It comes at too a high a cost when the biopolitical controls installed to ensure profit generation come at the expense of mutually respectful and supportive collegial relations. In other words, the cost is too high when ideas and people are compromised for the sake of money. The cost is fundamentally too high for the individual when the imperceptible complex controls installed to secure profit generation do away with the workers' ability to engage in ongoing practices of liberty, when these controls depoliticise individuals to such an extent that they are no longer able to claim or even be interested in claiming the right and obligation not to be governed like *that*.

We know all too well that the ingenuity and well-being of human capital and the synergy between knowledge workers are the fountainhead of knowledge generation. The right people in the right place surrounded by the right colleagues in a healthy and supportive work environment are the source of the ideas that generate the knowledge that drives organisational success. However, these knowledge workers are at risk. On the one hand, their work environment may attract and incentivise a disproportionally high percentage of individuals with Machiavellian, psychopathic, and narcissistic traits that pose a serious threat to healthy relationships within these organisations. On the other hand, their work environment is dominated by digital/social platforms that insinuate complex relations of control into every aspect of their lives—controls that predetermine their freedom of choice in predictable ways and hence greatly diminish their creative problem-solving, knowledge-generating capacities. As Törnberg and Uitermark (2020) point out, digital/social platforms may seem to create individual freedom, but they are in part doing so by concealing the pushing, nudging, and pulling that set the context and boundaries of individual freedom.

Let it not be forgotten that the complex control operative in and through digital/social platforms serves the profit incentive of the organisations behind those platforms, be it Google, Academia.edu, or LinkedIn, not the organisations that the knowledge workers work for. Instead, these platform organisations harness the thumotic drive for recognition and self-actualisation of the entrepreneurial knowledge worker to work to serve their own interests while the knowledge worker believes her-/himself to be working in her/his own interests. In the process, they severely compromise the knowledge worker's freedom to create truly innovative ideas. In addition, they diminish the knowledge worker's capacity for critique, which is crucial for the possibility of resistance, because these platforms actively steer their users to follow digital pathways that expose them to content that merely confirms their worldview, instead of questioning it.

It could be argued that in the era of complex control, the last two phases of what I have called the evolution that Foucault's notion of resistance have undergone, that is, creation and normalisation, have been rolled into one. On the one hand, the entrepreneurial knowledge worker as 'project' (Han 2017) is incited to and actively pursues creating her-/himself as an ever-increasingly efficient enterprise-unit (Foucault 2008). Self-creation has been co-opted by the neoliberal power/knowledge configurations in which it is inscribed, stripped of its critical, liberating potential, and normalised. Enterprising creativity is the new norm. Biopolitical control does not seek to normalise creative otherness, but seeks only to map how it is distributed around the norm. It thus 'tolerates' that which is alternative or otherwise and profits from it. Along the same line as Foucault's contention that power is not bad, but dangerous, I conclude that resistance in this context is not impossible, but improbable. In a context of constantly changing, flexible flows of complex control, the odds seem to be stacked against the working subject's ability to keep track of the governmentally imposed limits that have become increasingly imperceptible and elusive.

As Foucault points out, what should be questioned is the politics of truth that underlie these flows of control. The possibility thereof calls for a pessimistic activism,[3] a renewed and constant critical vigilance and awareness of just how dangerous power relations have become in our present information age in which the neoliberal theory of human capital has co-opted the supposedly free zone of resistance as self-creation (as the only space in which to practise liberty) with its injunction to (self-)invest in the entrepreneurial subject as a 'project-in-the-making'. What prevents us from surrendering to a complete fatalism is Miller and Rose's contention that '[g]overning is not the "realization of a programmer's dream". The "real" always insists in the form of resistance to programming; and the programmer's world is one of constant experiment, invention, failure, critique and adjustment' (Miller and Rose 2008, 39). In other words, the reality that the 'programmer', neoliberal governmentality, seeks to control invariably confronts that governmentality with forces removed from its access, capable of perhaps even deflecting or effectively blocking it (cf. Bröckling, Krasmann, and Lemke 2010, 11). Control, no matter how pervasive, is never complete. What is called for, however, is a critical consciousness of the operationalisation of truth/complex control that conditions the possibilities of our being, acting, and thinking in the present.

What I have attempted to offer in this study is an exercise of critique to unearth the governmentality to which knowledge workers are subject—the governmentality that orchestrates the possibilities of being and acting at their disposal, which nevertheless do not amount to domination. The aim is to throw the insidious danger of the present power/knowledge constellations into relief, which while recognising the necessity of reform, rejects the kind of blackmail that critique can only be taken seriously if it is the premise of a deduction that concludes with a practicable reform, that is, that does not dare to problematise without offering clear directives as to what is to be done. What is to be done is clearly dependent on the local and specific positionality of the knowledge worker. The utterance of critique, rather than premised on a solution, is presented as a resource, an instrument that serves to awaken consciousness, the consciousness of those who (must) seek to resist and to refuse what is. Critique, then, is a challenge directed to what is, and hence imposes a responsibility on the subject to mobilise his/her resilient agency, however minimal it may seem, to recognise and contest subjection. Only a critical awareness on the part of the knowledge worker of the exploitative machinations of the techno-capitalist order in which it is inscribed, can enable the worker to extricate him/herself to some extent from the ultimately ruinous cycle of self-exploitation and re-establish some semblance of that elusive work-life balance.

Notes

1. A version of this chapter has been published as Hofmeyr 2021c.
2. This section revisits the arguments put forward in Hofmeyr 2008.
3. According to Eagleton (1990, 387), Foucault exemplifies 'libertarian pessimism', an instructive oxymoron. Foucault's position is libertarian in that it advocates an aesthetics of existence, 'an existence blessedly free from the shackles of truth, meaning and sociality'. At the same time, however, it is pessimistic, 'because whatever blocks such creativity—law, meaning, power, closure—is acknowledged to be built into it, in a sceptical recognition of the imbrication of authority and desire'. Taylor (1984) points out that although Foucault wishes to discredit the very notion of a liberation from power, his own concept of power does not in fact make sense without the idea of such liberation.

References

Anthony, Peter D. 1977. *The Ideology of Work*. London: Tavistock.

Arendt, Hannah. 1958. *The Human Condition*. Chicago, IL: University of Chicago Press.

Arora, Sunit. 2019. 'The Golden Triangle and the Great Drug Game'. *Mint*, October 10. Last accessed July 1, 2021. https://www.livemint.com/opinion/columns/the-golden-triangle-and-the-great-drug-game-11570725896660.html

Ashton, Paul. 1999. 'Hegel and Labour'. Paper presented at the 'Legacy of Hegel' seminar, University of Melbourne, February 5, 1999. Last accessed June 29, 2021. https://www.marxists.org/reference/archive/hegel/txt/ashton.htm

Assiter, Alison. 2021. *A New Theory of Human Rights. New Materialism and Zoroastrianism*. Washington, DC: Rowman & Littlefield Publishers.

Audier, Serge. 2015a. *Penser le 'néolibéralisme': Le moment néolibéral, Foucault, et la crise du socialisme*. Lormont: Le Bord de l'Eau.

Audier, Serge. 2015b. 'Neoliberalism through Foucault's Eyes'. *History and Theory* 54, no. 3: 404–18.

Babiak, Paul, and Robert D. Hare. 2007. *Snakes in Suits. When Psychopaths Go to Work*. New York, NY: Harper.

Balibar, Etienne. 2002. *Politics and the Other Scene*. Translated by Christine Jones, James Swenson, and Chris Turner. London: Verso.

Ball, Philip. 2012. *Why Society Is a Complex Matter: Meeting Twenty-First Century Challenges with a New Kind of Science*. Berlin: Springer Science and Business Media.

Barnard, Chester I. 1938. *The Functions of the Executive*. Cambridge, MA: Harvard University Press.

Barnouw, Jeffrey. 2004. *Odysseus, Hero of Practical Intelligence: Deliberation and Signs in Homer's Odyssey*. Lanham, MD: University Press of America.

Bauman, Zygmunt. 2000. *Liquid Modernity*. Hoboken, NJ: Wiley.

Becker, Gary S. (1964) 1993. *Human Capital: A Theoretical and Empirical Analysis, with Special Reference to Education* (third edition). Chicago, IL: University of Chicago Press. [Foucault used the 1964 version, but my page references refer to the third revised edition of 1993.]

Becker, Gary S. 1965. 'A Theory of the Allocation of Time'. *The Economic Journal* 75, no. 299: 493–517.

Becker, Gary S. 1976. *The Economic Approach to Human Behaviour*. Chicago, IL: Chicago University Press.

Becker, Gary S. 1993. 'Nobel Lecture: The Economic Way of Looking at Human Behavior'. *Journal of Political Economy* 101, no. 3: 385–409.

Becker, Gary S., and George J. Stigler. 1995. 'De Gustibus Non Est Disputandum'. In *The Essential Becker*, edited by Ramón Febrero and Pedro Schwarz, 184–208. Stanford, CA: Hoover Institution Press.

Behrent, Michael C. 2009. 'A Seventies Thing: On the Limits of Foucault's Neoliberalism Course for Understanding the Present'. In *A Foucault for the 21st Century: Governmentality, Biopolitics and Discipline in the New Millennium*, edited by Sam Binkley and Jorge Capetillo, 16–29. Newcastle upon Tyne: Cambridge Scholars Publishing.

Bell, Daniel. 1973. *The Coming of Post-industrial Society. A Venture in Social Forecasting*. New York, NY: Basic Books.

Benkler, Yochal. 2002. 'Coase's penguin, or, linux and "the nature of the firm"'. *Yale Law Journal* 112: 369–446.

Benkler, Yochal. 2006. *The Wealth of Networks: How Social Production Transforms Markets and Freedom*. New Haven, CT: Yale University Press.

Bernstein, Paul. 1988. 'The Work Ethic: Economics, Not Religion'. *Business Horizons* 31, no. 3: 8–11.

Blunden, Andy. 2003. 'Fukuyama on Trust and Recognition'. Last accessed June 25, 2021. https://ethicalpolitics.org/ablunden/works/fukuyama.htm

Boltanski, Luc, and Eve Chiapello. 2007. *The New Spirit of Capitalism*. Translated by Gregory Elliot. London: Verso.

Bourdieu, Pierre. 1998. 'The Essence of Neoliberalism'. *Le Monde Diplomatique*, December. Translated by Jeremy J. Shapiro. Last accessed June 25, 2021, https://mondediplo.com/1998/12/08bourdieu

Bradley, Richard. 2008. 'Becker's Thesis of Three Models of Preference Change'. *CPNSS Working Paper* 4, no. 1. The Centre for Philosophy of Natural and Social Sciences (CPNSS), London School of Economics, London. Last accessed June 25, 2021. http://eprints.lse.ac.uk/27007/

Braude, Lee. 1975. *Work and Workers*. New York, NY: Praeger.

Bröckling, Ulrich, Susanne Krasmann, and Thomas Lemke. 2010. *Governmentality. Current Issues and Future Challenges*. New York, NY: Routledge.

Brown, Wendy. 2003. 'Neo-liberalism and the End of Liberal Democracy'. *Theory and Event* 7, no. 1: 1–29.

Brown, Wendy. 2015. *Undoing the Demos. Neoliberalism's Stealth Revolution*. New York: Zone Books.

Burke, Rory. 2007. *Project Management Leadership*. Cape Town: Burke.

Burrows, Dan. 2018. '10 Biggest Product Recalls of All Time'. *Kiplinger*, March 16. Last accessed July 4, 2021. https://www.kiplinger.com/slideshow/investing/t052-s000-10-biggest-product-recalls-of-all-time/index.html

Burud, Sandra, and Marie Tumolo. 2004. *Leveraging Human Capital*. Mountain View, CA: Davies-Black.

Butler, Judith. (2000) 2001. 'What is Critique? An Essay on Foucault's Virtue'. In *The Political: Readings in Continental Philosophy*, edited by David Ingram, 212–26. London: Blackwell.

Butler, Judith. 2002. 'Bodies and Power, Revisited'. *Radical Philosophy* 114: 13–19.

Cairns, Douglas. 2019. 'Thymos'. *Oxford Classical Dictionary*. Last accessed July 11, 2021. https://oxfordre.com/classics/classics/abstract/10.1093/acrefore/9780199381135.001.0001/acrefore-9780199381135-e-8180?rskey=ILhKQn&result=284

Castells, Manuel. 1996. *The Information Age: Economy, Society and Culture. Volume I: The Rise of the Network Society*. Oxford: Blackwell.

Castells, Manuel. 2009. *Communication Power*. Oxford: Oxford University Press.

Cherrington, David J. 1980. *The Work Ethic: Working Values and Values that Work*. New York, NY: AMACOM.

Choi, Thomas Y., and Glen H. Varney. 1995. 'Rethinking Knowledge Workers: Where Have All the Workers Gone?' *Organization Development* 13, no. 2: 41–50.

Clausewitz, Carl von. (1832) 1984. *On War*. Revised edition, edited and translated by Michael Howard and Peter Paret. Princeton, NJ: Princeton University Press.

Cohen, Don, and Laurence Prusak. 2002. *In Good Company: How Social Capital Makes Organizations Work*. Boston, MA: Harvard Business School Press.

Collins, Jim. 2001. *Good to Great: Why Some Companies Make the Leap . . . and Others Don't*. New York, NY: HarperBusiness.

Courpasson, David, Françoise Dany, and Stewart Clegg. 2012. 'Generating Productive Resistance in the Workplace'. *Organization Science* 23, no. 3: 801–19.

Cullen, Bernard. 1979. *Hegel's Social and Political Thought*. Dublin: Gill and Macmillan.

Daft, Richard L., and Richard M. Steers. 1986. *Organizations: A Micro/Macro Approach*. Glenview, IL: Scott, Foresman and Co.

Dardot, Pierre, and Christian Laval. 2009. *La nouvelle raison du monde*. Paris: La découverte.

Davenport, Thomas H. 2002. 'The Rise of the Knowledge Manager.' *Futurist* 36, no. 2: 14–15.

Davis, Nicholas. 2016. 'What is the Fourth Industrial Revolution?' World Economic Forum. Last accessed on June 25, 2021. https://www.weforum.org/agenda/2016/01/what-is-the-fourth-industrial-revolution/

De Lagasnerie, Geoffroy. 2012. *La dernière leçon de Michel Foucault. Sur le néolibéralisme, la théorie et la politique*. Paris: Fayard.

Dean, Michael C. 2018. 'Foucault and the Neoliberalism Controversy'. In *The SAGE Handbook of Neoliberalism*, edited by Damien *Cahill*, Melinda *Cooper*, Martijn *Konings*, and David *Primrose*, 40–54. Los Angeles, CA: Sage.

Dean, Michael C., and Daniel Zamora. 2019. *Le dernier homme et la fin de la revolution*. Québec: Lux Éditeur.

Deleuze, Gilles. (1992) 1990. 'Postscript on the Societies of Control'. *October* 59, Winter: 3–7.

Drucker, Peter, F. (1954) 2010. *The Practice of Management*. New York, NY: Harper Business.

Drucker, Peter F. 1959. *Landmarks of Tomorrow: Report on the New Post-modern World*. New York, NY: Harper and Row.

Drucker, Peter F. 1969. *The Age of Discontinuity: Guidelines to Our Changing Society*. London: Heinemann.

Drucker, Peter F. 1993. *Post-capitalist Society*. New York, NY: Harper Business.

Drucker, Peter F. 1999. 'Knowledge-worker Productivity: The Biggest Challenge'. *California Management Review* 41: 79–94.

Drucker, Peter F. 2003. *On the Profession of Management*. Cambridge, MA: Harvard Business Review.

Drucker, Peter F., Esther Dyson, Charles Handy, Paul Saffo, and Peter M. Senge. 1997. 'Looking Ahead: Implications of the Present'. *Harvard Business Review* 75, no. 5: 18–32.

Duménil, Gérard, and Dominique Lévy. 2011. *The Crisis of Neoliberalism*. Cambridge, MA: Harvard University Press.

Durkheim, Émile. (1893) 2013. *The Division of Labour in Society: A Study of the Organization of the Higher Societies*, edited by Steven Lukes. Translated by W. D. Halls. Second edition. London: Palgrave Macmillan.

Eagleton, Terry. 1990. *The Ideology of the Aesthetic*. New York, NY: Blackwell.

Ehin, Charles. 2000. 'Why It's So Critical That We Level the Top-down Organization'. *Journal of Quality and Participation* 23, no. 3: 61–64.

Ert, Eyal, Aliza Fleischer, and Nathan Magen. 2016. 'Trust and Reputation in the Sharing Economy: The Role of Personal Photos in Airbnb'. *Tourism Management* 55: 62–73.

Feenberg, Andrew. 2002. *Transforming Technology: A Critical Theory Revisited*. Oxford: Oxford University Press.

Fincham, Robin, ed. 1996. *New Relationships in the Organized Professions: Managers, Professionals and Knowledge Workers*. Aldershot: Avebury.

Flew, Terry. 2012. 'Michel Foucault's *The Birth of Biopolitics* and Contemporary Neoliberal Debates'. *Thesis Eleven* 108, no. 1: 47–65.

Flew, Terry. 2014. 'Six Theories of Neoliberalism'. *Thesis Eleven* 122, no. 1: 49–71.

Flynn, Thomas. 1994. 'Foucault's Mapping of History'. In *The Cambridge Companion to Foucault*, edited by Gary Gutting, 29–48. New York, NY: Cambridge University Press.

Folke, Carl. 2007. 'Social-ecological Systems and Adaptive Governance of the Commons'. *Ecological Research* 22: 14–15.

Foucault, Michel. (1963) 1977. 'A Preface to Transgression'. In *Michel Foucault. Language, Counter-memory, Practice. Selected Essays and Interviews*, edited by Donald F. Bouchard. Translated by Donald F. Bouchard and Sherry Simon, 29–52. Ithaca, NY: Cornell University Press.

Foucault, Michel. (1967) 1986. 'Of Other Spaces'. *Diacritics* 16: 22–27.

Foucault, Michel. (1971) 1984. 'Nietzsche Genealogy History'. In *The Foucault Reader*, edited by Paul Rabinow, 76–100. New York, NY: Pantheon Books.

Foucault, Michel. (1975) 1992. *Discipline and Punish. The Birth of the Prison*. Translated by Alan Sheridan. London: Penguin.

Foucault, Michel. (1976) 1990. *The History of Sexuality. Volume I: An Introduction*. Translated by Robert Hurley. London: Penguin.

Foucault, Michel. (1977) 1980. 'Power and Strategies'. In *Michel Foucault. Power/Knowledge. Selected Interviews and Other Writings 1972–1977*, edited by Colin Gordon. Translated by Colin Gordon, Leo Marshall, John Mepham, and Kate Soper, 134–45. Hassocks: Harvester Press.

Foucault, Michel. (1978) 1997. 'What Is Critique?' In *Michel Foucault. The Politics of Truth*, edited by Sylvère Lotringer, and Lysa Hochroth, 23–82. New York, NY: Semiotext(e).

Foucault, Michel. (1980) 1993. 'About the Beginning of the Hermeneutics of the Self: Two Lectures at Dartmouth'. *Political Theory* 21: 198–227.

Foucault, Michel. (1982a) 1988. 'Technologies of the Self'. In *Technologies of the Self. A Seminar with Michel Foucault*, edited by Luther H. Martin, Huck Gutman, and Patrick H. Hutton, 16–49. London: Tavistock.

Foucault, Michel. (1982b) 1986. 'The Subject and Power'. In *Michel Foucault. Beyond Structuralism and Hermeneutics*, edited by Hubert L. Dreyfus and Paul Rabinow, 208–26. London: Harvester.

Foucault, Michel. (1983) 1984. 'What is Enlightenment?' In *The Foucault Reader*, edited by Paul Rabinow, 32–50. New York, NY: Pantheon Books.

Foucault, Michel. (1984a) 1992b. *The History of Sexuality. Volume II: The Use of Pleasure*. Translated by Robert Hurley. London: Penguin.

Foucault, Michel. (1984b) 1990. *The History of Sexuality. Volume III: The Care of the Self*. Translated by Robert Hurley. London: Penguin.

Foucault, Michel. (1984c). 1988. 'The Ethic of Care for the Self as a Practice of Freedom. An Interview with Michel Foucault on January, 20, 1984'. Translated by J. D. Gauthier. In *The Final Foucault*, edited by James William Bernauer and David M. Rasmussen, 1–20. Cambridge, MA: MIT Press.

Foucault, Michel. 1997. *The Politics of Truth*, edited by Sylvère Lotringer and Lysa Hochroth. New York, NY: Semiotext(e).

Foucault, Michel. 2003. *Society Must be Defended. Lectures at the Collège de France 1975–76*. Translated by David Macey. London: Penguin.

Foucault, Michel. 2005. *The Hermeneutics of the Self. Lectures at the Collège de France 1981-82*, edited by Frédéric Gros, François Ewald, and Alessandro Fontana. New York, NY: Palgrave Macmillan.
Foucault, Michel. 2007. *Security, Territory, Population. Lectures at the Collège de France 1977–1978*, edited by Michel Senellart. Translated by Graham Burchell. New York, NY: Palgrave Macmillan.
Foucault, Michel. 2008. *The Birth of Biopolitics. Lectures at the Collège de France, 1978–79*, edited by Michel Senellart. Translated by Graham Burchell. New York, NY: Palgrave Macmillan.
Foucault, Michel. 2010. *The Government of Self and Others. Lectures at the Collège de France 1982-83*, edited by Graham Burchell and Arnold Davidson. New York, NY: Palgrave Macmillan.
Foucault, Michel. 2011. *The Courage of Truth. Lecturers at the Collège de France 1983–84*, edited by Frédéric Gros, François Ewald, and Alessandro Fontana. New York, NY: Palgrave Macmillan.
Fox, Alan. 1974. *Beyond Contract: Work, Power and Trust Relations*. London: Faber and Faber.
Fukuyama, Francis. 1992. *The End of History and the Last Man*. New York, NY: Free Press.
Gane, Mike. 2008. 'Foucault on Governmentality and Liberalism'. *Theory, Culture and Society* 25, no. 7–8: 353–63.
Gare, Arran. 1996. *Nihilism Inc., Environmental Destruction and the Metaphysics of Sustainability*. Como, NSW: Eco-logical Press.
Gilbert, James B. 1977. *Work Without Salvation*. Baltimore, MD: Johns Hopkins University Press.
Gordon, Colin, ed. 1980. *Michel Foucault. Power/knowledge. Selected Interviews and Other Writings 1972–1977*. Translated by Colin Gordon, Leo Marshall, John Mepham, and Kate Soper. Hassocks: Harvester Press.
Graeber, David. 2018. *Bullshit Jobs: A Theory*. London: Penguin Books.
Greenblatt, Stephen. 1980. *Renaissance Self-fashioning: From More to Shakespeare*. Chicago, IL: University of Chicago Press.
Guala, Francesco. 2006. 'Critical Notice – Review of "Naissance de la Biopolitique: Cours au Collège de France, 1978–1979"'. *Economics and Philosophy* 22: 429–39.
Gunderson, Lance, and Stephen S. Light. 2006. 'Adaptive Management and Adaptive Governance in the Everglades Ecosystem'. *Policy Science* 39: 323–34.
Guy, Jack 2021. 'Employees Working from Home are Putting in Longer Hours than Before the Pandemic'. *CNN Business*. Accessed July 19, 2021. https://edition.cnn.com/2021/02/05/business/working-from-home-hours-pandemic-scli-intl-gbr/index.html
Habermas, Jürgen. (1985) 1996. 'Hegel's Concept of Modernity'. In *The Philosophical Discourse of Modernity: Twelve Lectures*. Translated by Frederick G. Lawrence. Cambridge, MA: MIT Press.

Hallinan, Blake, and Ted Striphas. 2016. 'Recommended for You: The Netflix Prize and the Production of Algorithmic Culture'. *New Media Society* 18: 117–37.

Halpern, Orit. 2015. *Beautiful Data: A History of Vision and Reason Since 1945*. Durham, NC: Duke University Press.

Han, Byung-Chul. 2017. *Psychopolitics: Neoliberalism and New Technologies of Power*. London: Verso.

Hart, Robert. 2021. 'Working 55+ Hours a Week Kills 745, 000 People a Year—the Covid Pandemic, Gig Economy and Teleworking May Be Making It Worse, WHO Warns'. *Forbes*. Accessed on July 19, 2021. https://www.forbes.com/sites/roberthart/2021/05/17/working-55-hours-a-week-kills-745000-people-a-year---the-covid-pandemic-gig-economy-and-teleworking-may-be-making-it-worse-who-warns/?sh=504c975e5097

Hartmann, John. 2003. 'Power and Resistance in the Later Foucault'. Paper presented at the 3rd Annual Meeting of the Foucault Circle. Accessed on July 1, 2021. mypage.siu.edu/hartmajr/pdf/jh_fouccirc_03.pdf

Harvey, David. 2005. *A Brief History of Neoliberalism*. New York, NY: Oxford University Press.

Hayden, Patrick, ed. 2014. *Hannah Arendt: Key Concepts*. London: Routledge.

Hayek, Friedrich A. von. 1960. *The Constitution of Liberty*. Chicago, IL: Chicago University Press.

Hegel, Georg Wilhelm Friedrich. (1807) 1977. *Phenomenology of Spirit*, edited by Johannes Hoffmeister. Translated by Arnold V. Miller. Oxford: Oxford University Press.

Hegel, Georg Wilhelm Friedrich. (1820) 1991. *Elements of the Philosophy of Right*. Translated by Hugh Bar Nisbet. Cambridge: Cambridge University Press.

Heidegger, Martin. (1927) 1962. *Being and Time*. Translated by John Maquarrie and Edward Robinson. New York, NY: Harper and Row.

Helbing, Dirk. 2015. 'What the Digital Revolution Means for Us'. In *Thinking Ahead—Essays on Big Data, Digital Revolution, and Participatory Market Society*, edited by Dirk Helbing, 177–87. Berlin: Springer.

Herzberg, Frederick, Bernard Mausner, and Barbara Bloch Snyderman. 1959. *The Motivation to Work*. New York, NY: Wiley.

Heylighen, Francis, Paul Cilliers, and Carlos Gershenson. 2006. 'Complexity and Philosophy'. In *Complexity, Science and Society*, edited by Jan Bogg and Robert Geyer, 117–34. Oxford: Radcliffe Publishing.

Hill, Roger, B. 1992. 'Historical Context of the Work Ethics'. Last accessed July 3, 2021. http://workethic.coe.uga.edu/historypdf.pdf

Hilton, Margaret. 2001. 'Information Technology Workers in the New Economy'. *Monthly Labor Review* 124, no. 6: 41–45.

Hindess, Barry. 2009. 'A Tale of Origins and Disparity'. *Journal of Cultural Economy* 2, no. 1–2: 213–17.

Hobbs, Angela. 2006. *Plato and the Hero: Courage, Manliness and the Impersonal Good*. Cambridge: Cambridge University Press.

Hock, Dee. 1999. *Birth of the Chaordic Age*. San Francisco, CA: Berrett-Koehler.

Hofmeyr, A. Benda. 2005. 'From Usurpation to Subversion: Foucault Meets Cultural Capitalism'. *Andere Sinema* 175: 102–19 (English); 211–21 (Dutch).

Hofmeyr, A. Benda. 2008. 'The Contemporary Pertinence of the Later Foucault. Have His Strategies of Resistance Stood the Test of Time?' *South African Journal of Philosophy* 27, no. 2: 106–18.

Hofmeyr, A. Benda. 2011. 'The Culture and Subjectivity and Neo-liberalism Governmentality'. *Phronimon* 12, no. 1: 19–42.

Hofmeyr, A. Benda. 2021a. 'Foucault's Analyses of Neoliberal Governmentality. Past Investigations and Present Applications'. *Etica & Politica* 23: 589–616.

Hofmeyr, A. Benda. 2021b. 'The Relation Between Work and Thumos. A Critical Interrogation of the Motivation Behind Knowledge Work Compulsion'. *Filosofija Sociologija* 32, no. 3: 250-258.

Hofmeyr, A. Benda. 2021c. 'The Feasibility of Resistance in the Workplace: A Foucaultian Investigation'. *Indo-Pacific Journal of Phenomnology* 21: https://doi.org/10.1080/20797222.2021.1974283.

Hofmeyr, A. Benda. 2022a. 'Knowledge Work in the Age of Control'. *Acta Academica* 54, no. 1: page numbers not yet available.

Hofmeyr, A. Benda. 2021d. 'Neoliberal Governmentality, Knowledge Work, and Thumos'. *Journal of Philosophical Economics. Reflections on Economic and Social Issues* XIV (1–2): 33–62.

Hosken, Graham, and Wendy Knowler. 2017. 'Exposed: How Ford Was Warned About Burning Kugas But Did Nothing'. *Rand Daily Mail*, January 16, 2017. Last accessed July 4, 2021. https://www.businesslive.co.za/rdm/news/2017-01-16-exposed-how-ford-was-warned-about-burning-kugas-but-did-nothing/.

Huber, George P. 1984. 'The Nature and Design of Post-industrial Organizations'. *Management Science* 30, no. 8: 928–51.

Hunnicutt, Benjamin J. 1988. *Work Without End: Abandoning Shorter Hours for the Right to Work*. Philadelphia, PA: Temple University Press.

Jaggi, Bikki. 1988. 'A Comparative Analysis of Worker Participation in the United States and Europe'. In *Management Under Differing Labour Market and Employment Systems*, edited by Günter Dlugos, Wolfgang Dorow, Klaus Weiermair, and Frank C. Danesy, 443–54. Berlin: Walter de Gruyter.

Jones, Candace, William S. Hesterly, and Stephen P. Borgatti. 1997. 'A General Theory of Network Governance: Exchange Conditions and Social Mechanisms'. *Academy of Management Review* 22: 911–45.

Kant, Immanuel. (1784) 1997. 'Was ist Aufklärung?' In *Michel Foucault. The Politics of Truth*, edited by Sylvère Lotringer and Lysa Hochroth, 7–20. New York, NY: Semiotext(e).

Kelloway, E. Kevin, and Julian Barling. 2000. *Framework Paper 00-03. Knowledge Work as Organizational Behavior*. Kingston: Queen's School of Business.

Kiersey, Nicholas J. 2011. 'Everyday Neoliberalism and the Subjectivity of Crisis: Post-Political Control in an Era of Financial Turmoil'. *Journal of Critical Globalisation Studies* 4: 23–44.

Kitchin, Rob, Tracey P. Lauriault, and Matthew W. Wilson. 2017. *Understanding Spatial Media*. Thousand Oaks, CA: Sage.

Kojève, Alexander. (1947). 1991. *Introduction to the Reading of Hegel: Lectures on The Phenomenology of Spirit*, compiled by Raymond Queneau, edited by Allan Bloom. Translated by James H. Nichols. Cambridge: Cambridge University Press.

Kost, Danielle. 2020. 'You're Right! You are Working Longer and Attending More Meetings'. *Harvard Business School*. Accessed July 19, 2021. https://hbswk.hbs.edu/item/you-re-right-you-are-working-longer-and-attending-more-meetings

Leach, Desmond J., Toby D. Wall, and Paul R. Jackson. 2003. 'The Effect of Empowerment on Job Knowledge: An Empirical Test Involving Operators of Complex Technology'. *Journal of Occupational and Organizational Psychology* 76: 27–52.

Lemke, Thomas. 2000. 'Foucault, Governmentality and Critique'. Paper presented at the 'Rethinking Marxism' Conference, University of Amherst (MA), September 21–24, 2000. Last accessed July 23, 2020. http://www.thomaslemkeweb.de/publikationen/Foucault,%20Governmentality,%20and%20critique%2 0IV-2.pdf

Lemke, Thomas. 2001. 'The Birth of Bio-politics: Michael Foucault's Lectures at the College de France on Neo-liberal Governmentality'. *Economy and Society* 30, no. 2: 190–207.

Lipset, Seymour Martin. 1990. 'The Work Ethic – Then and Now'. *Public Interest* 98: 61–69.

Locke, John. (1690) 2007. *An Essay Concerning Human Understanding*. Keighley: Pomona.

Löwith, Karl. 1991. *From Hegel to Nietzsche: The Revolution in Nineteenth-Century Thought*. Translated by David E. Green. New York, NY: Columbia University Press.

Lundberg, Erik. 1992. Nobel Prize Award Ceremony Speech by Erik Lundberg. In *Nobel Lectures, Economics 1969-1980*, edited by Assar Lindbeck. Singapore: World Scientific Publishing. Last accessed July 21, 2021. https://www.nobelprize.org/prizes/economic-sciences/1976/ceremony-speech/

Maccoby, Michael. 1988. *Why Work*. New York, NY: Simon and Schuster.

Machlup, Fritz. 1962. *The Production and Distribution of Knowledge in the United States*. Princeton, NJ: Princeton University Press.

MacIntyre, Alisdair. 1988. *Whose Justice? Which Rationality?* London: Duckworth.

Marcuse, Herbert. (1941) 1970. *Reason and Revolution: Hegel and the Rise of Social Theory*. Boston, MA: Beacon Press.

Marres, Noortje. 2017. *Digital Sociology: The Reinvention of Social Research*. Hoboken, NJ: Wiley.

Marzocca, Ottavio. 2017. 'Foucault et la post-démocratie néolibérale. Au-delà de la 'critique inflationniste' de l'État'. In *La pensée politique de Foucault*, edited by Oratio Irrera and Salvo Vaccaro, 201–14. Paris: Éditions Kimé.

Maslow, Abraham. 1943. 'A Theory of Human Motivation'. *Psychological Review* 50, no. 4: 370–96.

Mattijssen, Thomas, Arjen Buijs, Birgit Elands, and Bas Arts. 2018. 'The "Green" and "Self" in Green Self-governance: A Study of 264 Green Space Initiatives by Citizens'. *Journal of Environmental Policy and Planning* 20: 96–113.

Maurer, Roy 2020. 'Remote Employees Are Working Longer Than Before'. *Society for Human Resource Management*, December 16, 2020. Last accessed on July 19, 2021. https://www.shrm.org/hr-today/news/hr-news/pages/remote-employees-are-working-longer-than-before.aspx

Maywood, A. G. 1982. 'Vocational Education and the Work Ethic'. *Canadian Vocational Journal* 18, no. 3: 7–12.

McCann, Jason Michael. 2016. 'Capitalism and Neoliberalism: What's the Difference?' Monday April 25. Blog. https://randompublicjournal.com/2016/04/25/capitalism-and-neoliberalism-whats-the-difference/

McDermott, Richard. 1995. 'Working in Public – Learning in Action: Designing Collaborative Knowledge Work Teams'. In *Advances in Interdisciplinary Studies in Work Teams. Volume II: Knowledge Work in Teams*, edited by Michael M. Beyerlein, Douglas A. Johnson, and Susan T. Beyerlein, 35–59. Greenwich, CT: JAI Press.

McKay, Brett, and Kate McKay. 2011. *The Art of Manliness – Manvotionals: Timeless Wisdom and Advice on Living the Seven Manly Virtues*. New York, NY: F+W Media.

McKay, Brett, and Kate McKay. 2013. 'Got Thumos?' Last accessed July 1, 2021. https://www.artofmanliness.com/articles/got-thumos/

Meyer, John P., and Natalie J. Allen. 1997. *Commitment in the Workplace: Theory, Research and Application*. Thousand Oaks, CA: Sage.

Michael, Robert T., and Gary S. Becker. 1973. 'On the New Theory of Consumer Behavior'. *Swedish Journal of Economics* 75, no. 4: 378–96.

Miller, J. 1993. *The Passion of Michel Foucault*. New York, NY: Anchor.

Miller, Peter, and Nikolas Rose. 2008. *Governing the Present. Administering Economic, Social and Political Life*. Cambridge: Polity.

Miller, W. F. 1986. 'Emerging Technologies and Their Implications for America'. *USA Today* 115: 60–65.

Milwaukee Public Museum. 'The Roman Empire: A Brief History'. Last accessed July 3, 2021. https://www.mpm.edu/research-collections/anthropology/anthropology-collections-research/mediterranean-oil-lamps/roman-empire-brief-history

Mincer, Jacob. 1958. 'Investment in Human Capital and Personal Income Distribution'. *Journal of Political Economy* 66: 281–302.

Mintzberg, Henry. 1993. *Structures in Fives: Designing Effective Organizations*. Englewood Cliffs, NJ: Prentice Hall.

Mitchell, Melanie. 2009. *Complexity: A Guided Tour*. Oxford: Oxford University Press.

Naisbitt, John. 1984. *Megatrends: Ten New Directions Transforming Our Lives*. New York, NY: Warner.

Newel, Sue, Maxine Robertson, Harry Scarbrough, and Jacky Swan. 2002. *Managing Knowledge Work*. New York, NY: Macmillan.

Newheiser, David. 2016. 'Foucault, Gary Becker and the Critique of Neoliberalism'. *Theory, Culture and Society* 33, no. 5: 3–21.

Nietzsche, Friedrich. (1874) 1997. *Untimely Meditations*. Translated by R. J. Hollingdale. Cambridge: Cambridge University Press.

Nietzsche, Friedrich. (1887) 2001. *On the Genealogy of Morals, A Polemical Tract*. Translated by Ian Johnston. Last accessed June 7, 2021. http://fs2.american.edu/dfagel/www/genealogy2.htm

Nobel Prize Dialogue. 2021. Nobel Prize Dialogue on the Future of Work Hosted by the University of Pretoria on May 18, 2021. Last accessed May 18, 2021. https://www.youtube.com/watch?v=J2o2VoI83Q0&ab_channel=NobelPrize

O'Dea, S. 2021. 'Smartphone Subscriptions Worldwide 2016-2026'. *Statista*, June 25. Last accessed July 4, 2021. https://www.statista.com/statistics/330695/number-of-smartphone-users-worldwide/

O'Mahony, Siobhán, and Beth A. Bechky. 2008. 'Boundary Organizations: Enabling Collaboration Among Unexpected Allies'. *Administrative Science Quarterly* 53, no. 3: 422–59.

Ohmae, Kenichi. 1991. *The Borderless World: Power and Strategy in the Interlinked Economy*. New York, NY: Harper Business.

Overbeek, Henk, and Bastiaan van Apeldoorn. 2012. *Neoliberalism in Crisis*. Basingstoke: Palgrave.

Owen, David. 1994. *Maturity and Modernity: Nietzsche, Weber, Foucault, and the Ambivalence of Reason*. London: Routledge.

Paltrinieri, Luca. 2019. 'Neoliberal Selves. Human Capital Between Bourdieu and Foucault'. In *Foucault, Neoliberalism and Beyond*, edited by Stephen W. Sawyer, and Daniel Steinmetz-Jenkins, 157–80. London: Rowman & Littlefield.

Paulhus, Delroy L., and Kevin M. Williams. 2002. 'The Dark Triad of Personality: Narcissism, Machiavellianism, and Psychopathy'. *Journal of Research in Personality* 36: 556–63.

Pelczynski, Zbigniew A. 1984. 'Introduction: The Significance of Hegel's Separation of the State and Civil Society'. In *The State and Civil Society: Studies in Hegel's Political Philosophy*, edited by Zbigniew A. Pelczynski, 1–13. Cambridge: Cambridge University Press.

Pestaña, José Luis Moreno. 2010. *Foucault, la gauche, et la politique*. Paris: Editions Textuel.

Pettman, Dominic. 2016. *Infinite Distraction. Paying Attention to Social Media*. Chichester, UK: Polity.

Pfeffer, Jeffrey. 1994. *Competitive Advantage Through People*. Boston, MA: Harvard Business School Press.

Pfeffer, Jeffrey, and Robert I. Sutton. 2000. *The Knowing–Doing Gap: How Smart Companies Turn Knowledge into Action*. Cambridge, MA: Harvard Business School Press.

Plant, Raymond. 1984. 'Hegel on Identity and Legitimation'. In *The State and Civil Society: Studies in Hegel's Political Philosophy*, edited by Zbigniew A. Pelczynski, 227–43. Cambridge: Cambridge University Press.

Plant, Raymond. 1993. 'Economic and Social Integration in Hegel's Political Philosophy'. In *Selected Essays on G.W.F. Hegel*, edited by Lawrence S. Stepelevich, 59–90. Atlantic Highlands, NJ: Humanities Press.

Plato. (circa 370 BCE) 2008. *Phaedrus*. Translated by Benjamin Jowett. Project Gutenberg Ebook.

Plato. (circa 375 BCE) 2008. *The Republic*. Translated by Benjamin Jowett. Project Gutenberg Ebook.

Porat, Marc U. 1977. *The Information Economy: Definition and Measurement Volume I*. Washington, DC: US Department of Commerce.

Price, Henry S. 2014. 'Interregnum? Understanding the Non-death of Neoliberalism'. Master's dissertation, University of Warwick. Last accessed July 23, 2021. http://www.academia.edu/10244810/Interregnum_Understanding_the_non-death_of_neoliberalism

Puschmann, Thomas, and Rainer Alt. 2016. 'Sharing Economy'. *Business and Information Systems Engineering* 58: 93–99.

Pyöriä, Pasi. 2005. 'The Concept of Knowledge Work'. *Journal of Knowledge Management* 9, no. 3: 116–27.

Quinn, Joseph F. 1983. 'The Work Ethic and Retirement'. In *The Work Ethic: A Critical Analysis*, edited by Jack Barbash, Robert J. Lampman, Sar A. Levitan, and Gus (F.) Tyler, 87–100. Madison, WI: Industrial Relations Research Association.

Reich, Robert B. 1991. *The Work of Nations: Preparing Ourselves for 21st-Century Capitalism*. New York, NY: Alfred A. Knopf.

Robin, Vicki, and Joe Dominguez. 2008. *Your Money or Your Life*. London: Penguin.

Rodgers, Daniel T. 1978. *The Work Ethic in Industrial America, 1850–1920*. Chicago, IL: University of Chicago Press.

Roetzel, Peter Gordon. 2019. 'Information Overload in the Information Age: A Review of the Literature from Business Administration, Business Psychology, and Related Disciplines with a Biometric Approach and Framework Development'. *Business Research* 12, no. 2: 479–522.

Rose, Michael. 1985. *Rewarding the Work Ethic: Economic Values and Socio-cultural Politics*. London: Schocken.

Rose, Nikolas. 1999. *Powers of Freedom. Reframing Political Thought*. Cambridge: Cambridge University Press.

Rousseau, Jean Jacques. (1762) 1920. *The Social Contract and Discourses*. Translated by G. D. H. Cole. New York, NY: Dent.

Rousseau, Jean Jacques. (1963) 2011. *Emile, or On Education*. Translated by Barbara Foxley. London: Dent.

Rozin, Paul, and Edward B. Royzman. 2001. 'Negativity Bias, Negativity Dominance and Contagion'. *Personality and Social Psychology Review* 5: 296–320.

Saad, Lydia. 2014. 'The "40-Hour" Workweek Is Actually Longer—by Seven Hours'. *Gallup*, August 29. Last accessed June 24, 2021. https://news.gallup.com/poll/175286/hour-workweek-actually-longer-seven-hours.aspx

Saraswathi, S. (2011). 'A Study on Factors that Motivate IT and Non-IT Sector Employees: A Comparison'. *International Journal of Research in Computer Application and Management* 1, no. 2: 72–77.

Scarbrough, Harry. 1999. 'Knowledge as Work: Conflicts in the Management of Knowledge Workers'. *Technology Analysis and Strategic Management* 11, no. 1: 5–16.

Schement, Jörge Reina. 1990. 'Porat, Bell, and the Information Society Reconsidered: The Growth of Information Work in the Early Twentieth Century'. *Information Processing and Management* 26, no. 4: 449–65.

Schulte, Brigid. 2014. *Overwhelmed: Work, Love, and Play When No One Has the Time*. New York, NY: Picador.

Schultz, Theodore W. 1961. 'Investment in Human Capital'. *American Economic Review* 51: 1–17.

Schultz, Theodore W. 1971. *Investment in Human Capital: The Role of Education and Research*. New York, NY: Free Press.

Schumpeter, Joseph A. 1942. *Capitalism, Socialism, Democracy*. New York, NY: Harper.

Senellart, Michel. 2007. Footnotes in Foucault, Michel. *Security, Territory, Population. Lectures at the Collège de France 1977–1978*, edited by Michel Senellart. Translated by Graham Burchell. New York, NY: Palgrave Macmillan.

Sennett, Richard. 1998. *The Corrosion of Character: The Personal Consequences of Work in the New Capitalism*. New York, NY: Norton.

Sennett, Richard. 2003. *Respect in a World in Inequality*. New York, NY: Norton.

Sennett, Richard. 2006. *The Culture of the New Capitalism*. New Haven, CT: Yale University Press.

Sennett, Richard. 2008. *The Craftsman*. London: Penguin.

Simon, Herbert A. 1971. 'Designing Organizations for an Information-Rich World'. In *Computers, Communications, and the Public Interest*, edited by Martin Greenberger, 38–72. Baltimore, MD: Johns Hopkins University Press.

Slobodian, Quinn. 2018. *Globalists: The End of Empire and the Birth of Neoliberalism*. Cambridge, MA: Harvard University Press.

Soete, Luc. 2001. 'ICTs, Knowledge Work and Employment: The Challenges to Europe'. *International Labour Review* 140, no. 2: 143–63.

Specter, Matthew G. 2015. 'Introduction: Forum: Foucault and Neoliberalism'. *History and Theory* 54: 367–71.

Srnicek, Nick. 2017. *Platform Capitalism*. Hoboken, NJ: Wiley.

Statista. 2021. 'Global Digital Population as of January 2021 (in billions)'. Last accessed July 1, 2021. https://www.statista.com/statistics/617136/digital-population-worldwide/

Suarez, Cyndi. 2017. 'With the Highest Inequality in Human History, Societies Are Ripe for Social Change'. *Nonprofit Quarterly*, November 22. Last accessed June 22, 2021. https://nonprofitquarterly.org/highest-inequality-human-history-societies-ripe-social-change/

Sundén, Jenny. 2002. *Material Virtualities: Approaching Online Textual Embodiment*. Oxford: Peter Lang.

Taylor, Charles. (1984) 1986. 'Foucault on Freedom and Truth'. In *Foucault. A Critical Reader*, edited by D. C. Hoy, 69–102. Oxford: Blackwell.

Thaler, Richard H., Cass R. Sunstein, and John P. Balz. 2013. 'Choice Architecture'. In *The Behavioral Foundations of Public Policy*, edited by Eldar Shafir, 428–39. Princeton, NJ: Princeton University Press.

Thompson, Kevin. 2003. 'Forms of Resistance: Foucault on Tactical Reversal and Self-formation'. *Continental Philosophy Review* 36, no. 2, 113–38.

Thompson, Paul, Chris Warhurst, and George Callaghan. 2000. 'Human Capital or Capitalising on Humanity? Knowledge, Skills and Competencies in Interactive Service Work'. In *Managing Knowledge: Critical Investigations of Work and Learning*, edited by Craig Pritchard, Mike Chumer, Richard Hull, and Hugh Willmot, 122–40. New York, NY: St Martin's Press.

Tilgher, Adriano. 1930. *Homo Faber: Work Through the Ages*. Translated by Dorothy Canfield Fisher. New York, NY: Harcourt Brace.

Törnberg, Petter, and Justus Uitermark. 2020. 'Complex Control and the Governmentality of Digital Platforms'. *Frontiers in Sustainable Cities* 2, no. 6: 1–11.

Trengrove, Iza. 2021. 'On Re-imagining Life and Work in South Africa'. *Daily Maverick*. Accessed on July 18, 2021. https://www.dailymaverick.co.za/article/2021-07-13-on-reimagining-life-and-work-in-south africa/?utm_medium=email&utm_campaign=Coronavirus%20Thursday%2015%20July%20NAF&utm_content=Coronavirus%20Thursday%2015%20July%20NAF+CID_401de667c11f5b9cdd9e160c5fa0e9e3&utm_source=TouchBasePro&utm_term=Iza%20Trengove%20finds%20out

Tribe, Keith. 2009. 'The Political Economy of Modernity: Foucault's College de France Lectures of 1978 and 1979'. *Economy and Society* 38, no. 4: 679–98.

Van Dijck, José, and Thomas Poell. 2013. 'Understanding Social Media Logic'. *Media and Communication* 1: 2–14.

Vatter, Miguel. 2018. 'Foucault and Becker: A Biopolitical Approach to Human Capital and the Stability of Preferences'. In *The Politics of Legality in a Neoliberal Age*, edited by Ben Golder and Daniel McLoughlin, 64–82. New York, NY: Routledge.

Verhaeghe, Paul. 2012. *What About Me? The Struggle for Identity in a Market-based Society*. Translated by Jane Hedley-Prôle. London: Scribe.

Walsh, Kate, Jean M. Bartunek, and Catherine A. Lacey. 1998. 'A Relational Approach to Empowerment'. In *Trends in Organizational Behaviour. Volume 5*, edited by Cary L. Cooper, and Denise M. Rousseau, 103–26. New York, NY: Wiley.

Walton, Richard E. 1974. 'Alienation and Innovation in the Workplace'. In *Work and the Quality of Life*, edited by James O'Toole, 227–45. Cambridge, MA: MIT Press.

Wattenberg, Ben J. 1984. *The Good News is the Bad News is Wrong*. New York, NY: Simon and Schuster.

Weber, Max. (1905) 1992. *The Protestant Ethic and the Spirit of Capitalism*. Translated by Talcott Parsons. New York, NY: Routledge.

Webster Family Encyclopedia. 1985. Des Moines, IA: Meredith.

Wilkinson, Richard. 2005. *The Impact of Inequality: How to Make Sick Societies Healthier*. London: Routledge.

Wilkinson, Richard, and Kate Pickett. 2010. *The Spirit Level: Why Equality is Better for Everyone* (revised edition). London: Penguin.

Winslow, Charles D., and William L. Bramer. 1994. *Future Work: Putting Knowledge to Work in the Knowledge Economy*. New York, NY: The Free Press.

Yankelovich, Daniel. 1981. *New Rules: Searching for Self-fulfilment in a World Turned Upside Down*. New York, NY: Random House.

Yankelovich, Daniel, and Sidney Harman. 1988. *Starting with the People*. Boston, MA: Houghton Mifflin.

Yankelovich, Daniel, and John Immerwahr. 1984. 'Putting the Work Ethic to Work'. *Society* 21, no. 2: 58–76.

Yusoff, Wan Fauziah Wan, Tan Shen Kian, and Mohammad Talha Mohamed Idris. 2013. 'Herzberg's Two Factors Theory on Work Motivation: Does it Work for Today's Environment?' *Global Journal of Commerce & Management Perspective* 2, no. 15: 18–22.

Zamora, Daniel. 2014. *Critiquer Foucault: Les années 1980 et la tentation neoliberale*. Brussels: Aden.

Zamora, Daniel, and Michael C. Behrent, eds. 2016. *Foucault and Neoliberalism*. Cambridge: Polity Press.

Zuboff, Shosana. (2018) 2019. *The Age of Surveillance Capitalism. The Fight for a Human Future at the New Frontier of Power*. New York, NY: Public Affairs.

Zuckerberg, Mark. 2019. *Facebook and Free Speech*. Last accessed June 19, 2021. https://www.youtube.com/watch?v=hcLSU17M3Lw

Index

www.ingramcontent.com/pod-product-compliance
Ingram Content Group UK Ltd.
Pitfield, Milton Keynes, MK11 3LW, UK
UKHW041838031026
15587UKWH00002B/855

9 781786 611727